Doctor with Big Shoes

Doctor with Big Shoes

Missionary Experiences in China and Africa

Henry S. Nelson

PROVIDENCE HOUSE PUBLISHERS
Franklin, Tennessee

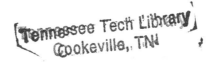

TENNESSEE HERITAGE LIBRARY
Bicentennial Collection

Printed in the United States of America

99   98   97   96   95   6   5   4   3   2   1

Library of Congress Catalog Card Number: 95-70539

ISBN: 1-881576-45-0

Published by
PROVIDENCE HOUSE PUBLISHERS
P.O. Box 158 • 238 Seaboard Lane
Franklin, Tennessee 37067
800-321-5692

To
our children and grandchildren

and to
our friends and colleagues in China and Africa,
with whom we have been privileged to serve.

Contents

Illustrations

Photographs

Foreword

I know of no other missionaries who have had such varied, fearful and fascinating experiences in different parts of the globe as Henry and Katie Nelson. Henry, a surgeon who was born in China, and Katie with degrees in nursing and international education, seemed to have the knack of being at home in different cultures and under conflicting political regimes and ideologies. When further medical service in one country was blocked, they asked for transfer to another one. Revolutions, political turmoil, wars and civil disturbances seemed to follow them. First, came the chaotic days of the Republican government of China following World War II. Then with the victory of the communist armies Henry served under the People's Republic of China. When further service here became impossible, they transferred to Africa and served under the colonial regime of the Belgian Congo. The transfer from Asia to Africa meant two new languages—French and Tshiluba— had to be learned. With the outbreak of tribal warfare came evacuation to Rhodesia. Then back to the independent Republic of Zaïre. Before their Africa days were finished, there were short tours in Malawi and Cameroon.

Now it was time to come home to the pleasant rolling hills of East Tennessee. But the itch to travel and serve struck again! Where would it be this time? The former mission hospital in Zhenjiang was seeking to reestablish relationships with the Presbyterian Mission Board that had founded the hospital in 1922. It would be the first opportunity for medical service in China since the Cultural Revolution. What better team could be appointed for this important and sensitive assignment than Henry and Katie Nelson? Following a two-year term in Zhenjiang came an opportunity to serve in the Beijing Medical University just in time to witness the Tiananmen Square massacre.

These memoirs have been enhanced by Henry's drawings and clarified by his maps. Descriptions of places and events are vivid and make the experiences come to life. Henry's recollections will form a valuable addition to the missionary medical history of post-World War II Asia and Africa.

During these tumultuous times some things never changed: the Nelsons' compassion for the sick and suffering, the willingness to serve under national leaders, the devotion to the church, optimism under trying circumstances, and always a cheerful witness to Jesus Christ. This tribute from Henry's colleague Dr. Zhang Zhi-Qing says it all:

> By the grace of God, Dr. and Mrs. Nelson have worked here in Zhenjiang for two years. They taught us English, medicine, nursing, and ethics. They taught us diligently, conscientiously, and selflessly. They not only taught with their mouths but with their hands too. They have done very good work for Jesus Christ (quoted by Sophie Crane, PCUS *Overseas Medical Missions*).

—G. Thompson Brown
Former Director and China Consultant
Division of International Mission
Presbyterian Church in the United States

Preface and Acknowledgments

I have been privileged to live in China and Zaïre through extremely interesting periods of history. In response to the urging of my friends and for the benefit of my children and grandchildren, I have described some of my experiences. I also hope to give some idea of the changing role of missionary service. Ability to adapt to changing demands and circumstances has certainly been one of the primary requisites in my life. Equally important has been the effort to develop a working knowledge of the language and appreciation of the culture of the people with whom we have lived and served.

Our service in China and Africa has been interdigitated. In order to make it easier for those primarily interested in one or the other of these two areas, I have divided the book into two sections, dealing first with all our experiences in China and secondly with all our African experiences. A chronology of our service abroad is included in Appendix A. We served with the Presbyterian Church in the United States (PCUS) prior to 1983 and with the Presbyterian Church (U.S.A.) thereafter.

In the section on China, Chinese words are spelled in the modern Pinyin phonetic alphabet, for example, Yangzi River. Many maps use the older spelling, Yangtze, though Changjiang is the name for the river that is used in China. Former equivalents are given for some of the other well-known geographical names. In Chinese, each syllable is represented by a single character. Many words and names are therefore made up of two or more characters. Chinese surnames come first, with the given name of one or two characters following. Some Chinese have retained the earlier romanization used for their names. This is the case with Bishop K.H.Ting, whose surname is the same as the artist, Mr. Ding Guanjia, who uses the modern Pinyin spelling.

In Zaïre, there was no written language until after the arrival of the Europeans, when the language was reduced to writing. Since those writing the language came from several different linguistic backgrounds, there was

13

some variation in the phonetic spelling. In the late 1950s, Catholic and Protestant missionaries got together for a joint revision of the translation of the Bible. At that time they agreed on a standardized spelling. Variations remain, however, especially in the spelling of names. I have attempted to follow the standardized spelling insofar as possible. With the change from colonial to independent status in the sixties, many new nations resumed the use of traditional African names. During the colonial era I have employed the names in use at that time. Following the name changes I have shifted to the names in current usage. The equivalent names are listed on the map of Zaïre.

Insofar as possible, I have used full personal names in the first reference to friends and colleagues, using familiar, abbreviated terms thereafter. We apologize to those esteemed friends who, for lack of full information, have been mentioned by a single name. We have occasionally used the Tshiluba term *tatu* preceding a man's name. *Tatu* means "father," but by extension, is often used as a term of respect for adult males in general.

I wish to thank the many who have given me encouragement during this project, including my brother Charles, Bill and Effie Rule, Bill and Virginia Pruitt, Bill and Annette Washburn, John and Aurie Miller, Paul and Sophie Crane, Lach and Winnie Vass, Walt and Nancy Hull, Ralph and Elsbeth Shannon, and others who have furnished information and given valuable suggestions. My wife Katie has done extensive editing in an effort to verify many of the facts to which I have referred. I take full responsibility for any errors that remain. My thanks to Betty Nelson for help in proofreading. Andrew B. Miller, publisher; Mary Bray Wheeler, managerial editor; Trinda Cole, Joanne Jaworski, Charles Flood and others of the Providence House staff have been an enormous help in bringing this book to reality. Special appreciation is expressed to Dr. G. Thompson Brown for his review of the manuscript and for his gracious contribution of the Foreword. I hope that my readers can share,in some measure, the challenge and inspiration that I have received, through the years, from Chinese and African friends.

Part I

China

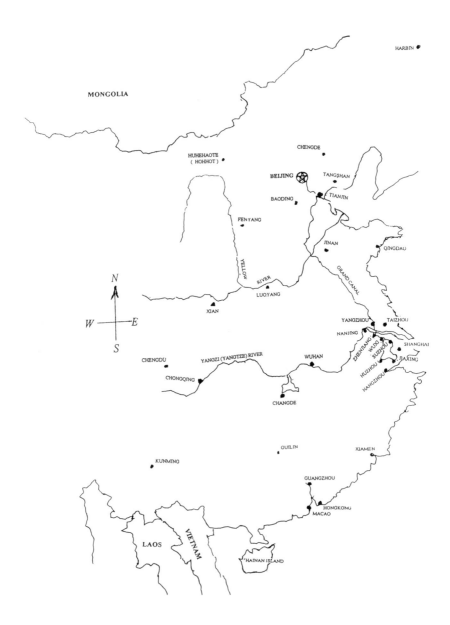

HARBIN

MONGOLIA

CHENGDE

HUHEHAOTE
(HOHHOT)

BEIJING ✪   TANGSHAN

BAODING   TIANJIN

FENYANG

JINAN   QINGDAO

YELLOW   RIVER

GRAND CANAL

LUOYANG

XIAN

YANGZHOU   TAIZHOU

NANJING

CHENGDU   YANGZI (YANGTZE) RIVER   WUHAN   ZHENJIANG   WUXI   SHANGHAI
                                                                    SUZHOU   JIAXING
CHONGQING   HUZHOU
                                                              HANGZHOU

CHANGDE

GUILIN   XIAMEN

KUNMING

GUANGZHOU

HONGKONG
MACAO

LAOS   VIETNAM

HAINAN ISLAND

China

1. China Calls: 1915-47

Roots

My father, Oscar Gustaf Nelson, grew up in Mobile, Alabama. Both his parents were born in Sweden and came to this country as children. My grandfather was a foundry worker. By placing first in a competitive examination, my father earned a scholarship to Vanderbilt University. This enabled him to go to university and continue on through medical school. While in school he met my mother, Henrietta Sperry, who was a native of Nashville. My father was a Methodist; mother was a Presbyterian. They volunteered to serve in China and were accepted by the Southern Methodist Mission Board. Mother was an undergraduate student at Vanderbilt, but did not complete her program and graduate. Instead, they were married just as soon as he graduated from medical school in 1915 and left immediately for the foreign field.

The trip to China was not without a memorable experience which my father liked to relate. They left Nashville in a Pullman. As the train passed through the Arizona desert, there was a derailment. Several cars including the diner overturned. Their car remained upright so they were not injured. A number of persons were badly injured, including one of the cooks, who was scalded when a kettle of boiling soup poured on him. Some of the people had to be pulled out of the windows of the overturned cars. There was another young physician on board. The two young doctors were hard pressed to care for all the injured, and first aid supplies were quickly exhausted. When they asked if anyone had any alcohol, many passengers opened suitcases to supply the need.

On arrival in China, they proceeded to Huzhou, Zhejiang (formerly spelled Huchow, Chekiang) where my father began as an understudy to Dr. Fred Manget. The following year my older brother, Oscar Gustaf Nelson, Jr., (Gus) was born. The usual term for missionaries with the Methodist Board at that time was seven years; however, since my father had come out directly from medical school, it was decided to send him home for surgical training so that he could cover for Dr. Manget's furlough. They returned to the States in 1918, as my father had obtained a surgical residency at New York General Hospital. Mother remained in Nashville with her family. In August 1919, Gus became suddenly ill with "infantile cholera." Electrolyte and fluid imbalance were little understood then, and the techniques to combat them had not been well developed. My father was summoned by telegram and took the next train, but Gus died before he could get back to Nashville.

After completing his surgical training, they returned to Huzhou. In November 1920, my sister Faith was born. My parents' joy quickly turned to dismay when they discovered that she was born with premature closure of the sutures of the skull, a condition later known as craniofacial synostosis. This necessitated two trips to Boston to be treated at Harvard by the renowned neurosurgeon, Dr. Harvey Cushing. He operated, removing portions of the skull, so that her head could expand to accommodate her growing brain. The condition left her with almost complete paralysis of both legs and her left arm, as well as with some speech abnormality due to the facial deformities.

I was born in Huzhou in January 1923. My brother Charles was born three years later, in August 1926, at Moganshan, a mountain resort near Huzhou where some of the missionaries went in the summer to escape the terribly moist heat of the coastal plain. I have very few memories of my early years in China. Apparently there were no other missionary children of my age at Huzhou and my playmates were Chinese. I spoke primarily the Huzhou dialect, one of the group of Wu languages which includes the Shanghai dialect. I used English with the missionary community. I am told that when my mother's mother, whom we called Munnie, came to visit early in 1926, I interpreted for her. When we went to Moganshan for the summer, I was placed in an English kindergarten to force me to use more English. I remember little of this, though I do recall knowing of Charles' birth. My most vivid memory of China is of a student demonstration or riot. Some students were displaying banners out of their dormitory windows. The firefighters were using hoses to break up the demonstration, pumping the water with hand-operated pumps.

Conditions in China were uncertain. Revolution was in the air. The Nationalists were trying to wrest control of the country from the various warlords. In fact, during one of my family's trips to the States, Huzhou had been taken by one of the warring factions. The missionary houses had been occupied. My father's medical books had been used for fuel by the soldiers. Their household staff had managed to save some of my parents' things by taking them to their own homes. Later, back in China, my parents became increasingly uneasy about their ability to assure Faith's health and safety under existing circumstances. In December 1926, the family returned to the States permanently.

Growing Up

Nashville became our stateside home. We stayed for a short while with Munnie, then moved into a small house on one of the taller hills of Nashville.

Frances Adams joined the family shortly after our arrival, to help take care of Faith. Frances had attended nursing school for a while and was a very caring person with many talents. She lived in our home and remained as Faith's nurse and companion for around forty years. She was virtually a member of the family and helped to rear both Charles and me.

Since Nashville was Mother's home, she returned to First Presbyterian Church, which had been her church home. My father attended the nearby McKendree Methodist Church, where he served as a steward. He later joined the family in First Presbyterian, where he taught a Sunday school class, became a deacon, and then for many years served as an elder. We always attended Sunday school and worship services. I joined the church at age eleven and became active in the young people's organization that met on Sunday evenings. I served in succession as treasurer, vice president, and president. At age fourteen, I began attending the Synod Young People's weeklong summer camp. For the first two or three years, this was held at Ovoca, a camp near Tullahoma, Tennessee. It was during my second year at Ovoca that I decided to devote my life to full-time Christian service. I also came to the realization that I was not inclined to be a preacher, but that I wanted to make my contribution as a medial missionary. This commitment was reconfirmed a couple of years later when I attended a Youth Mission Rally at which I heard Dr. Egbert Smith, the retired executive secretary of the General Assembly Mission Board, Presbyterian Church in the United States (PCUS). From that time onward, my goal was to become a physician and serve, hopefully, in China.

After attending Nashville public schools for the first three grades, I transferred to Peabody Demonstration School for the fourth grade. Peabody was on an eleven-year program, so I graduated from high school in 1939 at the age of sixteen. Just across the street was Vanderbilt University where I had been accepted for entrance.

College Days

The premedical program was concentrated into three years, after which I entered medical school as a "senior in absentia." Medical school entrance requirements included courses with laboratories four days a week for much of the time. The B.A. degree was awarded after finishing the first year in medical school. The war in Europe was much on our minds, as it was prominent in the papers and radio news broadcasts. The draft age was still twenty-one in December 1941. After Pearl Harbor the class ranks began to thin, with the departure of volunteers. I received my acceptance to Vanderbilt University Medical School in January 1942 and immediately enlisted in a Naval Reserve program for medical students. Shortly thereafter the draft age was lowered to eighteen. Since I was already enlisted, I could not register, so never had to deal with a draft board. The medical schools embarked on an accelerated schedule in order to produce more physicians for the war effort. It meant continuing around the year without a summer break; thus we graduated in three years instead of four. My B.A. degree was obtained in March 1943 at the end of my freshman year in medical school and my M.D. degree in June 1945, at twenty-two years of age.

In spite of the concentrated schedule, I found time to date a number of girls both in college and medical school, though none could be termed a steady girl friend. Finally during my senior year, lightning struck. Kathryn Wolff (Katie) was a student nurse whom I had seen occasionally on the wards. We both became involved in the Presbyterian youth group on campus. When we returned from a weekend mission trip to Big Lick on the Cumberland Plateau, I proposed. Not only was she the one with whom I wanted to spend the rest of my life, but she too was dedicated to full-time Christian service. Katie was from Bethania, North Carolina, a small Moravian community. She had been preparing to be a missionary nurse of the Moravian Church, expecting to go to Nicaragua. She agreed to go with me to China instead. Katie was in her junior year in nursing school. I had already been accepted for internship at Iowa City, Iowa, and would have to leave to go there in June 1945. I would be going on active duty with the Navy immediately after completion of the internship. Katie was in the Senior Cadet Nurse Corps, receiving tuition and a small stipend. I was in uniform in the Naval Reserve, receiving tuition and Able Seaman's pay. Sure of our mutual goal, and facing a time of separation, we decided to marry without delay. At that time my family belonged to Second Presbyterian Church. We were married there on January 27, 1945, by the pastor, the Reverend John Leith. We moved into an apartment a few blocks from school.

Internship: Iowa City 1945-46

Katie remained at Vanderbilt to complete her B.S. in Nursing. We were separated for much of the year following my graduation. Katie was able to come to Iowa City for a brief visit for our anniversary. At this visit, we began the custom of renewing our wedding vows each year, which we have continued throughout our wedded life. The last six months of Katie's program was an assignment with Senior Cadet Nurse Corps at Oak Ridge, Tennessee. When she was assigned there, no one knew what secret war program was going on at Oak Ridge. The atomic bomb was dropped before she went, and the secret was out. The war ended while I was still in Iowa. I contacted Dr. C. Darby Fulton, then executive secretary of the mission board, and he suggested that I ask the Navy for a discharge in order for us to go to China as missionaries. He then wrote to Representative Walter Judd, a former China missionary, asking for his support of the request for my release.

The Navy called me to active duty and assigned me to the Naval Air Station at Memphis. I had been there for a little over a month and obtained a weekend pass to visit my parents in Nashville. On my return to Memphis, I was informed that they had been looking for me, as my discharge papers had come. My internship lasted only nine months, while the first three months of military service were expected to fulfill the normal requirement for one year of postgraduate training. I was in a dilemma, since I had not completed a year. I called Nashville. My father was on the board of Protestant Hospital, later to become Baptist Hospital. The hospital was struggling along with practically no house staff. They had accepted some medical officers for the house staff who were due to be discharged from the service, and were glad to offer me a three-month appointment to fill the immediate need. The discharge center was across the street from the Naval Air Station. I was discharged the next day and caught a bus to Nashville. The following day, I began work at Protestant Hospital. I was not only the surgical resident, but had to cover the obstetrical service as well, and take call for the Florence Crittendon Home for unmarried mothers. This was located in the house in east Nashville which had formerly been the Sperry family home, where my mother had grown up.

Road to China

Katie was the top student in her class and earned the Founder's medal for the School of Nursing when she received her B.S.N. in 1946. I finished my service at Protestant Hospital shortly thereafter. We went to Montreat, North Carolina, for candidate school as new mission appointees. One of the most useful aspects of this was a linguistics course taught by Professor Esther Cummings, which proved to be invaluable in our later studies of languages. The World Missions Conference came at the end of candidate school. At the closing session we were commissioned, along with those going to Japan, Korea, Mexico, Brazil, and the Belgian Congo. The language school in China was not yet open, so we were sent to the Institute of Far Eastern Languages of Yale University for the school year.

Yale

The institute was under the direction of Dr. George Kennedy and his associate, Professor Gerard Kok. Professor Gardner Tewskbury, Annie Kok who later married the Reverend John Brady, and a team of Chinese drill masters were our very able teachers. Oral mastery of the language was the primary goal, with the study of characters receiving secondary emphasis. The spelling for Chinese characters in general usage at that time was the Wade system of romanization. This represented very poorly, to speakers of American English, the actual pronunciation of Chinese characters. A romanization had been developed at Yale that more closely represented the correct pronunciation for us. The lesson materials were still in mimeographed form. They were presented in general sessions. It was before the era of tape recorders, but we used Soundscriber discs and spent many an hour listening to the recorded lessons. Chinese drill instructors, who spoke Mandarin, held oral drill sessions with groups limited to six or eight students. At one of the sessions I was having difficulty producing an acceptable pronunciation. The instructor exclaimed that I was saying it like someone who came from a Wu speaking area. She had no idea that I had spoken a Wu dialect as a child. In spite of the fact that I had forgotten all my Huzhou dialect, its basis must still have been there in my subconscious mind.

Katie became pregnant shortly before we went to Yale. She continued in the language program until shortly before delivery. Dr. Grantly Dick-Read, author of *Childbirth Without Fear*, had lectured at Yale, and the house staff was interested in natural childbirth. This pleased Katie, and we prepared for delivery by this method. We were also pleased that there was a special "rooming-in" pilot project which we entered. The newborn babies stayed with the mothers, instead of in the nursery. In "rooming-in," the mothers cared for the babies from the very beginning. Henry Sperry Nelson, Jr. (Sperry) was born May 2, 1947. Following the end of the school year, we visited Katie's family in Bethania, stopped by Montreat during the World Mission Conference, then went on to Nashville to visit my family. Second Presbyterian Church undertook to share in our support as their missionaries and continued to do so throughout our missionary career. The church had a large going away party for us on the lawn of the church before our departure in the fall.

S.S. General Gordon

We left Nashville by train for San Francisco. There we boarded the *General Gordon* of the American President Line. We thought it quite a coincidence that the Captain was named Henry Nelson. The *General Gordon* was a "converted" troop carrier. Our accommodations were called "first class" though they were dormitory style. I was in a cabin which had been designated for the troop's officers. The bunks were three deep and there were eighteen men in my cabin, located on the boat deck, one deck above the promenade deck. Katie's accommodations were on the same deck toward the stern, in what had been the sick bay. The bunks were only two deep, but there were twenty-eight in her room, most of them occupied by mothers with babies or young children. There were a number of missionaries on board bound for China and Japan. Some had been at Yale with us. A number of them were in cabins one or two decks below the promenade deck. In addition to the "first class" passengers, there were many steerage passengers. These were mostly Chinese going back to the mainland. They were down in the holds. In good weather the covers were taken off the holds and we could look down on three decks, each with bunks stacked three deep.

The food was excellent. I often ate down the entire menu. Our first port of call was Honolulu. The ship was in port long enough for us to take a bus tour around the island, which we enjoyed very much. Crossing the International Date Line, we lost Sunday. To compensate, the missionaries on board divided Monday into two days. Services were held in the morning, and the afternoon became Monday.

We soon learned that the Pacific is not always smooth sailing. About halfway to Manila we encountered a typhoon. The seas became rougher and rougher, and the ship rolled and pitched. The pitching was the worst. When the propellers came out of the water, the whole ship would shudder and throb. It became so rough that we were confined to our cabins and told to wear our life preservers. No meals were served in the dining rooms, but sandwiches and coffee were brought to us. The captain decided to turn the ship 180 degrees and steam away from the storm for twenty-four hours. At the worst, the ship rolled over 30 degrees and seemed to hang there for an eternity before it righted and rolled the other way. Distress signals were received from a couple of Liberty boat freighters, but they were too far away for us to give assistance. As we entered Manila harbor, a freighter limped in, having lost one half of the bridge and the lifeboats from one side in the storm.

From Manila we sailed to Hong Kong. We took the cogwheel tram to the peak of the mountain on Hong Kong Island and looked down on the beautiful harbor. We also went over to Kowloon. Sperry, who was now five months old, was in my arms sitting on my camera bag. A newspaper boy ran up to me and slapped me on the chest with a paper. With his other hand he grabbed a pen out of my pocket. I realized immediately what he was doing, as one of our friends had the same thing done to him in Manila. I grabbed him with my free hand and started shouting at him in Chinese to give me my pen. Katie didn't realize what I was saying at first, but saw the pen drop and picked it up. A policeman was a few steps away, but he just turned his back and ignored the whole affair.

2. The Curtain Falls: 1947-51

Introduction to China

A full month after we had left the States, we arrived in Shanghai. We could see the Reverend John Minter and Mrs. Kitty Farrior on the dock awaiting us. Kitty's husband, the Reverend Stacy Farrior, was then the mission treasurer. There was mass confusion, with porters swarming aboard to carry the cabin baggage ashore. Our limited Chinese proved very useful in getting their attention. In the custom shed I heard my name paged; a Chinese gentleman from Mr. Farrior's office was bringing some money to help me get through the formalities. He handed me a stack of one million Chinese yuan. Welcome to inflation! At that time it was worth about U.S. $20.

Travel has always been an exciting part of the missionary experience, especially so in China in the forties. We traveled first to Jiaxing (formerly spelled Kashing) by train and were met by Dr. and Mrs. Mason Young. The Grand Canal was beside the railroad station, and we crossed over it and walked along a short section. On the canal bank was a squatter's shack with a roof of straw thatching. The streets were lined with tall walls of gray brick, and the buildings that were visible were of the same gray brick and roofed with a somewhat darker gray tile. We had hired rickshaws for the baggage and walked beside them to the mission station, which was only about a mile away. On the way, another rickshaw passed us with a Chinese gentleman who had between his legs a bale of unwrapped currency that was so tall he could not see over it. Another sign of inflation running out of control.

Several days later, I returned to Shanghai to get our freight cleared through customs. This required following the papers through the customs office to prod the officials at the various desks to apply the numerous red "chops" (seals) and pass them on to the next desk. In addition to our freight, there were also other items for Jiaxing. I decided to transport it all by road, rather than ship it by train. The Reverend Robert Henry, a former Methodist missionary and a friend of my parents, was director of China National Relief and Rehabilitation Administration (CNRRA). He was able to arrange for a couple of trucks. The crew, however, spoke Shanghai dialect. I only had a halting command of Mandarin that I had acquired during the year at Yale. One of the drivers could speak a little Mandarin, but with a decided Shanghai accent. Jiaxing is situated about sixty miles southwest of Shanghai on the Shanghai-Hangzhou rail line. The route we were to follow was considerably longer, as we crossed the Huangpu (Whangpo) River and went down the coast until we were opposite Jiaxing. This route was dictated by the fact that there were Communist guerrillas active in the countryside, whom we were attempting to avoid. After much delay in getting the trucks loaded, we left Shanghai early in the afternoon. When we arrived at the river crossing, my heart sank. We had to cross on a ferry which consisted of rusted metal tanks covered by a deck that was just big enough to accommodate our two trucks. As the trucks rolled onto the ferry, it tipped and rocked with the weight. There was no guardrail in front of the trucks, so I was afraid I was going to see one plunge into the river. A guardian angel must have been watching over us, as we negotiated the crossing without mishap. We were stopped numerous times by Nationalist soldiers who wanted to know our destination. The road was unpaved and was elevated, with irrigated fields on both sides. We were never out of sight of men, women, children, and water buffalo working in the fields. When we reached the coast, the road ran along the top of a high dike. On the seaward side, salt was being extracted from the sea. There were many large vats with low mud walls where the sea water was let in at high tide. These were at various stages of evaporation. In some, salt was being scraped up.

One of the trucks developed engine trouble and we finally ended up towing it with the other truck. We lost so much time, that it was getting late in the afternoon when we reached the small village where we were to turn inland toward Jiaxing. Here my driver said we would have to spend the night. There had been reports of guerrilla activity on the road to Jiaxing. He found lodging for us at the Haifeng Fandian (Sea Breeze Inn). This was my first experience sleeping on a Chinese bed, made with a surface of tightly strung cord, somewhat like a tennis racket, covered by a thin pad or blanket. On top of this, I rolled up in a comfort. Our crew had some difficulty communicating with the local people, as they spoke a variety of the Wu dialect so different from that of Shanghai that it was almost like another language. Even so,they were able to get food for us. I was served rice gruel with a fried egg and some soup. The next morning we traveled the remaining twenty miles to Jiaxing, still towing one truck. Katie was overjoyed to see us, as she had been concerned when we didn't arrive as scheduled.

Jiaxing

Jiaxing was cold in December. A *tanghu* (brass hot water bottle) wrapped in a flannel cover was used as a bed warmer. The house did not have running water, instead there was a washstand and pitcher in the room. The water would freeze in the pitcher at night. The water in the *tanghu* would still be hot enough to use for shaving in the morning.

The Reverend Jack Vinson and his wife Lucy were also stationed in Jiaxing. They had been in China before World War II and had been interned in the Philippines by the Japanese. They had suffered much and had many tales to tell of their experiences there. They lived in a residence at the school, a couple of blocks from the hospital. They had the luxury of a Japanese bathtub and occasionally invited us to come to their house to bathe. The tub was oval, made of wood, and just big enough to sit in, but not big enough to lie down in. There was a stove in one end, for heating the water. One would first take a sponge bath, then get in and soak. We would take turns, ladies first, in order to conserve fuel.

While at Jiaxing, we acquired our Chinese names. Jack asked Mr. Gu, principal of the school, to help us. My father's name, Ni Erxun (humble), was a transliteration of Nelson. I wanted a name with a Christian connotation and wished to keep the same surname, Ni. Mr. Gu suggested that the given names should approximately transliterate Henry and Kathryn. The names he chose were En Yi (kindness and justice) for me and Ke Ren (able and sensitive) for Katie. The term for "righteous" commonly used by Christians combines the two characters, *ren* and *yi*, which occur in our names. Our life-long struggle toward fulfillment of the meaning continues.

The hospital, having suffered during the Japanese occupation, was not yet in full operation. The main hospital building was nearing completion of the repairs and restoration. Carpenters were active in the hospital yard, building furniture for the wards, such as bedside tables and stools. One day Mr. Nigel McDougall, a New Zealand electrical engineer, was sent by International Relief Committee (IRC) to check equipment and give technical advice. He installed a U.S. Army portable X-ray unit that had been given to the hospital. I stayed with him to help and learn all I could about the installation and upkeep of the machine.

The house that was to be our home had been repaired and the floors had been finished with a very hard Ningpo varnish. This is made from sumac and is very allergenic. It must cure for weeks, or months. It was dry enough to walk on, but when we stepped into the house our skin tingled from the fumes. While waiting for the house to become habitable, we stayed with Dr. and Mrs. Mason Young, who were nearing retirement. Before the war, Dr. Young had been in Suzhou, where he had pioneered a psychiatric service. Miss Elinore Lynch also shared the house with us. We enjoyed very much our association with them. The three senior missionaries were infinitely patient with us and seemed genuinely pleased to have a baby in the house.

The Reverend and Mrs. George Hudson occupied the house next door. He did a great deal of itinerating by canal boat; later, in Taiwan, he was famous for his evangelistic tent meetings. One day, he invited me to go with him on a day trip. It was my first canal trip in a small motorized sampan. We went out to one of the congregations not far from Jiaxing. The village had been destroyed during the war and much was still in rubble. The first building to be rebuilt by the Christians was the little chapel. We visited the pastor, who was living in a small hut adjacent to the chapel. On the return trip to Jiaxing, we stopped for tea on an island in a lake. Here we enjoyed cracking and eating water chestnuts along with our tea.

Reassignment to Taizhou

Not long after our arrival in China, mission meeting was held in Suzhou. Katie didn't attempt to attend, as she was occupied taking care of Sperry, who was then about six months old. The meeting was held in the old Presbyterian Hospital which had not been reopened following the war. It was located outside the old city. While there, I went into the city with a couple of other missionaries to see the Methodist school. Charlotte Dunlap was in the party. We rode in rickshaws, which I discovered is not without danger. As we went into the city, we passed over an arched bridge. The man pulling Charlotte stumbled and fell, pitching Charlotte out onto the street. She suffered a small cut on the chin, scrapes, and bruises, but fortunately no broken bones.

Following our departure from the States, Dr. Robert Price, who was scheduled to return to Taizhou (formerly spelled Taichow), had died suddenly while itinerating. He had opened the medical work in Taizhou, built the hospital, and had been repatriated during the Japanese occupation. Repairs had already begun on the Taizhou hospital. We were reassigned to Taizhou, but were to go first to Beijing (then called Beiping) for six months of language study.

Marguerite Mizell, one of the evangelistic missionaries, suggested that I go to Taizhou with her to look over the situation and get some idea of what was needed to reopen the hospital. We traveled by train to Zhenjiang (formerly spelled Chinkiang), where we spent the night with Dr. Alex Moffett and his family. The next morning we boarded a river launch to go down the Yangzi (Yangtze) River. I was a bit concerned, because the launch had very narrow decks only about six inches above the surface of the water. We entered the cabin through a narrow door and descended three or four steep steps to sit on long benches that ran lengthwise on the ship. The cabin was packed, and I knew there was no way to escape, in case of an accident. Marguerite entered into an interesting conversation with an old lady who said she had never heard of the Gospel. Though she could not read, she was given a copy of John's Gospel and she promised to have someone read it to her. The trip took several hours with some intermediate stops before we arrived at the little river port named Longkou (Dragon's Mouth) situated about seventeen miles south of Taizhou. It was also referred to as Kouan (Port). We arrived late in the day, and no vehicles would start for Taizhou for fear of Communist guerrillas who were active at night, so we spent the night in a Chinese inn. Next morning, Marguerite haggled with drivers for a car to take us to Taizhou. I could not begin to guess what make of car it was that took us. It seemed to have been put together from several different vehicles. I sat in the rear seat between two Chinese passengers. In front of us on a sawhorse were three more passengers. Two passengers sat on the front seat beside the driver. Standing on the running boards were two of the crew of the car, plus a couple more passengers. Baggage was tied on the front fenders. The rear window right behind me was missing. The road, of course, was unpaved, very rough, and very dusty. By the time we arrived in Taizhou, the back of my head was caked with dust. I was most grateful for the custom that provided a hot bath as soon as we arrived. The houses had no hot running water, but hot water was brought in tin containers from a nearby hot water shop.

The hospital buildings had suffered much during the Japanese occupation. The furnace, boiler, pipes, and radiators had all been removed and sent to Japan as scrap metal for their war effort. Many of the windowpanes were broken. The water system and electric wiring needed to be totally redone and put back into working order by Tang Da, the hospital maintenance man. There were metal cots, many of them lacking springs; however, the hospital had received from war surplus one hundred Gatch frames with a backrest and a foot section that raised to support the feet and legs. These frames could be placed on the cots, converting them to usable hospital beds. Another piece of equipment from war surplus was a U.S. Army portable X-ray machine. It was packed in four boxes and similar to the unit I had just helped to assemble at Jiaxing. To my dismay, I found that there were two boxes of the head containing the X-ray tube, but no box containing the control unit. I decided to stop in Shanghai to see Mr. Henry, director of CNRRA, to ask if he could help me locate the missing control box.

The war surplus supplies and equipment were all being distributed through CNRRA. Mr. Henry was not sure, but thought that there was a single box containing an X-ray part at Zhenjiang, in a warehouse which was soon to be closed. He wrote a letter authorizing me to get it, if it was what I needed. I took the overnight train to Zhenjiang. It was bitterly cold and the train floor had cracks through which I could see the tracks, and which allowed a gale to blow up under my feet. I arrived in Zhenjiang at daybreak, nearly frozen, and walked a mile or so to Goldsby King Memorial Hospital. The cook was up and let me into the Moffetts' house. He had already lighted a roaring fire in the fireplace in the living room. I lay down on the floor in front of the fire and immediately fell asleep. That was where the family found me when they came down to breakfast. To my great fortune and delight, the box proved to be the missing control unit. I was able to arrange with Charlotte Dunlap, who was the nurse and administrator of Goldsby King Memorial Hospital, to send it on to Taizhou. I also discovered that she had the portable generator designed to power the X-ray unit. Zhenjiang had reliable city power, so she really did not need it. I made a deal with her to swap the generator for ten of our Gatch frames which she needed.

Language Study in Beijing

We spent Christmas and January in Jiaxing before traveling to Beijing. The middle of February we went first to Shanghai, where we stayed a couple of days with Dr. and Mrs. Robert Price Richardson (Pete and Agnes), waiting for the weather to clear so that plane service to Beijing could be resumed. We finally got off, only to have the pilot report that, because of the weather, we would be unable to land at Beijing and that he was diverting to Qingdao (old spelling Tsingtao), the former German concession on the Shandong peninsula. The houses and other buildings were all in German architectural style. One might have thought he was in Europe. We were able to obtain a room in an old hotel, though there was no provision for Sperry and no heat. We rigged a makeshift crib for him, using a big armchair pulled up against the side of the bed, and huddled under comforts for warmth. The next day the flight resumed, and we finally arrived at our destination, having seen very little of Qingdao.

Beijing (formerly spelled Peking) means northern capital. In 1948, under the Nationalist government, it was called Beiping, which means northern peace. Huawen Xuexiao,the language school, was located in the northeast sector of the city near Dongsi Pilou. This was a prominent intersection surrounded by four memorial arches that bridged the intersecting streets. The street going east led to one of the magnificent gates towering above the enormous wall that surrounded the city. The west street passed behind the Forbidden City and led to Xisi Pilou, the four west memorial arches, which were at a similar intersection in the northwest sector of the city. There were few motor vehicles in Beijing in those days. We often traveled about the city by pedicab, a three-wheeled vehicle like a rickshaw, except that instead of a man pulling between shafts like a horse, he rides in front pedaling the front part of a bicycle. There were always several of these pedicabs at the gate of the school. We became quite familiar with the men who were regulars there. I also bought a bicycle and would often ride it beside the pedicab carrying Katie. There was a Presbyterian hospital on Ertiao Hutong in the northern part of the city. I arranged to work in the outpatient department once a week in order to have an opportunity to speak Chinese in a medical setting. I would cycle out there on the afternoons when I attended clinic and was fascinated by the activity on the streets. Two-wheeled carts drawn by men, donkeys, or horses were the common means of transporting goods. One often saw a cart piled high with pink carcasses of freshly slaughtered hogs being pulled along the street. In the evenings, we often heard a hawker going by in the street crying, *"Liurou,"* meaning donkey meat. We joked that they must be selling meat from donkeys that had died in the traces that day. Camel caravans bringing sacks of coal into the city from the north were not infrequently seen in our sector of town. Men and women, balancing loads hung from the ends of shoulder poles, joined the mixture of bikes and pedestrians.

Beijing was subject to terrible dust storms. The climate was very dry, and when the wind blew steadily for several days from the west, it would bring fine dust from the Gobi Desert, enough to cut visibility to less than a hundred yards. It filtered into the rooms, even though windows were closed, leaving a film of dust everywhere. On occasion, we would go up to the flat roof of the dormitory to watch a dust storm approaching like a dense dark cloud.

Beijing is a windy city and the Chinese love to fly kites, which they make in all shapes and sizes. I bought one in the form of a hawk, one of the popular shapes. It was designed so that the kite flew almost directly above me, making it easy to get the kite up in a small space. I was able to fly it from the top of the dormitory roof.

Our days were very busy with language study, though we were able to get in a few excursions. Trips within the city were organized to the Forbidden City, Beihai, Temple of Heaven, and Lama Temple. One visit to the Lama Temple in the spring was especially interesting. There was a ceremony for exorcising the devils. I went out with one of the other missionaries to see it and take pictures. The courtyard of the temple was packed tightly with the mob. We could barely squeeze inside. The priests came out with much clanging of gongs and cymbals. Several doll-like figures, each about six or eight inches long, were thrown down on the pavement. The priests proceeded to beat the dolls, at the same time chanting and banging their instruments. The excitement of the crowd was at high pitch as they applauded the whole procedure.

There were also several trips outside the city. The Summer Palace, northwest of the city, was reached by a road that passed through cultivated fields and was lined by stone steles standing atop stone tortoises. Another trip took us further out to the Western Hills. We went by truck through the northwest gate and visited first the Jade Fountain, from which springs fed the stream that furnished water for the moat and lakes of Beijing. We climbed the hill to the Jade Fountain Pagoda and went on to visit a couple more temples in the area. One was famous for a pavilion containing the statues of one hundred Luohan (Buddhist saints), one of which was said to represent Marco Polo. Another was the Sleeping Buddha Temple. The reclining statue of Buddha was about seventeen feet long. The statue had bare feet. Hundreds of pairs of shoes donated by the Buddhist faithful were on display in the temple. While returning from this excursion, we became quite concerned that we might get caught outside the wall. The city gates closed at sundown, and it was getting late. We had left Sperry in the care of his Chinese amah. To our relief, we finally made it with less than a half-hour to spare.

Our most exciting excursion outside the city was to the Great Wall. At that time Beijing was a Nationalist stronghold, but there was a lot of guerrilla activity in the region. A train left every morning for Badaling, the most accessible site on the wall, and returned in the afternoon. We arranged for someone to keep Sperry for the day and left early in the morning. The wall was magnificent, even though it had not yet been repaired and restored. It was also devoid of hordes of tourists. We climbed up one side from the pass and picnicked on the wall. We could hear sporadic gunfire in the distance. Whether or not this was just target practice, it was unnerving. Knowing that the station where we got off the train was different from where we were to catch the train for the return trip only added to our unease. If we missed the train, there would be no way back until the next day. We finally located the right place and were much relieved to get back to Beijing without any trouble.

Baoding

At the end of June, there was a break in classes for several weeks. Two evangelistic missionaries and I decided to spend time at a Presbyterian mission station at Baoding, which is located about seventy miles south of Beijing, on a strategic rail line leading to Luoyang and farther west to Xian. The rail line had been cut by Communist guerrillas, so we knew it was not going to be an easy trip. We started by train and about halfway to our destination came to the end of the line. Sizhang was a small dusty market place where we waited. Finally the "convoy" from Baoding began to arrive. First came a truck loaded with soldiers, with a light machine gun mounted on top of the cab. Then fifteen trucks, a couple loaded with pigs and the rest each carrying a few people, straggled in at intervals over the next couple of hours. The trucks arriving late were so far behind the lead truck that they were afforded no protection at all. We started trying to locate places on one of the trucks. First they had to take on their loads. Only after being fully loaded would they talk about taking "yellow fish," as extra passengers were called. We finally obtained places along with eight or ten Chinese on a truck piled high with sacks of beans.

Our truck was apparently paired with another truck, each of which was manned by a driver and a mechanic. Just when we thought we were ready to depart, they began consulting about one of the tires on the other truck. They finally decided to change it for the spare from our truck. Apparently there was just one spare between the two trucks. While they were changing the tire, I looked a little more closely at the tire they were removing. I could not believe my eyes. The tire consisted of parts of two tires bolted together. To protect the inner tube, they had used boots inside, where there were joints. My place was at the rear, sitting on the sacks with my feet braced on the tailgate. Shortly after starting out, we saw why the train could go no further. Bridges had been destroyed, both for the rail line and the road. We detoured down and forded the stream, which was almost dry. As we came up the other bank we could see a small fort with a couple of pillboxes manned by Nationalist soldiers. Our two trucks stopped and, after another consultation, the crews decided to change one of the tires on our truck, replacing it with the tire they had originally rejected. This certainly did not ease our minds.

The road was unpaved and was intersected by bumps at frequent intervals, where guerrillas had dug trenches halfway across the road. These had been filled in with dirt which had settled, making shallow ditches on one side and causing the truck to tip. The road paralleled the rail bed and one could see where the tracks had been torn up, the crossties stacked and burned, with the rails laid across them so that they became twisted and unusable. Once we stopped. In response to our queries, we were told that there were soldiers up ahead. We finally spotted a line of soldiers walking across the fields to intersect the road ahead of us. The truck with our soldier escort had gone on long before.

After a few tense moments, it was determined that this was a friendly patrol of Nationalists and not guerrillas. We passed a truck that had been caught and burned a few days earlier. For the last few miles, there were frequent groups of soldiers guarding the road.

Baoding at that time was still surrounded by a city wall, though it was not as large and imposing as the one surrounding Beijing. We were met at the gate by one of the Presbyterian missionaries and taken to the mission with much rejoicing at our safe arrival. The normal hospital schedule had been modified. Normally operations were scheduled for the morning, with outpatient consultations in the afternoon. This had been reversed because wounded began to arrive from the countryside about midday, due to the previous night's skirmishes. Gunshot wounds and wounds from land mines made up the bulk of cases. After about a week, rumors were rife that the city would fall to the Communists any day. My two companions decided to return to Beijing, since what they were doing was not essential. I felt that I was helping and also learning, so I decided to stick it out and stay as originally planned. The days were full, but in the evenings we sometimes had a moment to relax. The mission station was in the northwest corner of the city. They kept goats in order to have fresh goat milk. We would sit up on the city wall above the goat pen and watch the sunset, as Nationalist patrols came in from the countryside. There were trenches and barbed wire entanglements below us outside the wall. The city gates were closed and no one was allowed in or out of the city at night.

For the return trip to Beijing, our local missionary friends were able to arrange for a place on a more reliable truck that was loaded only with passengers. The road was swarming with Nationalist soldiers, and at one narrow bridge our truck had to back off to give right of way to an army convoy.

Coastal Voyage: Tianjin to Shanghai

Following my safe return to Beijing, we continued with our Chinese studies through the summer term, which ran until the end of August. When the time came for us to leave Beijing, Katie and Sperry flew down to Shanghai and I followed by boat with the baggage via Tianjin, Beijing's port. About halfway to Tianjin, the train came to a sudden stop. We weren't near a station, so everyone was curious about the reason. I was told that someone had committed suicide on the track.

My sailing was delayed a couple of days, so I stayed at a hostel for transient missionaries. First class accommodations on the coastal boat were reserved for Chinese. Foreigners could only get second class booking. My cabin had six bunks which were all occupied by men. This was not the case with the other cabins, in which no attention was paid to gender. The ship had been built in Canada as a mine sweeper. It was completed only at the close of World War II and had been given to the Chinese. It was a mixed cargo-passenger service and there were large wicker baskets of dried fish stacked on the deck. I had taken some provisions with me to supplement the diet on board, but did not need them. The seas became increasingly rough and the little ship rolled and pitched unmercifully. The second day out I showed up for breakfast and found that I was the only passenger not seasick. The breakfast consisted of rice gruel and something that I did not recognize. I made the mistake of asking what it was and was told it was pig's intestine (chitterlings). If it hadn't tasted so good, that might have lost it for me. We were in the edge of a typhoon. In order to get away from the high seas, the ship put in at Qingdao and waited until the next day. The ship was a day late arriving in Shanghai, where there was a happy reunion with Katie and Sperry.

Taizhou

Pete and Agnes Richardson were returning to Taizhou in the fall of 1948. They had been missionaries there before the war. Pete, who was Dr. Robert Price's cousin, had been working in Shanghai with United Nations Relief and Rehabilitation Administration (UNRRA), funneling war surplus and relief supplies through CNRRA. Returning to mission work, he arranged for a freight car from Shanghai to Zhenjiang to take all the baggage for Taizhou. Gu Er, the Richardsons' cook, rode on the freight car to keep an eye on things. During those times, nearly every freight car had someone riding on it to protect shipments from pilfering. We all spent the night in Zhenjiang. Arrangements were made to send the freight by canal boat from Zhenjiang to Taizhou. Pete had been able to get a war surplus U.S. Army personnel carrier for Taizhou hospital. The Bridgman family and Marguerite Mizell were in Zhenjiang, returning to Taizhou. Agnes, Katie, and Sperry joined them on a twelve-hour launch trip to Taizhou. Pete and I crossed the Yangzi by ferry and drove to Taizhou in the personnel carrier. The road was narrow and elevated, passing through irrigated fields. The whole area was crisscrossed by canals. It was startling to see a sail gliding across a field, until one got close enough to see that there was a boat in a canal beneath it. The streets of Taizhou were not made for motor traffic. They were so narrow that our vehicle could barely squeeze through at places and it was impossible to turn a corner. Fortunately the street we entered led straight to the back gate of the hospital, so no turns were necessary. The streets were often used for other activities, since space in the homes was so limited. At one point, we had to stop and let them gather up peanuts that had been spread out to dry on mats in the street, before we could pass.

We shared the house in the hospital compound with the Reverend Harold Bridgman, his wife Eleanor, and their sons, David and Stewart. The house was a large two-story residence which had a central hall on both floors. Upstairs there were two bedrooms on each side and a large screened sleeping porch over the front porch, so it was not difficult to divide the living space.

Katie was pregnant, and while we were thinking of names, we asked our friends to help us with Chinese names also. They came up with a list of ten names, all of them having the character *li* (truth) which also occurs in the combination *daoli* (doctrine or belief). We eventually used five of the names. The first three names were from I Corinthians 13: faith, hope, and love. We gave Sperry the name Aili, "love the truth."

I was pleased to find on arrival in Taizhou that the hospital repairs were almost completed. Pete was invaluable in helping round up some of the old staff. The most important were Chen Zi, the head nurse and operating room supervisor, and Tang Xiaojie, the pharmacist. A couple other nurses were also available. We planned to open the hospital on October 21 with a memorial service for Dr. Price, as this was his birthday. The service was held with a tremendous crowd attending. The opening was delayed, however, because I did not yet have a license to practice in China, and we needed a licensed local physician to give legitimacy to the institution. Another physician was needed, in any case, as it was too big a task for one doctor. It was finally decided that I should go to Nanjing and see if I could recruit someone to come to Taizhou.

It had been raining steadily for several days, so the roads were impassable. Trucks and cars were not attempting to travel. The best option was to travel by rickshaw to the river, take a launch to Zhenjiang, then ride the train to Nanjing. Because of road conditions, it was necessary to have two men, one to pull and the other to push the rickshaw. I started off in the morning. The rickshaw had the hood up and a waterproof curtain stretched in front of me, that offered a little protection from the steady drizzle. The road was beyond my wildest imagination. At places the mud came almost up to the hub caps and the men sank almost to their knees. It was slow and difficult progress. We stopped midway for bowls of hot noodles and then continued on our way. I really felt like a filthy imperialist, but knowing that I had to make business calls in Nanjing, I dared not get out and slog through the rain and mud. We finally reached Longkou, the river port, late in the day. To my disappointment, it was too late to catch that day's launch. I obtained a bed in a Chinese inn. The proprietor sent out and got a new comfort for me. The bed was solid wood with a thin pad, but after the long day, I had little trouble falling to sleep. The launch trip on the river and train trip from Zhenjiang to Nanjing were uneventful.

I visited the Gulou (Drum Tower) Christian Hospital, but no one could give me any encouragement. The Communist forces were already drawing near Taizhou and no one was willing to risk going north of the river to work. I returned to Zhenjiang somewhat discouraged. There I received word from Pete that he had been able to persuade Dr. Zhuo Jingtai to work part time. Dr. Zhuo, an internist, had formerly been on the staff and was an elder in the church. He did not want to give up his private practice in Taizhou, but agreed to lend his name to the institution and to work afternoons in the outpatient department.

The water system was another problem. The hospital had two diesel engines, one large horizontal engine and a smaller upright engine. Both needed overhauling. These operated two pumps. One blew air into an artesian well, forcing water up into a surface tank. The other was a force pump that took the water from the surface tank up to a tank in the attic of the three-story hospital building. I made a trip to Shanghai to get a freight shipment of hospital supplies cleared through customs and also to try to arrange for the overhaul of the diesel engines. With great difficulty, I was able to persuade Jardin Matheson, the engineering firm that had originally installed the

Hospital maintenance man Tang Da with assistant Sen Liu, Taizhou 1949.

engines, to send two men to do the work. This time on the return trip to Taizhou from Zhenjiang, I took a canal boat. It was an all-day trip. I left early in the morning. Toward dark we were still some distance from the city. We heard some gunshots ahead and the crew became quite concerned. They made me go into the cabin and hide while they slowed and tried to determine if it was safe to continue. They finally decided the danger had passed and we proceeded into the city. The mechanics were able to overhaul the smaller diesel. The larger engine required reboring of the cylinder and new larger rings. They had to take the cylinder back to Shanghai with them. I never could get them to return. The company shipped the cylinder back to us and faithful Tang Da, our very able hospital mechanic, managed to reassemble the engine and put it in service again.

After the diesel motors for our water system were repaired, we still had a problem The inner pipe of the five hundred foot deep artesian well went down four hundred feet. Scale had built up in the pipe, constricting the lumen. Pete had obtained some replacement pipe when he was at UNRRA, but we could not persuade the engineers of Jardin Matheson to come up to install it for us. Once again Tang Da came to the rescue. He told me he was present when it was originally installed, and he thought he could do the job. We gave him permission to try. He rigged a tripod of logs and with a block and tackle pulled the pipe up one section at a time. He fashioned a clamp to hold the lower section while he used two large pipe wrenches to disconnect the pipes. By doing one section at a time, he removed the old pipe and then reversed the procedure to install the new pipe. The increased water flow allowed us to run the engines a much shorter time each day, reducing the amount of fuel required for pumping.

There were no mattresses for the hospital beds. I asked Mr. Henry at CNRRA if he had any ticking that we could use to make mattresses. He said he had none. On second thought he remembered he had a couple bales of heavy cloth that was impregnated with a gummy anti-mustard gas material. No one wanted it. I jumped at the opportunity. It turned out to be very useful. The gummy material washed out easily. We had mattress bags made from the material, which we filled with straw. When a mattress became soiled or infested with bedbugs, the straw was burned, and the bag was washed and refilled with fresh straw.

Reopening the Hospital

The hospital in Taizhou had two names. The Chinese name, Fuyin Yiyuan, was "Good News (Gospel) Hospital." The English name was Sarah Walkup Hospital, named for the mother of Mr. William Henry Belk of Belk Department Stores, who had financed its construction.

The Sarah Walkup Hospital compound consisted of three walled enclo-

sures. The front enclosure contained the oldest hospital building and the gatehouse. The front brick wall on the street had originally been only about four feet high with an additional six foot iron fence on top. The brick wall had later been raised to about seven feet, still with the iron fence on top. In the past, there had been all sorts of wild rumors about "Foreign Devils." The iron fence allowed people to look in and see that there was nothing to hide, but still allowed us to maintain control of the compound. A big double wrought iron front gate was closed at night. A small door to one side allowed entry after clinic hours. The gatehouse was manned to control the traffic. Originally this enclosure had been separated from the back enclosure by a canal and a wall. During the Japanese occupation, the canal had been filled in, though there was still a

Sarah Walkup Hospital (Fuyin Yiyuan) front gate, Taizhou 1949.

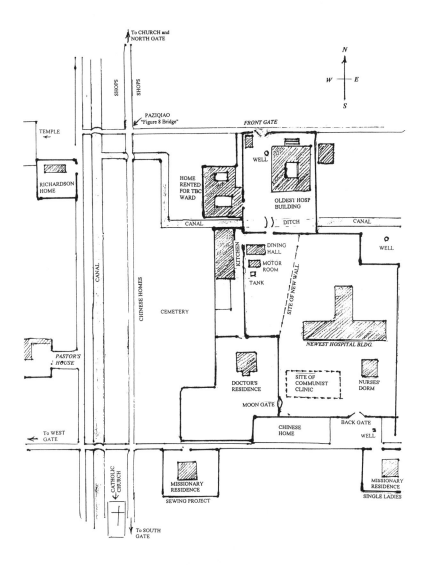

Taizhou
Sarah Walkup Hospital
1950

depression marking its site. A bridge passed over this ditch and led to a gate in the wall for entry into the back compound.

The largest building in the back compound was the newer three-story hospital building. There was also a two-story residence for nurses, a dining hall, the artesian well, a surface tank, and the engine house containing the diesel engines and pumps. In the back west corner, a moon gate let one pass into the large L-shaped enclosure containing the doctor's residence and a large vegetable garden. Outside the back gate of the hospital compound, one passed by a community well and crossed the street to the compound where the single lady missionaries lived. Further down the street to the right, was another missionary residence, known as the Lancaster house, where Agnes Richardson later had her sewing project.

The older hospital building in the front compound was built in a hollow square with a small courtyard in the center. A basement floor, which was only partially underground, had three large wards and some storerooms. The main floor was reached by stairs rising to the front door, which opened into a lobby, with the registration office to the left and the pharmacy at the rear of the lobby. On either side of the lobby were large waiting rooms. Leading back from each waiting room was a hall with windows facing the courtyard and doors opening into consultation and examining rooms. Across the back of the building, connecting the two wings, the laboratory had access from both halls. On the second floor were inpatient rooms. Above this was an attic used for storing supplies.

The newer hospital building in the back compound was built in the shape of a T. It had three floors plus a large attic storage space. The top of the T ran east and west. The patient wards and rooms occupied all the southern exposure on the three floors; taking advantage of the sun in winter for some warmth, and being shielded from the afternoon sun in summer, they were reasonably comfortable. The north side of the halls contained the nurses' stations, toilets, and workrooms. The leg of the T had offices on the first floor, X-ray and an apartment for the head nurse on the second floor, and the surgical suite on the third.

We planned to open first the outpatient department, and then follow in a couple of weeks with the inpatient wards, one or two at a time, as demand and staff allowed. On November 1 we finally had the grand opening. It was a gala occasion. A number of dignitaries of the city were invited, and quite a crowd gathered. A Chinese band came parading down the street with gongs and cymbals clanging, accompanied by a large red banner with congratulations and good wishes. A number of speeches were made and long strings of firecrackers erupted in explosions. The festivities lasted all morning. Clinic was scheduled to begin at 1 o'clock. After a hurried lunch, I rushed back to start consultations. People had been looking forward to the day for a long time. There were sixty people registered, many of them having paid extra to see the foreign doctor. It was one of the most difficult days I have ever experienced. The Mandarin spoken in Taizhou is of the north Jiangsu variety and is strongly influenced by the Wu dialect. I had to use a nurse as interpreter, as the patients often did not understand my "Beijing Mandarin" tinged with a southern U.S. accent. Every patient was a new patient who required at least an abbreviated history. I saw over forty patients; Dr. Zhuo saw the rest. It was after dark before clinic was finished. Needless to say, I fell asleep exhausted that night. We had planned to open the inpatient department after a couple of weeks, but only one week later, we were forced to admit our first patient with acute appendicitis. Other patients requiring admission soon followed.

Exodus Begins

By the middle of November 1948, the collapse of the Nationalist government (Guomindang, Kuomintang) was imminent. The U.S. consular service gave repeated advice for women and children to evacuate. The missionaries then at Taizhou were the Richardsons, the Bridgman family, Marguerite Mizell, and Gussie Louise Fraser, with Katie, me, and Sperry, who was then eighteen months old. Katie was seven months pregnant. The Bridgmans and the single ladies felt strongly that we should not stay under the Communist regime. Everyone felt it was best for Katie to leave before the changeover, despite her desire to stay. It was decided that the Richardsons and I should stay to close things up and follow later. On November 22, I drove the personnel carrier down to the Yangzi, to transport those who were leaving. When we arrived at Longkou, we again found that the launch would not leave until the next morning. We spent the night in the same hotel I had used before. The next morning at daybreak we went to the dock. There was a heavy fog. Watching Katie and Sperry on the deck of the launch, fading into the mists, was one of the hardest things I have ever had to do. The future seemed desperately uncertain.

At Yangzhou, about forty miles west of Taizhou, there was a Baptist Mission Hospital and also a district hospital. In Taizhou there was a small city hospital, hardly more than a clinic, that had about twenty beds. Nantong was about seventy miles to the east, where there had been a Dutch Reformed Mission Hospital, but it had not reopened. One had to go a hundred and twenty miles north to Huaiyin to find another hospital, but I am not sure that it was in operation at that time. There were said to be three million people in the three counties surrounding Taizhou. With Katie and Sperry safely out of harm's way, and after much prayer and thought, I decided that I could not leave, having just reopened the hospital. I was living in the house in the hospital compound, but had arranged to have my meals with the Richardsons. They lived about a block away across a canal. I went over to breakfast to announce my decision. I found that Pete and Agnes had also made a decision to stay and see what work could be done under the Communists.

Katie and Sperry were staying in Shanghai with Dr. Frank Brown, Jr. and his family. Mission officials sent repeated telegrams to Taizhou urging me to evacuate to Shanghai. Katie finally decided that to relieve the pressure on me, and to ease the minds of those concerned, she would return to the States. She left by plane early in December. Rumors grew more and more persistent that

Taizhou would soon fall. Finally in mid-January, its fall became sure.

The city fathers had been negotiating with the Nationalist garrison to leave the city without looting. Most of the troops had withdrawn. Our second son, States Lee, was born in Nashville on January 14 (the 15th in China) and Katie sent me a cablegram announcing his arrival. The cable arrived the last day that the telegraph-post office was open. That evening most of the soldiers were out of the city. When I left the Richardsons after supper to return home, it was pitch dark. As I started up the street, I saw a spark and heard someone challenge me. It was a civilian patrol organized by the businessmen of the city. They were armed with spears and knives. I had seen the spark caused by a spear point striking the cobblestones. The next day the city fathers divided into two groups. One accompanied the last of the Nationalist troops to the west gate and paid ransom for the city. The other group went to the east gate to welcome the arriving Communist troops.

Life in Taizhou

Taizhou was a county seat and was located in the Yangzi River delta about seventeen miles north of the river. There was no modern industry; the only "factory" was a flour mill with machinery made in Wisconsin, located three kilometers west of town. The bricks of the city wall had been dismantled, though a mound of earth and a canal still surrounded most of the city. Pete, Agnes, and I occasionally took walks on these remains of the old city wall. At the southeast corner there was a tower called Wanghailou (See the Sea Tower). Legend had it that one could formerly see the ocean from the tower. This was a bit hard to believe, as Taizhou was now about sixty miles from the coast. It must have taken centuries for the delta to build up sufficiently to put the ocean that far out of sight.

Taizhou was a strong Buddhist center. The principal temple was one of the few in China where Buddhist priests were consecrated. It had an altar where they laid their heads when incense was burned on them, leaving the scars seen on the priests' scalps. When the first missionaries came to Taizhou, they were not allowed to spend the night in the city. For a time they had to live in houseboats outside the city walls. At the time we arrived, Buddhism was still strong. We often heard the clanging of gongs as priests came to bless a home or conduct a funeral. The society was structured on a feudal system. The land was largely in the hands of landlords, much of it in the control of Buddhist temples, funded in large part by the rent from their lands. The various trades were organized into guilds, in which master craftsmen each had several apprentices.

The church was located about a mile from the hospital. The walk down the main street en route to church was always interesting. The route was lined by stores and workshops, all open to the street. At the bakery, one could see the big Dutch oven made of brick, in which a fire was built, then raked out, and the bread put in to bake by the heat radiated from the bricks.

Hot water shop, Taizhou 1949.

A smaller version of the Dutch oven could be seen on the street corner, where the typical Taizhou *xiaobing* were baked. Here the oven was a barrel lined with firebrick and clay, in which a fire was built. The flat sesame rolls were slapped against the inner walls and peeled off after they were baked.

Water stoves were scattered about the city. These sold hot water for tea and baths. The stove was fueled with straw or rice hulls. In the latter case, the hulls had to be fed to the fire a handful at a time through a hole in the top of the stove. The water was boiled in small deep woks set into the stove's top surface, over the firebox. At one end of the stove, there was another much larger wok with tall barrel staves fastened around it to form a reservoir. This preheated the water that was used to fill the smaller woks. People came bringing their kettles or thermos bottles to get boiling water for tea. Tin containers shaped like large watering cans might be brought to get water for baths.

Among the city's small shops, one had four or five hand-operated machines for knitting stockings. Another shop fluffed the cotton or raw silk filling for comforts and padded garments, using a long bow with a tight string. This was done by laying the padding out on a flat surface. The string was struck to make it vibrate as it beat the padding. The paper stores made paper flower funeral wreaths, paper models of houses and furniture, and paper money shaped like gold bars to be burned at Buddhist funerals. One of Taizhou's specialties was candle making. The candlesticks had a spike which was inserted into the candle. The special Taizhou red candles were square in shape, with intricate carvings on the four sides. They were made especially for use on the family altars and in the temples. When we returned in 1986, we were interested to find that candle making was still a Taizhou specialty. Candles, however, are now made in the shape of figurines of the old man representing long life and wisdom, and of Santa Claus!

Taizhou also had public bathhouses. One, which I passed daily, was located a few doors from the hospital. I could hear animated conversations coming from within as I passed by. I regret that I did not have the courage to go in and experience it at least once.

The carpenter shop was fascinating to watch. They did such beautiful work with primitive tools. Their planes were made of wood, with a slot in which the blade was held in place by a wedge. The drill bits were placed in the end of a round spindle, with a handle on top, in which the spindle could turn. A bow, the string of which was wound around the spindle, was drawn back and forth, causing the spindle and bit to spin first in one direction and then in the other. Primitive, but it worked. Carpenters used wooden mallets to strike their chisels. On occasion, when we had furniture made for the hospital, the carpenters would come and work on site. Boards were unavailable, so lumber was purchased as logs. The carpenter would mark out the various size boards he needed, by stretching an inked string along the log and snapping it to mark a line. The log would then be propped up at an angle. A two-man saw was used, one man above and the other below, to saw the planks.

At the jeweler's shop, another type of drill was used. Here the spindle was smaller. The bow was broader and had a hole in the center, through which the spindle passed. A string ran from each end of the bow and attached to the top of the spindle. After winding the strings on the spindle, one could make it spin by pressing down on the bow and then releasing the pressure to let the string rewind in the opposite direction. This allowed one to use the drill with one hand, leaving the other hand free to manipulate the object being worked upon. This same drill was used by the artisan who came around to repair broken china. He carried all his paraphernalia on a shoulder pole and came to the house to repair broken bowls and vases. Pairs of holes were drilled on each side of the break. The pieces were then put together with little brass clips cemented into the holes to hold the pieces securely.

Other craftsmen were itinerant, coming around at intervals. One repaired cast-iron woks, which often burned out or cracked. The bad section was chipped out and the hole fitted with a piece big enough to fill the defect, leaving a small crack all around it. This piece was held in place with slivers of bamboo. A small crucible filled with scraps of iron was heated over a charcoal stove. A wooden bellows was used to fan the fire hot enough to melt the iron. The bellows was an oblong box with a piston that was pushed back and forth. Valves in the box were so arranged that on both strokes, air was forced out a pipe extending from the center of the box to the charcoal brazier. When the metal was white hot, the craftsman would ladle out a small drop and slap it on a spot in the crack. He then held a leather pad underneath the crack while striking the drop on top with a small hammer. This would cause the drop to flatten out like a brad on both sides of the crack. By continuing around the edge of the piece until the entire crack was filled, the wok could be made watertight once again. Burned out pots and kettles were repaired by tinsmiths. They would cut out the damaged bottom and replace it with a new one.

Some craftsmen preferred to pick a spot on the street where they stayed and let people come to them, instead of going house to house. This was usually true of the shoe repairman, who was equipped with a small anvil and with a sewing machine, operated by hand or by foot pedal. He also had pieces and straps of leather to make repairs on all sorts of leather goods. Repairs were often made on unexpected items. Zippers, for example, would be repaired by replacing the slides instead of replacing the entire zipper. Tailors also used hand- or foot-operated sewing machines, though much of their work was done by hand.

Some itinerant tradesmen sold items to eat. They often had a stove slung from one end of a pole and the items for sale on the other end. Various kinds of dumplings, fritters, or noodles were brought by on the street this way. Each tradesman had a distinctive way of letting people know he was passing down the street. Some banged a gong or a triangle. Others used a rattle or a temple block to call attention to the cries of their wares.

Some itinerants directed their talents to entertaining children. There were some who made small figures out of colored dough. We saw two different kinds of puppet shows. One was like a Punch and Judy show, with the puppets operated from below with sticks. Another was a kind of shadow show. A translucent screen

Puppet Show, Beijing 1948.

was used. The puppets, made of thin oiled leather which had been colored, were held against the screen with sticks and illuminated by a light which shone from behind, so the image was visible through the screen.

The residential streets were lined with long expanses of blank walls with only occasional doors allowing entry into courtyards. The rooms in the houses faced into the courtyards, with no windows opening on the street. The streets were often used for drying grains, sunning blankets and clothes, or other activities, among which was the manufacture of rope, twine, and thread. The strands would sometimes stretch for a city block, while hand spinning wheels twisted them together. Taizhou was famous for its fish nets. Much of the heavy cord that was made on the streets went into the manufacture of these nets. Boats came up from the south coast to buy nets for sale to the fishermen down there.

The streets of Taizhou were not only narrow, but were paved with small cobblestones and were very rough. The most common vehicle for transport in the city was the wheelbarrow. The wheelbarrow used in our area of north Jiangsu was very interesting. The iron-rimmed wheel was about two and a half feet in diameter There was a frame that covered the wheel and a platform on either side just above the axle. Handles extended back from the platform. Usually there was a strap that passed from the end of the handles up over the shoulders of the man pushing the wheelbarrow. Loads were balanced on the platforms so that the center of gravity was over the wheel; thus the man pushing the load carried little of the weight, but used his strength to guide it. Water was brought into the city on wheelbarrows equipped with oval tubs occupying the two platforms, and similarly, night soil (human excreta) was carried out to vats in the fields for use as fertilizer. Sometimes a seat was placed on one side and the barrow was used to transport a person, with his belongings strapped on the opposite side to balance him. Patients were frequently brought to the hospital in this manner. Stones about two feet long laid end to end down the center of the street made a path for the wheelbarrows. These became grooved by the metal rims. When two barrows met, there were often loud arguments over which one would have to move out of the groove to let the other pass. The rule was that the most heavily loaded barrow had the right of way. Pedestrian traffic filled the streets most of the time. There were a few bicycles and rare rickshaws. A bedridden patient brought to the hospital might be transported on a makeshift stretcher consisting of a door or a shallow wicker drying tray slung on ropes from a pole carried on two men's shoulders.

After the other missionaries left, the Richardsons and I, along with the French Catholic priest, were the only foreigners in the city. We didn't have a great deal of contact with the priest, though he, or one of the Chinese nuns, would occasionally bring patients to the clinic. We invited him for dinner on special U.S. holidays, July Fourth and Thanksgiving. Conversation was a bit difficult, as we didn't speak French and he didn't speak English. We had to converse in Chinese, he with a strong French accent superimposed on the north Jiangsu dialect, and we with our southern American accents.

Culinary Delights

Rice is the principal staple in south China, whereas wheat products, such as dumplings, breads, and noodles, predominate in north China. Around Taizhou we had both. Many of the fields produced three crops a year, winter wheat, beans, and rice. Buckwheat, millet, and rape were also widely grown, the latter for production of rapeseed oil, commonly used for cooking. For breakfast cereal we often had cracked wheat or millet. Puffed rice was also available. This was produced on the street by a man using what looked like a short mortar, a short fat cylinder with one end closed and rounded. The other end had a pressure cover that was secured with quick release clips. The rice was placed inside, and the cylinder was tilted up so that the rice was in the closed end. This was heated with a kerosene pressure stove. A gauge indicated when the pressure in the mortar had risen to the proper point. The mortar was then tilted down into a reinforced bag. With the quick release of the lid, there was an explosion and the bag filled with puffed grains of rice, literally shot from a gun.

I enjoyed Chinese breakfast on occasion. This consisted of a bowl of soupy rice gruel which was eaten with a number of condiments, including shredded dried meat or fish, pickled or dried turnips, pickled or boiled peanuts, "thousand year" eggs (lime eggs), duck eggs pickled in brine, or *doufujiang* (soybean cheese). The first really gourmet and unusual dish we enjoyed after arriving in China was at Jiaxing. Here we were invited to a dinner where we were served *yipinggu* (all in one pot). This was said to be the traditional dish served to Confucian scholars on successful completion of their examinations. It consisted of a large tureen of hot soup in which was swimming a whole chicken, a fresh pork roast, and a ham. They were all so tender that they were falling apart. As we were the guests of honor, the choice pieces were fished out and placed in our bowls. These consisted of the chicken's head and big chunks of fat. Katie kept slipping the fat out of her bowl into mine. Etiquette required that I eat it all, which was difficult to accomplish.

In Beijing, "Peking duck" is a well-known delicacy. We became equally fond of a Mongolian dish called *cauyangrou* (grilled lamb). The Beijing restaurant that served this was on the third floor above an arcade, with a lot of little shops and tables of goods, like a flea market. We reached it by means of a flight of narrow wooden stairs, not without concern about the fire hazard! The lamb was cut into thin strips and marinated in a mixture of wine, soya sauce, and herbs. We cooked the lamb on a grill over a charcoal brazier that was set in the middle of the table. Then the mixture was placed in a sesame seed bun and eaten like a hamburger. Flavor and aroma were out of this world!

Some of the fruits were special. In Beijing, big sweet persimmons, resembling large tomatoes, were stored and lasted well into the winter. In Taizhou we enjoyed a crisp pear that came from Shandong Province. There was also pomelo, which is similar to grapefruit, but with a loose skin that is easily peeled. The segments can be separated like a tangerine.

The principal meat available in Taizhou was pork. Each spring, the hospital purchased a couple of shoats and fed them on table scraps. At Christmas and at China New Year, one of the hogs was slaughtered for a feast for the hospital staff. Zhenjiang and Yangzhou both had Moslem communities. Beef was available there, since the Moslems did not eat pork. Some of our Chinese friends knew we liked beef, so occasionally when they went to Yangzhou, they would bring us some. Chicken, duck, wild pheasant, fish, and freshwater shrimp were usually available. The seasonal shad came up the Yangzi in the spring to spawn. This tasty fish, filled with tiny bones, was not protected by law and was thus fair game for the fishermen.

One of Taizhou's specialties is *shizitou* (lions' heads). These were large, fatty meat balls, made with a mixture of crab and pork, that were served with Chinese cabbage. Xiao Gu, the hospital chef, was always coming up with new dishes, but one dish that was repeated at nearly every special dinner was *babaofan* (eight precious foods). This was a dish of very sweet glutinous rice which contained dried fruits and lotus seeds. Another special dish was similar to Mongolian hot pot, but instead of having the fire come up through a chimney in the center, there was a large tureen with a trough around the bottom into which alcohol was poured, then burned. The flame curled up around the outside, giving it the name of "chrysanthemum dish." Slivers of meat, chicken, and shredded vegetables were cooked in the boiling soup by the diners, using their chopsticks.

Xiao Gu also prepared a very good shrimp toast, a dish one sometimes sees in Hong Kong when one eats *dim sum* (in Mandarin, *dianxin*, meaning

Kitchen crew, hospital chef Xiao Gu on left, Taizhou 1949.

"little hearts"). This is a collection of small finger foods such as dumplings, chicken wings, ribs, and the like.

It may sound as if we were living like kings, but these foods were only eaten on special occasions. This was not the usual fare. At times food was scarce and expensive. In fact, because of this, some of the staff contracted to have some soybean milk brought in about midmorning each day. I joined them in this. To make it more palatable, I would add some ice cream powder mix from war surplus goods to make a milk shake, which I had to drink warm. At the Richardsons, on rare occasions, we had real ice cream. This depended on getting ice from the icehouse. In winter, ice was harvested off the canals and stored in underground depots. The ice was used primarily to chill fish for shipment. One section of the icehouse was opened at a time. Sometimes we could get enough ice to use the ice cream freezer.

Sarah Walkup Hospital

Many problems arose relative to the operation of the hospital. I have already mentioned the difficulty of assembling a staff. As time went on, several more nurses joined us. The first year, I was able to recruit Dr. Wang Hulun, a newly graduated young woman. Dr. Miriam Li had been in the States for study. On her return, she and her friend Sarah Pan, a laboratory technician, joined the staff. The second year, Dr. Huang Siren was lent to us by Zhenjiang hospital and decided to stay. He had been a classmate of Dr. Wang, and had studied for two years in Bible school before going into medicine, so was a great addition to the staff. We could not meet the requirements for a nursing school, but did recruit eight young women to train as nurses' aides. At the beginning, we employed a couple of cooks who had worked for missionaries. Soon we had an application from Xiao Gu, the son of a former employee of one of the missionaries. He had been trained as a hotel chef, but wanted to work for the mission. This was a real godsend. The quality of the food improved

Doctors Zhuo, Nelson, and Wang, Taizhou 1949.

tremendously. Any time anyone connected with the mission or the hospital gave a dinner or a feast, they would borrow Xiao Gu to prepare the meal.

The major hospital problem was financial. Inflation was so rampant that exchange rates changed not daily, but hourly. Charges for hospitalization and for operations were based on the price of rice. We provided food for the patients. There were three rates. Third class patients who were in the large wards received a very basic diet. Second class, who were in two- to four-bed wards, received somewhat better food. First class, or private patients, were in two-bed rooms, in which a family member occupied the second bed. Both patient and attendant received hospital food. We had to send out to obtain the current price of rice twice a day, when someone was ready to settle accounts. Sometimes patients paid in actual rice. For outpatients the charges were based on the price of a *xiaobing* (the common sesame seed bun). A new chart was the price of three buns, return visit one bun. One could pay the price of five buns and be put up at the head of the line. Some patients demanded to see a specified doctor, most often the foreign doctor; this cost ten buns. We didn't change this price daily, but when there began to be too many of the higher paid visits, we knew it was time to adjust the price. I would then send out to learn the current price of a bun.

Money was losing value so fast that I also had to adjust the way we paid salaries. We began paying salaries twice a month instead of monthly. The first week of the month, the hospital bought needed fuel, rice, and drugs. The second week we would try to accumulate enough to meet the mid-month payroll. The third week we would again buy frantically, and the fourth week again save for the end of the month payroll. I felt we had planned correctly, if there was not quite enough to meet the payroll when it was due, as there were always a couple of the staff willing to wait a day or so to be paid.

There were three men in the accounting department. Mr. Liu, the chief accountant, was an old Chinese merchant. The two others were in the admitting office and collected the outpatient fees. When a patient registered, he was given a stick numbered in sequence. The sticks for different fees were of different colors. In this way, we could take them in order of registration, seeing first the ones who had paid extra. At the end of each clinic day, the fees of each doctor were tabulated according to the sticks. This had to tally with the total at the admitting office. Everything that involved finances or supplies had to have a system of checks and balances. I took accounts with Mr. Liu every day. We had an old adding machine that was very cumbersome and I used it only when I had to have a tape record for monthly reports. Ordinarily I would add figures with paper and pencil. Frequently my total would not agree with Mr. Liu's and I would have to add again. He would rapidly whip out the answer on his abacus and wait for me to finish. One day I became exasperated and asked him, "How long would it take you to teach me to use the abacus?" "Oh," he replied, "you could learn in a day or so." I immediately asked him to buy me one. True to his word, he showed me a little exercise that let me learn to add and subtract quickly and with ease. From that day on I used the abacus, even after we went to Africa, until it was replaced by the hand-held electronic calculator.

From time to time, when taking accounts with Mr. Liu, an item appeared irregularly for a contribution to the volunteer fire department. I questioned this a couple of times, but as it was a small amount, I let it pass. One day while making rounds, I heard the dinner bell ringing frantically. Since it was not mealtime, I hurried out to see what was the matter. The brick stoves in the kitchen were built against one wall, and the fires were fed straw from a room back of the stoves. This room had been stacked high with newly bought straw. A spark had popped out and started a fire. Flames were reaching to the roof. About the time I got there, the volunteer fire brigade arrived, pulling the hand-drawn pump, which resembled an old railroad handcar, with a rocker handle pumped by two men, one on each end of the handle. The kitchen was adjacent to the old canal which was just outside the wall. The intake hose was thrown into the canal and the firemen started pumping furiously. In a very short time, they had put out the fire, saving our kitchen building. I never did complain again about contributions to the fire department. I now understood that it was the custom for everyone in the neighborhood to pay a little each time anyone needed the volunteer firemen's services.

Mr. Liu bought straw for fuel for the hospital kitchen, weighing it with the old Chinese balance stick. A weight was moved along the graduated stick to achieve a balance. Rice was bought in the hull by volume, since it kept better that way. We had it hulled and polished, a little at a time, as needed. To store the rice, long mats about two to three feet wide were used. One was

The accountant, Mr. Liu, buying straw for kitchen fuel, Taizhou 1949.

placed on edge and secured to form a circle, and the rice was poured into the middle. Before it reached the top edge, another mat was placed inside, overlapping with the lower mat, and more rice was poured in. This could be repeated several times so that the rice was contained in a round cylinder five or six feet tall and eight to ten feet in diameter.

Pete Richardson was a constant help as my able mentor. Knowing the local people and their ways, he helped to assemble some of the old staff and to screen and choose the accountants and some of the other workers. Initially, I used a committee of key personnel to advise me with major problems as they arose—Mr. Liu, chief accountant; Chen Zi, head nurse; Tang Xiaojie, pharmacist; Tang Da, maintenance man; and later Dr. Li and Sarah Pan, lab technician. As time went on, it became apparent that our days as missionaries were numbered. We decided to set up a hospital board, separate from the staff, to oversee the hospital. There was no Christian medical doctor in town who was not associated with the hospital. There were a number of men with various levels of preparation who were practicing Western-style medicine. The largest number had been trained as nurses at Sarah Walkup Hospital. The early nurses had all been men. A couple of them were asked to serve on the board along with the pastor and the director of the school. Dr. Zhang Zhiqing, pediatrician on the staff at Zhenjiang, was also named to the board, being a native of Taizhou. When the board first met, he was elected chairman. The board met twice before I left in February 1951. At the second meeting, a few months before my departure, Dr. Miriam Li was named director of the hospital and I became her associate.

Weather in Taizhou tended toward the extremes. Being in the coastal plain and close to the Yangzi, it was nearly always very humid. In summer I carried a fan and used it constantly. At night it was hard to sleep on a sheet, so a rush mat was laid over the sheet and I would go to sleep fanning. Winters were cold and damp. There was no heat in the houses or hospital, with the exception that, at the hospital, a small kerosene space heater was placed in the dressing room adjacent to my examining room. It was moved into the X-ray room on the days I took X-rays. This allowed the patients to disrobe sufficiently to be examined. We also had a potbellied stove in one end of the operating room to take the chill off. Since we used primarily spinal and

Doctor with Big Shoes (author), left, and the Reverend R. P. Richardson on steps of Morningside, Taizhou, Winter 1949.

local anesthesia, we got by with that. At the Richardsons, we ate breakfast and lunch in the dining room, the meal being cooked in an outside kitchen on a Chinese stove. I can recall eating breakfast with the temperature below freezing in the room. In the evening, we had a small stove in an upstairs bedroom where Gu Er, the cook, would heat up the supper. There we could relax in a little warmth. During the winter, I wore a long Chinese robe that reached to my ankles and was padded with raw silk. In addition, I wore "long handled underwear" with heavy pants and a sweater underneath the robe, and a Russian style fur hat. On my feet I wore ski boots that I had bought in a war surplus store in New Haven, Connecticut. These had box-shaped toes and soles almost an inch thick. They came with two pairs of thick felt inner soles which could be changed and worn on alternate days. I thus became known as the "doctor with big shoes" or "the doctor with boxes on his feet." On rounds I carried a hot water bottle in a flannel cover to warm my hands so that I could examine the patients. Clothed in their thickly padded garments and covered with heavy comforts, their examination was difficult, even at best.

Taizhou nurses, Chen Zi, Feng Da, Wang San, and Feng Liu, Taizhou 1949.

There was a generator in town that provided electricity for a few hours each night. We subscribed to the service, which left much to be desired. The circuits were so overloaded that the voltage, which was supposed to be 110, was usually only about 80. We had a small suction machine for use in the operating room. I needed a transformer in order to step up the voltage sufficiently to run the machine. None was available in town and I could not go to Shanghai. Tang Da came up with the solution. He found a man in town who had been trained as an electrical engineer. When he came, he assured me that he could build a transformer that could do the task, and he did! We also ran a line from the portable X-ray generator to the operating room to give us power when the city generator was not in service.

In 1949, when the Communists took over the newer building, the operating room had to be moved to the old building. Shortly thereafter, I noticed that the floor was shaky when we rolled the operating table to a new position. I checked and discovered that the wall was sagging outward and the floor joists were pulling out of the wall. This room faced the open courtyard. To correct the problem, we got some logs that were a little longer than the width of the courtyard, and placed them at the level of the floor of the second story, forcing them into place and bracing this wall against the wall on the other side of the courtyard. This forced the wall back into place and supported it, making the floor firm again. We also moved the operating room to one of the larger ward rooms.

Medical Problems

A few medical patients stand out in my memory. We had initially planned to open the inpatient wards a couple of weeks after beginning the outpatient

Pharmicist Tang Xiaojie, Taizhou 1949.

clinic. We had to admit the first inpatient ahead of schedule for an emergency appendectomy. We first opened the patient rooms on the second and third floors of the newest building. Later we opened the patient rooms on the top floor of the old building, for tuberculosis patients. When we first started treating tuberculosis, no specific medication was available. Bed rest and supportive medications were the only treatment. Later we began to get streptomycin.

One day in clinic I was seeing a patient and suddenly realized he must be suffering from leprosy. Our laboratory technician, Mr. Song, had trained in Nantong at the Dutch Reformed Mission Hospital, where there had been a leprosy treatment program, before World War II. I called him in to see the patient, and he confirmed my impression that it looked like leprosy. He knew how to take the proper smears. They were positive. I had met Dr. Eugene R. Kellersberger when he passed through Shanghai on his trip around the world for the American Leprosy Missions. I wrote to him and he put me in contact with the British Leprosy Mission in Hong Kong which furnished drugs for China. Sulfones were just beginning to be used. When we received the drugs and began treatments, more and more patients with leprosy appeared at the clinic. Finally, to relieve the regular clinic and to allay the fears of other patients, I started a separate clinic for the treatment of leprosy once a week in a basement storeroom, accessible from the back of the hospital building. As far as I could determine, these were the first leprosy patients to receive treatment in Taizhou. By the time I left, I had diagnosed over two hundred patients, most of whom came regularly for treatment.

Cholera was endemic. Cases occurred annually with the advent of hot weather. The main treatment was to replace the fluids lost, until the infection ran its course. Intravenous fluids were difficult to transport, as plastic containers had not yet come into use. They were also expensive, so we had to produce our own. We did not have a proper autoclave and were using a large pressure cooker, heated by a charcoal brazier, fanned with a wooden bellows.

*Orderly Sen Er sterilizing
with pressure cooker heated by
charcoal brazier and wooden
bellows, Taizhou 1949.*

I had sent Katie a picture of Sen Er, the operating room orderly, using this to sterilize operating room supplies. She showed this picture to one of the women's groups where she was speaking, at First Presbyterian Church in Greensboro, North Carolina. The ladies were appalled and immediately gave the money for a new autoclave. I ordered a larger upright autoclave from Shanghai that could be heated by charcoal or by a kerosene pressure stove. It arrived just in time to be put to use sterilizing I.V. solutions for the treatment of an outbreak of cholera.

Cholera immunizations needed to be repeated annually. Each spring I obtained vaccine and tried to immunize all the staff, as the risk of coming into contact with patients was great. One summer, one of our orderlies came down with a severe case of cholera. He had avoided getting immunized. We saved him by the hardest. It would have been impossible without the fluids provided by the new autoclave.

I had received very little training in surgery. I had assisted my father a great deal and had rotated through general surgery, gynecology, and urology during my internship. My father had given me his twelve-volume set of *Nelson's Practice of Surgery*. This was an invaluable aid. Whenever I had a problem that I had not faced before, I would make a careful study of it. I had a stand built similar to a music stand, so that I could have an anatomy text and the surgery text in the operating room for reference. This enabled me to perform some rather complex major operations with success.

One day a twelve-year-old boy came with an old fracture of the right elbow. He had come about one hundred miles, from the northern part of Jiangsu Province. He had fractured the lower end of the humerus, but it had not been set. It healed in such a way that a fragment was blocking the joint from bending, leaving his arm straight out in complete extension. He asked if I could fix it so he could eat and write. I told him to come back the next day after I had a chance to study the problem. A complete description of an arthroplasty (remaking the joint) of the elbow was in the surgery set. I told him I would try, but could not guarantee how good the results might be.

Girl writing letter home,
Sarah Walkup Hospital,
Taizhou 1949.

I thought that at worst he would be left with his arm flexed at an angle, instead of straight. The operation was quite complicated, requiring a graft of fascia from the thigh, excision of the fragment blocking the joint, reshaping of the joint surfaces, and then lining them with the fascia. When I was in the middle of the operation with the joint wide open, Chen Zi looked at me as if she thought that I would never get it put back together. To my joy and the satisfaction of the boy, it worked. In fact it worked so well that several months later he sent me another patient with a somewhat similar problem.

Not all our efforts ended happily. There was a man who baked *xiaobing* at the street corner near the Richardsons, where I passed him every day. One day he came to the hospital because he had been in a fight over a bucket of ashes. He had been struck in the side and was complaining of tenderness over the spleen. I had never done a splenectomy and was hesitant to operate. I took the "conservative" approach of observing him, having him return daily for examination. Everything seemed all right for several days. One day he did not show up for clinic and someone came to say they could not arouse him. I immediately sent our orderlies with the stretcher to get him. We rushed him to the operating room, forced I.V. fluids, and operated immediately. Unfortunately he had lost too much blood from a ruptured spleen and died on the table.

Shortly after the Communists took Taizhou, a woman in uniform came to the clinic. She had suffered a wound of the calf in north China. This had healed, leaving her with a shortened heel cord (Achilles' tendon). She was unable to put her foot flat on the ground, and asked me to fix it. Theoretically, I knew how to do a heel cord lengthening, though I had never seen one done. Considering the patient's identity, I was hesitant to attempt the procedure. She insisted, so I tried it with fear and trembling. Happily it was successful.

A number of "tropical diseases" were endemic in the area. Intestinal parasites such as ascaris and hookworm, were common. We occasionally saw profound anemia due to the latter. We saw a few patients with malaria, but most of them had acquired the infection further south. The Yangzi River was roughly the dividing line between the areas where schistosomiasis (liver fluke

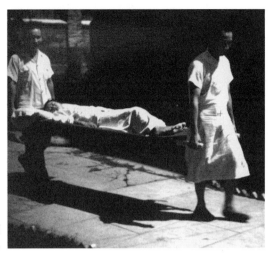

*Sen Er's daughter transported
on stretcher, Taizhou 1949.*

infestation) and kala-azar (sandfly fever) were endemic. Schistosomiasis was prevalent south of the river. The intermediate host was a small snail that lived in the canals. A person became infected with the parasite, which can penetrate the skin, by coming in contact with infested water. The Goldsby King Memorial Hospital in Zhenjiang was on the bank of the Grand Canal, which was heavily infested with the snail and the parasite. They treated large numbers for this disease, but we saw only occasional cases at Taizhou. Kala-azar, a parasite transmitted by the sandfly, was endemic in north Jiangsu and Shandong Provinces and we saw a few of these cases as well. Superficially, the patients were somewhat similar, as they both developed very large livers and accumulated large quantities of abdominal fluid. Even rarer in our area were two other flukes that were diagnosed in our laboratory. They were the two flukes that live in the gall bladder and bile ducts, which are transmitted by eating raw seafood. These are endemic in south China. They were found in fisher folk who had come to Taizhou to buy fish nets.

Another uncommon disease attacked the daughter of Sen Er, the O.R. orderly. This was a strange ascending paralysis, which I diagnosed as Guillain-Barré Syndrome. The cause was unknown. Fortunately for her, the condition arrested before her respiratory muscles were affected and she eventually recovered.

We did not have the facilities to do a lot of bacteriology examinations, so some of our diagnoses had to be presumptive. One case showed up with all the symptoms and signs of bubonic plague, which is a flea-borne disease. I placed him in a small ward that we had just prepared to open, and kept him isolated. I became really concerned when he developed pneumonia, because if it were plague, it could become an air-borne infection in this stage. We increased the isolation to include gowns, gloves, and masks, and restricted access to his ward. Fortunately, no one else came down with it, and he recovered.

Sometimes the doctor gets sick, too. The first time for me was before the Communist takeover. I developed an infection in my right wrist. The only antibiotics we had were sulfa drugs and limited quantities of crystalline penicillin. This type of penicillin must be given intramuscularly every four hours and is quite painful. It would bring tears to my eyes for the nurse to step into the room with the next injection. The infection became a large abscess, and then started to spread up my arm with a couple of smaller satellite abscesses. I became concerned that I might develop septicemia and decided that I needed to have the abscesses lanced. Dr. Zhuo declined to do it, as he was afraid he would be blamed if anything went wrong. Finally I persuaded Chen Zi to help me. For anesthesia, she froze it with ethyl chloride and I had to lance it myself, using my left hand. The second time I became ill, I had a high fever and terrific bone and joint pains. I suspect it may have been a case of dengue fever, also known as "breakbone fever" because of the pains. During both illnesses, the staff was very supportive and concerned.

One incident gave me a big boost. An old gentleman, blind with cataracts, came to my consultation. He began with the traditional polite phrases, "What's your honorable name?" I replied, "My name is Ni," giving my Chinese name. He then said , "Where is your honorable old home?" I replied, "My old home is Huzhou," where I was born. We continued with the consultation and I wrote out a prescription. Before leaving, he turned to the young nurse aide who was helping me and said, "But I paid to see the foreign doctor." I can't claim that my Chinese was that good. He must have attributed my accent to the fact that I had told him I was from an area that does not speak mandarin.

The most harrowing experience occurred one afternoon after the Communist takeover. A teacher from the Communist school with a group of his students rushed in bringing a student who was struggling to breathe. He was very cyanotic and almost comatose. Something was obstructing his airway, allowing only a small amount of air to pass into the lungs. We rushed him to the operating room, but could not see the obstruction, using the laryngoscope. The boy's family was not available so we had to rely on authorization of the teacher to proceed. I quickly performed a tracheotomy. To my dismay the obstruction was below the tracheotomy site. We had no bronchoscope, so I was in a dilemma. We had been in such a rush that we had not stopped to pray before starting the surgery. I paused and asked Chen Zi to pray. While she was praying, I remembered that in our sigmoidoscope set, there was a metal child's sigmoidoscope that was small enough to fit into the trachea. I asked Chen Zi to get it and sterilize it quickly. Using the sigmoidoscope, I could see a pale flesh colored object. Using a long probe, I was able to dislodge the object and push it to one side, allowing air to pass more freely. I had no instrument that I could pass down the sigmoidoscope, with which to grasp the object. I finally gave up and withdrew the sigmoidoscope, since he was getting sufficient air and his color had improved. Suddenly he became completely obstructed and unable to exchange any air. I quickly reinserted the scope, but had some difficulty opening the airway again. Chen Zi went out and told the teacher and his classmates that the boy seemed to be dead. Finally, the object was dislodged sufficiently for him to breathe, but there was still no way to remove it. Once again I withdrew the sigmoidoscope. Suddenly he gave a cough and woke up, exclaiming, "It's in my mouth, Doctor." The object was the inner part of a water chestnut. When enough air had gotten behind it, he was able to expel it. The students had been swimming in the canal. The chestnut was floating in the water, and he had inadvertently aspirated it.

Behind the Bamboo Curtain

When the Communist troops first came into the city, they displayed the red flag with hammer and sickle that appeared to be identical with the Russian flag. This did not go over well with the people, since one of their chief Communist slogans was "Down with imperialism." Other slogans which appeared as posters on walls throughout the city were, "Equality," "Protection of industry," "Freedom of religion," and "Down with capitalism." The church was not spared. The Communists made everyone attend indoctrination sessions. They demanded the use of the church for their meetings. The elders could not refuse the use of the building, but insisted on retaining it for worship on Sunday morning, so we continued to have services there, though the walls were placarded with slogans.

Shortly after the city was taken by the Communists, we attempted to call on the official in charge of the city, as we had called on the mayor when we first arrived. We were told he was busy and to wait. We waited about two hours, and then we were told he was too busy to see us that day. We tried a second time, with the same results. This remained the pattern. No one in authority would see us in an official capacity. I did see a number of Communist patients in consultation. They all wore the same uniforms, with no insignia. They would usually come in a group. I could tell by the reaction of my staff that there was someone of importance among them, but could never tell for sure which one it was. They were often difficult to treat, as they carried the slogan of "equality" to the extreme, and did not seem to put much faith in my advice or knowledge of medicine.

Propaganda posters on wall in front of hospital, Taizhou 1951.

A few days after the turnover, I was called to the front gate because soldiers were demanding to be quartered in the hospital. The officer in charge was a short fellow about five feet tall. I argued with him that the hospital was a place for the sick, but he was adamant. He threatened to use his pistol to blow the locks off the doors if I wouldn't open them. So I lost that round. At that time we had opened the top two floors of the newer building for patients. The soldiers took over the ground floor and stabled their horses in the dining pavilion. We had to pass by the rooms they were occupying to go upstairs to the patient rooms. This group stayed about a week or ten days.

Soon another group demanded to be quartered in the hospital. This group of young boys and girls was to be trained for six weeks as medical workers. We had just cleaned up the wards in the basement of the old building. They took over these wards for a month, with all of them sleeping there.

One dark moonless night, after an evening at the Richardsons, I stepped out of the front gate. I heard a voice challenging, "Who goes there?" I replied that I was the hospital director and was returning to the hospital. I advanced a few steps, and again was challenged, "Who goes there?" I repeated my reply and took a few more steps, almost reaching the corner. For a third time I received the same challenge. I held up the kerosene lantern I was carrying so that it shone on my face and finally located where the voice was coming from. A young soldier, who appeared to be in his early teens, was sitting on a window sill with a big rifle pointed in my direction. I again explained in more detail who I was and where the hospital was located. I turned the corner and walked across the bridge and on toward the hospital as slowly and deliberately as I could, conscious all the while of the rifle at my back. The next morning, I found out that a new company of soldiers had come into town and were quartered in the temple behind the Richardsons' house. Sentries had been placed in all the streets surrounding the bivouac.

The Communists had taken all the territory down to the Yangzi River. We could hear the cannons shelling back and forth across the river at night. The Nationalists started daily air raids. A couple of planes would come over just about the time clinic was to begin in the afternoon. The soldiers in the city would start shooting rifles and machine guns, though I don't think they really had any antiaircraft weapons. They made an awful din. We had to shift our clinic hours to later in the day. Even so, whenever the water pipes started knocking, people would dive under the tables, thinking the planes were coming. The planes dropped incendiary and fragmentation bombs, usually in the northern sector of the city around the canal docks. We had a number of burned and wounded patients to treat as a result. Fortunately, no bombs were dropped near the hospital. The building was so prominent that I am sure the Nationalist pilots were aware that it was the hospital.

Soldiers kept wandering through the hospital at all times of the day. I even had to chase them out of the operating room. We finally complained to the official in charge. He replied that many of the soldiers had come from the countryside and had never seen a multistory building. A new company had just arrived in town and had not had an opportunity to visit the hospital. He arranged to have them come all at one time and get it over with.

The next morning about six hundred came and camped in the hospital yard, taking turns in groups of twenty-five to visit the hospital. I was afraid of what might happen if the Nationalist planes came over while they were in the yard, but they left before the daily air raid.

Before attempting to cross the Yangzi and take the big industrial cities south of the river, the Communists took time to regroup and consolidate their territory. They drafted young men into their army and set about putting their soldiers in new uniforms. To do this, they required contributions from the local population. Each work unit and guild was given a quota, and they in turn set quotas for the individuals. Individuals who failed to meet their quotas were harassed until they complied.

Getting funds for the hospital was a problem, since the treasurer's office in Shanghai was still using the Nationalist *yuan* and we were using Communist *renminbi*. This currency problem was somewhat alleviated when Mr. Farrior, the treasurer, was able to send us a few small gold bars. Some patients also paid us in gold, so we had to have a jewelers' scale to weigh it. The hospital accounts for the year 1949 were a mess. They were in U.S. dollars, Nationalist *yuan*, Communist *renminbi*, and gold.

Regular communications were cut off until the Communists moved south of the river. We received letters once, which were weeks old, when a post office was captured that had some mail sacks for Taizhou. When the Communists moved south of the river, the collapse of the Nationalists was rapid and complete. The most able and talented Communist officials were busy gaining control of the big industrial centers. It was interesting to see how the local officials went about getting control. Everyone was assigned to a work unit or guild and required to attend meetings for indoctrination. In many units, such as schools, all the teachers were put in uniforms. Then a couple of the teachers were chosen and sent off to an indoctrination course for a month. When the training was completed, they were sent back, not to their original schools, but to other schools. Suddenly the teachers were confronted with new faces, in Communist uniforms, quoting the Communist line. Everyone was afraid to express his real opinion. Children were encouraged to report any reactionary speech or conduct of their teachers or their parents.

"Kangaroo courts" were held, accusing landlords and other affluent people of exploiting the proletariat. Many were summarily condemned and executed by firing squads. The schoolchildren were sometimes required to witness the public executions. Mr. Li, the owner of the flour mill, lived next door to the hospital. He had the mill taken from him and was harassed, but was still living when we left Taizhou. He was a friend, and the last time I saw him, I was distressed to see how much weight he had lost as a result of his constant difficulties and worries.

Following the flight of the Nationalists from south China, the Communists immediately began preparing for an invasion of Taiwan, assembling an armada of junks to transport the troops. They realized that a number would be sunk by the Nationalist planes. Many of their troops came from north China and did not know how to swim. They began to teach them to swim in the streams and canals, without considering the fact that these waters were heavily infested with schistosomes (flukes), mentioned earlier. One stage of the parasite is a free-swimming larva which enters through the intact skin when one comes in contact with infested water. The adult fluke lives in the veins of the liver. They soon had so many troops suffering from acute schistosomiasis that it upset their timetable, and they had to cancel the invasion. Many hospitals throughout the country were required to send at least one physician to aid in the treatment. I saw some of the soldiers who had been discharged because of the disease.

Another facet of the preparation that affected our area was the stocking of grain to feed the invasion force. Large granaries were built. Such heavy levies of grain were placed on the farmers, that there was not enough food for the population during the winter. I saw many starving and malnourished at that time. In fact, we saw several with intestinal obstruction from eating clay, just to have something in their stomachs. In nearby towns there were several food riots, with mobs attacking the granaries. With the delay in invasion plans, the rice that had been stored was then dumped on the market at the time of the spring rice harvest, depressing the price of rice and adding insult to injury for the farmers.

Before an invasion could be mounted, the Korean war broke out. President Harry Truman interposed the U.S. fleet between Taiwan and the mainland. The Communists then began to shift their troops to the north and prepared to enter the war on the side of North Korea.

Occupation of the Hospital

One night, government authorities came to one of the teachers in the mission school saying that they planned to take over the newest hospital building. Yangzhou had been the Nationalists' district headquarters. When they fled south of the Yangzi, they took with them the staff and all the movable equipment of the district hospital. When the Communists took over south of the river, they captured the hospital intact. The Communists had moved the district headquarters to Taizhou, and were now planning to bring the district hospital back north of the river and place it at Taizhou. Since they had all their staff and equipment, they would require only the building. Negotiations went on for several days. They never approached anyone in the hospital directly, but always came at night to the schoolteacher. It became obvious that we would have to comply. We proposed several conditions.

> (1) That we build a wall separating the two hospital buildings. We had stocked brick that had come from the demolition of the old city wall, which could be used for this purpose. We asked that they help defray the expense of the labor.

(2) Our nurses' dormitory would be in their compound. We suggested that they swap it for the missionary residence across the street which they had occupied.

(3) Since the water tank was in the attic of the new building, we asked that they share in the cost of diesel fuel to operate the pumps.

(4) We asked for a written statement acknowledging the fact that we were freely lending the building.

We were led to believe that they agreed to these conditions. Finally, one afternoon they informed us that the district hospital would arrive to take possession of the building after three days. We could remove all of our equipment and leave the building empty. Anything left after three days would be confiscated. They claimed that the district official who would sign the paper we had requested was out of town, and that he would give it to us later. This never happened. Neither did they contribute to the cost of the wall, nor swap buildings as requested.

When they announced their plans to move in, I immediately called the contractor who frequently worked for us, and showed him where I wanted the wall. I sited this carefully, so that the well and pump house were on our side. I asked him how long it would take to build the wall. He estimated it would take "150 man days work." I said, "Fine, you have three days. Can you have 50 men on the job in the morning?" He looked at me in disbelief. I assured him I meant what I said, and he agreed to do it.

We were using the wards on the top floor of the old building for tuberculosis patients. I immediately discharged all of them. We started cleaning up those rooms and began moving equipment from the new building to the old. We moved operating room, X-ray, beds, and furniture all during the daylight hours. At night, we closed the gates of the compound and moved stores from the attic to the attics of the old building and the doctor's residence. We were able to accommodate all the general patients in the basement wards and top floor rooms of the old building. There was an old operating room on the top floor. I converted one of the consultation rooms on the main floor to an X-ray room and built a dark room adjacent to it. The work on the wall went on while we were

Wall constructed in three days to divide compound, Taizhou 1949.

doing the moving. A gap was left in the wall through which we moved equipment and supplies. Late on the third day, we moved the last bed through the gap. The workmen quickly put up the rest of the wall. After things had settled down, we were able to reopen a tuberculosis ward by renting two courts of a Chinese residence next door to the hospital. We simply opened a door through the wall to allow access from our compound.

The morning after the wall was closed, a group of Communist officials came marching in the front gate and were brought abruptly to a halt at the wall, which prevented them from going back to the new building. They were astonished to find a solid wall where three days before there had been a walkway. They had to go back out the front gate and around the block to come in the back gate. We began pumping water only into the surface tank and stopped pumping into the tank in the top of the new building, waiting for them to supply some diesel fuel. We had to carry all our water in buckets to the hospital. This went on for a couple of weeks. One night we had a terrific rain. It was reported that some of the wall surrounding their portion of the compound had collapsed. I still felt responsible for the mission property, so I called the contractor again. We made an inspection tour around outside of the walls. We ended up on the east side near a well beside the old canal. The Communists had opened a gate in the wall and one of their workmen was drawing water from the well. I was discussing with the contractor the repairs that needed to be done. The workman began complaining in a loud voice, so I could hear, that he had to carry water from the well, though the hospital had nice plumbing which was useless because there was no water. I finally turned and told him that there could be water any time that his hospital decided to fulfill their agreement to supply some diesel fuel. That afternoon, a barrel of fuel appeared. Thereafter, whenever we began to run low, we would let them know and they would send more fuel.

Interaction with the New Regime

After the district hospital moved in, we could see over the wall into their compound from the rear of the old building. Their doctors and nurses were required to do manual labor in the yard of the hospital and to dig a garden as part of the policy of equality. One day the medical director sent a request for us to take some X-rays for them, as they did not have a machine in operation. We had very limited supplies of film and I was having to resort to using fluoroscopic examinations for most of the cases. One afternoon a week, however, I scheduled routine X-ray examinations, so I agreed to do cases for them as well. This worked out satisfactorily.

At another time the doctor sent me a request to come for a consultation. I went over and they showed me a young man on whom they had done an appendectomy. He continued to run fever and was not doing well. I examined him and there seemed to be a tender mass in the area of the appendix. I asked whether or not they routinely counted sponges. They said they didn't, but were confident that nothing had been left behind. I observed that it appeared as though he had an abscess and advised an exploration to drain it. Several days later I was making rounds when one of the nurses came running very excitedly saying that there were some Communist soldiers downstairs asking for me. I went to see what they wanted. It was a group of six young men. They said they were engineers and were classmates of the young man for whom I had been consulted. They had come from Shanghai to see what had gone wrong. They said they understood I had advised an operation, but the doctor would not do it without a transfusion. They wanted to know if we had a professional donor list. I said we didn't, but required families to provide donors. I asked what type blood was needed. They said the patient was type O. I asked if one of them could give blood. They claimed that none of them were the right type. I knew this wasn't likely, since O is the most common type. In any case, I told them I would see what I could do. I discouraged our staff from giving blood routinely, since they were exposed to so much illness and nutrition was a problem. I knew I was type O. I talked it over with the Richardsons, and we decided that all of us should offer blood. We went to our laboratory and had our blood tested. Neither of the Richardsons was type O. I had a sample of my blood drawn and sent it with a note saying I had found a donor, and, if it cross matched, the donor was willing to give the blood.

Several days later, I received a note saying they would like to give the transfusion the following afternoon at three o'clock. This was in the middle of my clinic hours, so I was concerned about how I was going to manage it. The next day was rainy and clinic was light, so I had finished by three. I slipped out the back of the hospital, went through the moon gate in front of the doctor's residence, and over to their building. When I walked in, there were a lot of astonished stares. I asked for the doctor and was taken to where they were making rounds. I inquired as to the condition of the patient. They said they had operated that morning and denied finding any foreign body. I asked if they still wanted to give the transfusion. They said, "Yes, where is the donor?" I replied, "I am the donor." Now there was general consternation. They said they would have to ask the patient if he was willing to accept my blood. We went to see the patient and they let me examine him. Finally they hesitatingly told him that I was the donor and asked his permission to proceed. I have never witnessed such an expression of joy and thanks on a patient's face. Now they were in a bind. They said they would have to get permission from the Communist administrator who was in charge of the hospital. We went to his office. At first he was unwilling to give permission without clearing it with the district officer. When he found that the district officer was out of town, he finally reluctantly gave permission.

The patient and I were taken to the operating room. We lay on stretchers side by side. The transfusion was accomplished by using 50 cubic centimeter syringes into which they drew up a small quantity of anticoagulant. They used two syringes, drawing blood from me with one and injecting it slowly into the patient while drawing another syringeful from me. They took a total of about 300 cc. instead of the usual 500 cc.

As they were about to finish, Sen Er, our O.R. orderly came looking for me. Our staff had missed me and were getting worried because I had been away so long. Whether as a result of the exploration or the transfusion, I was relieved to learn that the patient began to improve from that day on.

The next day, while I was making rounds, again a nurse came excitedly saying the Communists were back asking for me. I went down to see them, but they had gone. They had brought a gift of a basket containing four live chickens, a ham, a large Mandarin fish, and forty delicious pears. I didn't feel I could accept it and sent it back with a letter.

> Dear Friends,
> I wish to thank you for your expression of gratitude which moved me greatly. However, what I did was not for any praise for myself. Any other follower of my Lord Jesus Christ would have done the same. Certainly he gave his life for us dying on a cross, why should we not give a little of ourselves to help a brother in need? Please accept it as an expression of the friendship and love that exists between the American people and the Christians in America for the people of China.
>
> I am returning the food—your gift—to be used for the patient, as I am sure that it will do him more good than it will me. We are earnestly praying that the efforts of all concerned in his behalf will prove successful and that he will recover.

They returned the basket with a letter.

> Dearest Dr. Nelson,
> We express our deepest thanks for your enthusiastic and generous help.
>
> That you came yesterday unexpectedly to "The People's Hospital" as a voluntary donor very much astonished and moved us. We were moved to tears. We do not know how to thank you. A debt of conscience among us will never be vanished. Your noble personality lives forever in our memories and our friends! You not only help our schoolmate materially and spiritually, but also teach us an important lesson of human love— a real force cosmopolitan.
> Herewith we present you a bit of gift for nourishment after transfusion. Wish you accept that widow's coin.

Following this incident, the staff of the district hospital was forbidden to have any contact with our staff. The Communist administrator who had given permission was dismissed from his job. The moon gate was locked at night, so our nurses could not change shifts at the usual eleven o'clock hour in the evening. This forced us to readjust the shift schedule.

Late in the fall, we began to hear rumors that the district hospital was going to move back to Yangzhou. When it became pretty sure that this was the case, Pete and I paid a visit to the hospital and talked to the new Communist administrator who was in charge. We asked, since the district hospital was moving, that the building be returned to us. Interestingly, the transfusion patient was in the room, as he was being used as a messenger during his convalescence. We were told that it would not be possible to return the building, as the city hospital was to take its place.

During a Christmas party for the staff, I was surprised to see the young transfusion patient come in. He was leaving town to return to his work. He came to thank me again before leaving. He stayed to enjoy the Christmas carols and party.

One day while I was at clinic, a Communist in uniform came asking me to make a house call. It was a very busy day and there were still a number of patients waiting to be seen. I inquired as to the nature of the illness, and it sounded as if some laboratory tests were needed. I suggested that, because of this, it would be better if the patient were brought to the hospital, and I offered to send a stretcher. They declined the offer. During the night, Dr. Miriam Li, our obstetrician, called me to help her with an emergency operation for an ectopic pregnancy. Instead of coming to us, the patient had gone to the Communist hospital behind us, which was now the city hospital. The doctors of the city hospital were not as competent as those of the district hospital had been, and were afraid to operate. The patient had steadily become worse. When it became apparent that she was in danger of dying, they hurriedly brought her through the back moon gate, into our compound. I rushed to the operating room where Dr. Li was about to begin. We operated and found the abdomen full of blood. We bailed the blood out, filtered it, and gave it back as an autotransfusion. The patient recovered. It turned out that she was a high Communist official in charge of the granaries. While in the hospital, she became interested in Christianity. Dr. Li and Sarah Pan were both excellent evangelists and spent a lot of time with her. The Communists often had meetings on Sunday. In any case, because of her position, she could not come to church. Long after there was any medical need, she would come to clinic to see Dr. Li and have her explain the Bible to her.

As time went on, we became uneasy about the personnel carrier. It was painted in army colors and we were afraid that it would be an embarrassment to our Chinese colleagues after we left. It was stored in a shed that we had built against the motor room. It had not been driven since I had used it to evacuate the other missionaries. There was a flood in the north and relief supplies were being gathered for the flood victims. We took this opportunity to get rid of the truck. We offered to give it for transport of the relief supplies. Our offer was accepted. When they came to get the truck, I was afraid that we would have a hard time getting it started since it had been sitting for months.

We charged the battery and soon got it going. The wall separating the hospital compound had been built since we parked the truck in the shed. We tried driving the truck out the front gate. It would go through the gate, but the street was too narrow. It was impossible to turn into the street. We tried going through the gate forward and backward without success. There was no way except to tear a hole in the wall and build it back after the truck was gone.

One day I heard gunshots in the hospital yard. The only trees for miles around were in the mission compounds and many birds came to roost in them. I went out and approached the soldier who was shooting at the birds, telling him it was disturbing the patients. It was not until we were getting ready to leave and were called to get our travel permits that I discovered I had reprimanded the chief of police!

Christian Witness

Evangelistic witness in the hospital was accomplished in a number of ways. A daily morning worship service was attended by staff and ambulatory patients. This was led by Christian members of the staff, who took turns. All the Christians on the staff, doctors and nurses, spent time with the patients, telling them of the Gospel. Bibles were made available at the bedside. Bible study groups were organized, and those members of the staff who were not Christians were encouraged to attend. A number of them became Christians through the loving efforts of their colleagues.

Becoming a church member was not quick or easy. The church required a prolonged period of study. The session examined inquirers a couple of times a year. They considered not only their knowledge of the Bible and understanding of Christian doctrines, but they also examined their manner of life. They required the candidates to cleanse their homes of idols and to seek actively to bring others to Christ. Candidates were often turned down once or twice, before they were deemed ready for baptism. It usually took a year or more for admission to the church. Because of this policy, the strength of the church was a dedicated laity.

The Reverend R. P. Richardson (Pete) and Pastor Sang, Taizhou, Summer 1949.

Pete Richardson was no longer preaching, but he was able to continue a very effective ministry. The pastors and evangelists came to him constantly for encouragement and guidance. He was able to send Christian literature to those working in the countryside. A village north of Taizhou had their Bibles confiscated and burned and were not allowed to worship in their church. They continued to meet in the homes, reciting to each other passages of scripture they had memorized. Later a more lenient official came to their village, and Pete was able to send Bibles to them. There was great rejoicing that they once again had the Word of God.

Several families in Taizhou started having services in the home, inviting their neighbors to attend. Already they were anticipating the "house churches" that were to keep the church alive and growing during the Cultural Revolution that was to come.

The Chen family had been ruled by a matriarch who was a devout Buddhist. She had prevented the family from contact with the church while Chen Zi's older brothers were growing up. After her death, Chen Zi entered nurses' training and became a Christian. Gradually other members of the family also became Christians. Her oldest brother and his wife had long resisted. Not long before we left, he and his wife were the last members of the family to become Christians. The Chens had a service of thanksgiving and testimony at the pastor's house. Many came to rejoice with them and testify. I was amazed at how many persons credited the hospital and the witness of the staff with bringing them to Christ. It made me realize that all the troubles and agony were truly worthwhile.

Near the end of our time in Taizhou, a procession arrived at the hospital accompanied by a Chinese band, with clashing of cymbals. In contrast to the biblical one of ten, a large group of leprosy patients had come to present long silk banners, expressing thanks to "the latter day Luke."

Preparing to Leave

We had determined to stay as long as we could be effective and were not a hindrance to the Chinese Christians. They kept insisting that they wished us to stay. We had even requested permission for Katie to return. The U.S. was involved in the Korean war, however, and after the Chinese entered on the side of North Korea, conditions changed. We became enemy aliens. Reluctantly, our Chinese friends agreed that it would be in their best interest for us to leave. We requested travel papers and were required to advertise in the regional and local papers that we were leaving. Anyone with claims on us was urged to come forth. No one, however, brought charges. We had almost forgotten that we had requested permission for Katie to return, and we were astonished to receive an entry permit for her. By this time, of course, her return was no longer feasible.

Early in December 1950, we heard that our travel papers had arrived in the city. Unfortunately, this coincided with the start of a month-long anti-American campaign. The travel permits were held up until the campaign was over. The Communists had held frequent demonstrations and parades in the past, and the route had been pretty well fixed through the main streets. During this month, the routes were changed in order to pass in front of the hospital and mission school. All organizations were required to send delegations to march in the parades, so there were always a few of the hospital employees sent to the parades. I stood at the hospital gate to watch the parade pass. Spaced among the marchers were Communist cadres who would lead the chants. I recognized some of them as patients I had seen in consultation. As they passed by the hospital, they would shout, "Down with American imperialism," and then nod to me and march on.

Journey Home

The day for our departure from Taizhou finally arrived. It was a bitterly cold January day in 1951 and the ground was frozen solid. I had packed things to be shipped home and sent them to Shanghai. Before we could leave though, our hand luggage had to be inspected. We had been told that we could not take our cameras, so I had sold mine. They went through my bags with "a fine-toothed comb" to make sure that I did not take away any of the hospital instruments. We had arranged for two cars. Due to the blockade of China, gasoline was very scarce. The cars had been converted to run on wood! There was a metal contraption attached to the back of the car in which small blocks of wood were jammed into one compartment. Under this was a small firebox, the heat from which drove gases out of the wood. Frequent stops were necessary to replenish the wood in the chamber and to stoke the fire. A pipe about an inch and a half in diameter led from the top of the apparatus, over the roof of the car, and down through a hole in the hood to the carburetor. I was amazed, but it worked. Because of all the delays, we started off late in the day. As we approached the first canal, we found that the bridge had been dismantled in order for larger canal boats to be brought in to haul out grain. We had to cross the canal on a small ferry that was poled across. The ferry would only carry one car at a time, so the car with the Richardsons went on ahead. When my turn came and the driver started the car, I discovered another peculiarity of the vehicle. The transmission was stuck in gear. Before starting, the driver had to take a plate off the gearbox and knock the gears apart. There were several more canals; at each crossing the whole process had to be repeated. Our travel documents read that we were to go by way of Yangzhou to Zhenjiang. With all the delays, it was late in the afternoon by the time my car approached Yangzhou. The Richardsons were nowhere to be seen. The road turned south to the river just outside Yangzhou, so I continued on, without going into the city, to avoid missing the ferry, which did not run after dark. I arrived at the ferry almost frozen. A hot bowl of noodles at one of the restaurant stalls did wonders to warm me up. One ferry left, and the Richardsons still had not shown up. Finally, just before the last ferry was to leave, their car came. They had gone into Yangzhou, and had been held there, waiting for me to arrive. Pete had finally persuaded the officials to let them proceed.

We spent the night in Zhenjiang with Ruth Worth and Charlotte Dunlap, the Moffetts having left before the Communist takeover. The next day we continued on to Shanghai by train. Every time we got on or off a ferry or train, our papers were scrutinized, and often our baggage examined as well. Commerce in Shanghai was limited to local goods, as there was virtually no international shipping, due to the blockade. The streets were still crowded with pedestrians, bicycles, and rickshaws. The buses were running on coal. Every bus pulled a small trailer carrying an apparatus that looked like a still, which produced the coal gas. As we could not sail from Shanghai, we spent a couple of days there before we could travel on by train to Guangzhou (Canton). There had been restrictions on the amount of money that could be brought into China for us. I had spent as little as possible, in order to save enough to pay for travel out of the country. After we had bought our tickets, I found I had some left over. I purchased a set of carved tea tables, a carved camphor wood chest, and a set of rice china, which was packed in the chest. These were all crated and added to the freight I was sending home. We had shipped some other things when Katie left, but the trunk with our most precious items, including photographs, had been lost in New York. Shipping freight out of Shanghai in 1951 was a big gamble, but I thought it was worth a try. Fortunately, everything arrived intact.

The Chinese sleeper cars on the trains have four bunks to a compartment. They make up into two benches facing each other during the day. There is a table between the benches. Hot water is brought in from time to time to fill a large thermos so one can have tea. Berth assignments ignore gender, and the berths are without curtains. One has to dress and undress under the covers. Pete, Agnes, and I were in a compartment with a Chinese gentleman. The trip to Guangzhou took two days. We were not allowed to get off at any of the stops. The Chinese gentleman was from Hong Kong and was a representative of Philippine Air Lines (PAL). In those days, missionaries usually traveled to and from the Far East by ship. He soon convinced me that flying would not only be quicker, but actually cheaper, because the days of waiting for passage on a ship would add costs for food and lodging. He was able to give me a tentative reservation for a flight to the U.S.

When we arrived in Guangzhou, we were taken under guard to a hotel for the night. The next morning we were escorted to the station for the train that shuttled back and forth to the border. There we had to disembark and go through inspection of our papers and baggage. The train was not allowed to cross the border. We had to walk across the railroad bridge carrying all our baggage. We were greeted warmly by the British police officers, who were a welcome sight indeed. We went to a hotel on Hong Kong Island. After getting settled, I went to the telephone-telegraph office to try to call Katie. No luck, the phone lines to the States were booked solid for three days, so I sent a cable to Katie, telling her we were out of China, and giving her the phone number of the hotel. Certain hours of the day were allocated for calls to be placed from Hong Kong, and other times for calls to be made from the States. Katie did not have to wait, and her call came through without delay. It was wonderful to hear her voice. I explained the situation to her, and asked her to relay a request for my mother to seek permission for me to fly home. Katie and the boys were in Richmond, Virginia, but my parents lived in Nashville where our mission headquarters were located. Katie called Mother, who then tried to track down Dr. Darby Fulton, the executive secretary. He was out of town, but she finally contacted a secretary who knew he had a speaking engagement in Selma, Alabama. She called the church where he was speaking. He was called out of the pulpit and immediately gave permission. Mother placed a call to me, just before the lines closed down for calls from the States, to tell me I was authorized to fly home. Dr. Fulton was able to announce to the congregation that three more missionaries were now out of China. Only six or seven others still remained on the mainland. The last remaining missionary of the Presbyterian Church U.S., Dr. Frank Price, was finally allowed to leave in December 1951.

I can't remember what kind of plane the PAL used for the flight across the Pacific. It was the only plane I have been on that was like a Pullman. I flew first to Manila. From Manila to Honolulu, I took sleeper class. To save money, from Honolulu to San Francisco, I booked tourist class. I was still wearing winter clothes. It was very warm in Manila, and even hotter when we landed on Guam and Midway. I slept both of those legs of the journey. It was late evening, on arrival in Honolulu. As this was the first U.S. port of call, we had to go through immigration and customs. By this time I was really hot and sweaty. My clean clothes were all in my checked luggage. The only thing available at the airport store was some Hawaiian shirts. I purchased a sport shirt, bright orange with pictures of palm trees, with a matching blouse for Katie. The showers were about to close. I persuaded the attendant to stay open long enough for me to get a quick shower and put on the clean shirt. When we boarded the plane, I told the stewardess that I was supposed to be in tourist class for the remainder of the flight. She said she didn't have a place for me there, so she put me back in first class.

Richmond, Virginia

I had booked flights to go via Nashville, hoping to see my parents at the airport as I passed through. On arrival at San Francisco, I was told that the eastern U.S. was gripped in a winter storm. Nashville airport was closed, and half the city was without power due to the ice storm. I had to reroute my flights through Chicago and Washington to Richmond. I drew quite a few stares in Chicago, as I was wearing a Russian type fur hat, a heavy winter overcoat, and the bright orange Hawaiian shirt. Katie met me with the boys. She was a bit concerned about our two-year-old's acceptance of the father he had never seen. Lee had just passed his second birthday, and knew me only from pictures. She had prepared him well. He jumped into my arms immediately. It was a joyous reunion with Katie and the boys.

I had hardly gotten home before I received a call from Nashville. Dr. Fulton was scheduled to speak at a meeting of the Women of the Church in Second Presbyterian Church in Richmond. He was unable to leave Nashville, as the airport was still closed due to the ice storm. He asked me to speak in his place. Dr. Fulton was one of the most effective speakers I have been privileged to hear. I took the assignment with great trepidation. I was suffering from the worst case of culture shock I have ever experienced, and was having difficulty expressing myself in English. I had been speaking nothing but Chinese, except at meal times, for two years. Katie couldn't understand my Chinese, as I had shifted to the north Jiangsu dialect of Mandarin spoken in Taizhou. I had come from a city where the fastest modes of transportation were wheelbarrow, rickshaw, and bicycle. The fast pace of vehicles of all sorts on Richmond streets was just too much to adjust to in such a short time. I spoke at the meeting, struggling for words to express my thoughts, and made it through my message with great difficulty.

Shortly after I came home, the mission board met in Nashville. At a preceding meeting, they had granted Katie permission to return to China; now they had to decide what to do with us next. Dr. Fulton discussed the possibilities with us, stressing the urgent need for doctors and nurses in the Belgian Congo, now the Republic of Zaïre. At the time, Korea was out of the question. Our church did not yet have medical work in Taiwan. Dr. Frank Brown, Jr. had been designated to initiate a medical program in Japan. In order to practice in Brazil or in Mexico, doctors had to be educated in that respective country. Africa had been our second choice of an area in which to work when we first applied for missionary service, so we gladly accepted Dr. Fulton's challenge. Our new assignment required a year in Belgium studying French and Tropical Medicine. Thus began a long hiatus in our experience in China, but that story will be told in Part II.

3. China Near End of Cultural Revolution: 1975

U.S.-China People's Friendship Tour

Following President Richard Nixon's visit in 1972, China began to admit a limited number of tour groups. In 1975, we were living in Maryville, Tennessee, and were active in the Knoxville chapter of the U.S.-China People's Friendship Association, when we learned that the association was planning a China tour. The cities of Knoxville and Nashville were each to be allowed two representatives. I was, at that time, working as an emergency physician in Knoxville and Katie was teaching at Maryville College. We both applied. Katie and Marilyn Jacobson were chosen, and I was named as an alternate. Marilyn was a member of the Knoxville School Board and an active Catholic layperson. Her husband was a professor at the University of Tennessee.

In preparation for the trip, we contacted the University of Tennessee and found that they had an excellent language laboratory with tapes of spoken Chinese. The lessons followed closely the Yale system. We were accorded the privilege of using the tapes at the laboratory. We were delighted to find that even after years of working in French and the African language, Tshiluba, we could recall much of our Chinese. When Katie was instructed to get her passport and immunizations, we both followed all the instructions. There was an orientation meeting held at Highlands, a rural community center north of Knoxville. I attended this, too. There were to be twenty-two persons on the tour. Shortly before time for the trip, one of the persons chosen to go from Nashville withdrew. Since I had all my papers in order and was ready, I was awarded the spot.

The members of the group were all civic leaders from various walks of life. The tour leader was Dr. Allyn Rickett, professor of Chinese at the University of Pennsylvania. He had arrived in Beijing shortly after we were there in language school. After the Communists took Beijing, he was accused

Henry and Katie before U.S.-China People's Friendship Tour 1975.

of spying. He spent some four years in prison in Beijing. During part of this time, his wife Adele was confined in another Beijing prison. Prior to our trip, she had already led a U.S.-China Friendship tour; now it was his turn. I was the only physician and Katie the only nurse in the group. There was a dentist, who was also an anesthesiologist. The retired executive secretary of the Family Planning Council was one of the members. There were two journalists; one was the medical reporter for a New York paper and the other taught journalism in Atlanta. There were a couple of school teachers, a music teacher, and a former YMCA secretary, who had served in Shanghai before Liberation (the term used for the Communists' consolidation of control of the mainland). James Bond, Julian Bond's brother and an Atlanta city councilman, was the only Afro-American on the tour. The only other couple was a psychologist and his wife who were into acupuncture research and *taiqi*. Aside from Allyn Rickett, whose Chinese was flawless, there were only a few members of the group who had any command of Chinese. The itinerary had been set, but we were all given the opportunity to request what we would like to see at the various cities we were to visit. The tour lasted three weeks. Ground transportation was used for travel in China, with the tour ending in Shanghai and departing by air.

Beijing

We were under the impression that the Beijing Hotel where we stayed in 1975 was then called the "Friendship Hotel," but when we returned to Beijing in 1986, we found that the latter name referred to a large hotel establishment that had formerly provided housing for Russian "foreign experts." The present Beijing Hotel was relatively new in 1975. One of the main shopping streets ran by its east end. Tiananmen Square was just a block to the west. This huge square in front of the "Forbidden City" had been opened up after Beijing became the Communist capital. It extended all the way to the south gate of the city and was bordered on the west by the Great Hall of the People and on the east by large museum buildings. These new buildings were built in Russian style architecture. Both Mao Zedong and Chou Enlai were living at the time, so the mausoleum in the southern end of the square had not yet been built. At our arrival, the main street, Changan Boulevard, was festooned with flags to welcome some foreign dignitary. As we entered the hotel, there was a huge mosaic proclaiming "Welcome to Our Friends from all over the World."

The format of the tour was explained to us. Many requests for particular visits were included. We had asked if it were possible to visit Taizhou or Zhenjiang, but were courteously told that it was not possible to deviate from the cities included in the itinerary. Each day we were to visit several sites in the morning. After lunch there were more visits. After dinner, some form of entertainment was often provided. A head guide and two interpreter guides accompanied us for the entire trip. In each city, a local guide made presentations. When we visited an institution, we were first taken to a reception room. There someone gave us an orientation in Chinese which was translated into English. We then had an opportunity to ask questions through the interpreter. At the conclusion of each visit, we returned to the reception room where we were again allowed to ask questions to clarify our ideas and impressions. This proved to be a marvelous opportunity for us to review Chinese, as we heard everything in both languages. I shall not attempt to cover all the places we visited, but rather, try to pick out items of special interest and give my impressions.

We were taken to see a few of the tourist attractions, such as the Forbidden City, Temple of Heaven, Lama Temple, Summer Palace, and the Great Wall at Badaling. These were not new to us, but we enjoyed seeing them again. There was an interesting encounter as we left the rear entrance of the Forbidden City with an old gentleman who was rolling a young child in a stroller. The stroller was made of bamboo, a familiar sight in Beijing. I started to take a picture, but he objected. We talked to him and found out that before Liberation, he had worked for foreigners. He was afraid to have anything to do with us, as he had suffered much for his association with "capitalists."

The first institution we visited was the Children's Hospital. The medical director, who was a pediatric surgeon, gave the orientation. He had been trained in Western medicine. Chairman Mao had decreed that Western

Bamboo baby buggy, Beijing 1975.

medicine and traditional Chinese medicine should be integrated, so in hospitals and medical schools throughout China, there was a mixture of the two. Someone asked about the use of acupuncture as anesthesia. Our host said that in his hospital, the parents were allowed to choose either Western anesthesia or acupuncture. He said about half chose acupuncture. They were not doing surgery that day, but we were to have an opportunity to see surgery later in our tour. During the tour of the hospital, I asked our host in Chinese for his opinion as to the indications for acupuncture, other than as anesthesia. He replied that he felt it was best used for diseases for which there were no specific medications and for functional (psychosomatic) illnesses. We went to the acupuncture treatment room. The elderly doctor in charge had been trained in traditional medicine. He had three children there under treatment. One was suffering from bed-wetting, another from a nervous tic, and the third from nightmares, all possibly psychosomatic complaints.

We were in Beijing on a Sunday. Several in the group expressed interest in attending church. We were told that two churches were open in Beijing, one Protestant and one Catholic. They could arrange to take those who wished to go to one of the churches; the rest of the group would go on one of the visits that had already been scheduled. Katie and I decided to split up. She went to church and I went with the others. The church they attended was the Catholic cathedral. The mass was in Latin. The priest was Chinese, but the congregation was small and all seemed to be foreigners. We have since been told that these first churches were opened because some of the African students in Beijing asked why there was no Christian church they could attend, since the Chinese constitution guaranteed freedom of religion. Marilyn Jacobson and Katie talked with the priest after the service. Marilyn pointed out that in the rest of the world, the vernacular was being used for the mass. She asked why they were still celebrating the mass in Latin. He replied that the church in China was no longer under the Pope and that they were retaining the traditions of the church.

The Beijing subway was under construction. Only the southern section of the loop around the city and part of the extension to the west were open. We were taken to ride from one station to the next and back. We had a little free time, so Katie and I went for a walk one afternoon. We walked out to Dongsi Pilou. The memorial arches were still there in 1975. We talked to some of the people who were sitting at the entrance to the little street that led to the language school. One old gentleman recognized the name, Huawen Xuexiao, but a building blocked the street about halfway down to the school, so we didn't get to see it. We went into some of the stores in the shopping district by the hotel just to see what they offered. We found that the prices charged were about the same as those in the Friendship Store for similar items. In the bookstore, I was delighted to find a book on Chinese birds. It was all in Chinese, and the pictures were good, so I purchased it. I was disappointed that we did not see more birds on the tour. This may have been related to the fact that there were many more trees than before, so the birds were more widely scattered. There had also been heavy use of insecticides during extermination campaigns.

Tianjin

On the train trip from Beijing to Tianjin, one of the group remembered that she had put her alarm clock under the mattress and had forgotten to retrieve it. She told one of the guides and, sure enough, it eventually caught up with us in Tianjin, where we visited several schools. One was a school of instrumental music using the traditional Chinese instruments— the *erhu*, a two-stringed violin with a bow, the strings of which pass between the two strings of the instrument itself; the hammer dulcimer; the flute; and other stringed instruments. We visited a high school where the buildings resembled those of a former mission school. We asked, but could not get a definite answer about the history of the school before Liberation. In one class they were teaching students to give themselves acupuncture to treat their near-sightedness. I was standing in the rear of the group. One of the guides, who was very nearsighted, sidled up to me and whispered, "But it doesn't help if you have had it a long time." We also visited an athletic program where they were training young girls for Olympic gymnastic events.

Tangshan

Tangshan is a mining community northeast of Tianjin which, the year after our visit, was the center of a devastating earthquake that caused thousands of deaths, some even as far away as Beijing. We saw pictures of the remains of the hotel where we had stayed in *Time* magazine's news report of that quake. The air in Tangshan was very polluted; everything was stained with coal dust. Our guide told us that miners received higher wages than most other workers, because of the job's importance and the hazards involved. We did not go down into the mines; instead, they took us to a museum. The local guide told of all the atrocities suffered at the hands of the British and President Hoover of the U.S. The local guide was speaking in Chinese and our interpreter failed to translate a lot of the criticism of the U.S. One of the Chinese complained that she didn't translate what the guide had said. The local guide repeated it all, but the interpreter again failed to translate the harshest criticisms of the U.S. The local guide was not following the new line of "friendship to America" and "opening to the West." The museum contained some pictures purported to be of persons who had suffered mutilations at the hands of

Farmer on commune near Tangshan 1975.

the foreigners. There was speculation among the observers as to whether some were, rather, pictures reflecting the ravages of leprosy.

We also visited a rural commune in an area where the very hilly land had been deemed unsuitable for agriculture. They had terraced the hills for fields and built irrigation systems. The pumps that we saw in the countryside were either electrical or diesel. We saw none that were powered by men or animals. I was impressed by the homes. The farmers had more living space than the apartments of those who lived and worked in the cities. They had electricity for a few lights, but did not have enough to be used for stoves.

Yellow River

Our next stop as we traveled south was at the Huanghe (Yellow River). During some centuries, this river ran into the sea north of the Shandong peninsula, and in other centuries, the mouth was south of the peninsula. Fine yellow dust from the arid western provinces makes the water a murky yellow and gives the river its name. Levees along the banks have to be built higher and higher as silt deposits on the riverbed. After a time, the riverbed becomes higher than the surrounding fields. This has resulted in devastating floods when the levees break at high water, justifying the sobriquet, "China's Sorrow." They showed us the famous Jinan dikes and described their attempts to control erosion and dust in the western provinces by reforestation projects, in an effort to reduce the amount of silt.

Jinan

The most exciting experience of the trip for me was the morning we spent in the operating room of a hospital in Jinan. This was one of two leading medical centers in the use of acupuncture for anesthesia. The first patient we observed was a young nurse who had mitral stenosis. This is a heart condition that requires an open-heart operation to break apart the leaves of the mitral valve. She had received mild sedation, but was still able to talk to us. Acupuncture needles were inserted at four points and were connected to an electrical stimulator. I couldn't believe that they were able to open the chest without having an endotracheal tube in place, with which to control respiration and prevent the lungs from collapsing. When the left chest was opened, there were some adhesions of the lung that prevented it from collapsing completely. They then started giving her oxygen by mask, while they released the adhesions. By stabilizing the mediastinum, they permitted the right lung to function. A rubber dam was sewed to the left auricle and an opening made in the auricle. The pressure in the auricle is always low, so the blood just welled up in the dam. They were able to break open the valve through the incision in the heart, which was then closed. Chest tubes were put in place and closure of the chest wall was done in the usual manner. After the muscles of the chest wall were closed, while they were still placing stitches in the skin, a nurse brought the patient a compote of canned pears and fed her. After we had seen the next three cases, we went to visit her in the ward. She was sitting up cheerfully in the bed. The doctors claimed that following acupuncture anesthesia, there was much less need for postoperative pain medication.

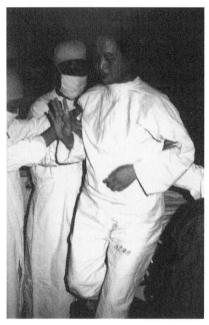

Patient getting off operating table after thyroidectomy under acupuncture anesthesia, Jinan 1975.

The second patient had a goiter. They were just completing this operation when we entered the operating room. After dressings were applied, the patient got off the operating table and walked to the ward. The third patient was being operated upon for a tumor of the pituitary gland at the base of the brain. They used a frontal approach. The patient was draped in such a manner that we could look under the drapes and see the patient's face. He was awake and answering the doctor's questions during the procedure. The last patient had an abdominal operation for an ovarian cyst. I tried to observe closely the placement of the acupuncture needles for the anesthesia. One insertion point was common to all four procedures. This was the *houku* point, on the back of the web between the thumb and index finger, beside the middle of the metacarpal of the thumb. I have found that I can use accupressure on myself, massaging this point to relieve headaches, pain of arthritis, and other aches. The placement of the other needles varied according to the body part affected.

We spent the second Sunday of our tour in Jinan. We asked, but no one would admit that there were Christians in the city. In any case, there was no church open. We visited a pencil factory and then took a bus trip out into Shandong peninsula. We visited a Buddhist temple that was a tourist attraction and did not seem to be actively used for worship. On the way, we passed through hilly farmland. Instead of draft animals, small diesel-powered tractors were being used. In some areas these were small four-wheeled tractors. In other areas they were two-wheeled tractors, like oversized garden tractors, which were hitched to trailers, making them in effect four-wheeled, with a joint in the middle. The motor was a single cylinder diesel driving the tractor by a belt. Sometimes, in the fields, the belt was shifted to power a threshing machine. The same type motor was seen at times powering irrigation pumps. These ubiquitous motors were also used to power barges on the canals.

Nanjing

The train passed over the Yangzi on the Nanjing Bridge, which was then, one of the first places they took us to visit. The Chinese were very proud of the bridge. It was originally designed, and construction begun, by Russian engineers. When relations between Russia and China cooled, all the Russian engineers were withdrawn, taking the plans with them. The Chinese engineers took over, reconstructed the plans, and completed the bridge. It stands very high over the river, allowing the passage of large oceangoing vessels beneath it. The lower level has a double railroad track and the upper level, a road for vehicles. On the Nanjing end, we entered a reception center. The antechamber had one of the massive statues of Chairman Mao that were then prevalent. We saw similar statues at institutions of higher learning and many other public places. The cult of Mao was at its height. Everywhere we visited on the tour, signboards and neon signs proclaimed, "Chairman Mao ten thousand years" (Long live Chairman Mao). In the reception room, we were shown a fifty-foot architect's model of the bridge and given an account of its construction.

On a hill overlooking the city was the famed Nanjing observatory. There were several modern telescopes, but the most interesting items on display were some of the old instruments used for celestial observations, introduced by Jesuit priests. Our visit to the tomb of Sun Yatsen was also noteworthy.

The former Jinling Women's College had become Jiangsu Provincial Teachers' College. On our visit there, we met a number of the teachers. Several had been on the staff when it was a mission institution. They were very wary and reluctant to admit the former relationship with the church. We also met several students who were from Taizhou. They recognized the name of Fuyin Yiyuan, the old Taizhou hospital, but could give me no news of any of my former staff. They were friendly and interested to know that I had worked there during the early days after Liberation. At the time of our visit in 1975, there was a tremendous statue of Mao on the Jinling campus, which was removed prior to our return in 1986.

Shanghai

The Bund stretching along the Huangpu River had been the financial capital of China. The banks, office buildings, and custom house were familiar. The traffic on the Bund and in the adjacent shopping district was much lighter than I had remembered. We were taken to the Friendship Store, a large department store for foreign tourists, located in the compound that had been the British Embassy, beside Suzhou Creek at the north end of the Bund. While the group was shopping, Katie and I walked around the block. We saw the building where our mission treasurer's office had been, on the street behind the British Embassy. On the corner by Suzhou Creek was a small Methodist Church where I had worshiped a couple of times on my trips to Shanghai. We found that it was being used as a welding shop. We had seen a number of churches during the tour, none of them open. Some had been boarded up, others were being used as schools, stores, or workshops.

Early in our Shanghai visit, the group was taken to a work unit in the city. Here we gained some insight into why the streets downtown were not terribly crowded. Factories, schools, hospitals, and other work units were all required to furnish housing for their workers, so nearly all the workers lived close to their workplaces. There was therefore no tremendous rush of workers into the central city every day. Also, we were told that most factories were on a seven-day work schedule, with one seventh of the workers off each day. This accounted for the fact that we had observed large numbers of people in the parks and at tourist attractions seven days a week.

At the work unit, we visited their clinic. As this was a fairly large urban work unit, the clinic was like a large outpatient department with several specialists. There were pediatric and medical departments, a small maternity unit, and also a dental unit. When we entered, the dentist had just finished an extraction under acupuncture anesthesia. The dental anesthesiologist in our group wanted to see where the needles had been placed. The dentist did not want to stick the patient again, so he demonstrated by sticking himself. I noted that one of the insertion points was again the *houku* point. This was the largest and most complete medical setup we had seen in a work unit.

Most of the work units we visited had small one- or two-room dispensaries manned by minimally trained medical workers, often referred to as "barefoot doctors." These workers usually had been given only a few months of training. They had a small stock of drugs, such as worm medicines, laxatives, and a few antibiotics. They treated minor illnesses and referred more complicated cases to the next level of care, usually a city or district hospital. They also gave acupuncture treatments. The main impact the "barefoot doctors" made on the health of their units was in the realm of public health. They were in charge of sanitation in the unit, kept records to be sure all the children received their immunizations, and kept careful check on all women of childbearing age with respect to their menstrual periods and birth control. In 1975, families were limited to two children. They admitted that abortions were being done, but declared that these were used mainly in case of birth control failure.

Work units also provided child care, often beginning while the child was still in the cradle. We visited a number of these care centers. In one, children of kindergarten age lived there and only saw their parents once a week, on the parents' day off. Over and over again, we visited kindergartens and primary schools and were entertained by song and dance programs of the children.

We had an interesting visit to Shanghai School for the Deaf. There was a very high ratio of teachers to students and they did not use any hearing aid devices. They were teaching the children lip reading and some sign language. We were given a talk and demonstration by a Chinese acupuncture specialist who was treating the deafness. My impression was that the results were attributable to intensive teaching and efforts to help the children use their residual hearing to the best advantage. The students put on a program for us which included some group singing!

We also visited Shanghai's industrial exhibition hall, built in the Russian style. Here we saw examples of some of China's heavy industry. Trucks, cars, farm machinery, and plastic molding machines were on display. Then a bus trip south of Shanghai took us toward Jiaxing to a mixed commune. Here, in a farm commune with a dairy, they were also producing canal barges out of fibrocement. They laid wire mesh over a mold and plastered it with the cement, then turned it over, and the deck was added in a similar manner.

Impressions

First things first! The food on the entire tour was great! We were given the choice of Chinese or Western style breakfast. Katie chose Western and I chose Chinese. With the usual rice gruel and condiments, I received the same eggs, yogurt, and fruit that Katie had on her breakfast. All the other meals were Chinese. We feasted all the way, usually having at least four main dishes at both lunch and supper. Since we were moving from one region to another, we had dishes from a number of different styles of cuisine. In fact, during the whole three weeks, there were not more than two or three dishes that were repeated. We were especially impressed with the quality and variety of the dishes that we were served at the two meals we had on the farm communes. We were impressed that the population, in general, was well nourished. We witnessed neither obesity nor malnutrition. Could this be the same China we had known in the past?

Most of the farmhouses had at least a few lights. Irrigation pumps were electrified or run by small diesel engines. The major changes in the country-side, apart from rural electrification, were the presence of trees and the absence of graves. During the forties, the countryside was practically treeless, especially in the Yangzi valley. Trees had since been planted along the canals and roads. Windbreaks of trees divided many of the fields. In the past, many graves dotted the landscape. In the Yangzi valley, these were often large cone-shaped mounds; around Shanghai, coffins were placed on the ground, then encased in brick and roofed with tile. These graves had all disappeared. Cremation was the order of the day. Shanghai had grown and incorporated many surrounding areas into the city. Apartment buildings now stood where there had been graveyards in the past. In the countryside, land once occupied by graves had been returned to agriculture. The single-story farmhouses were being replaced with two-story buildings, often built as row houses.

All of China's progress was continually extolled as a triumph of the socialist system. I recognized the economic progress and rejoiced at many of the achievements. In 1951, I left China at a time of conflict and turmoil. During the intervening twenty-four years, the mainland had been under a unified regime. I should have been sorely disappointed had progress not occurred. I was acutely aware, however, of the toll in human suffering, the regimentation, and the loss of personal freedom through which these results had been achieved.

4. Curtain Rising?: 1986-89

China after the Cultural Revolution

Duntil the so-called Cultural Revolution (1966-76), all places of worship, Protestant, Catholic, and Buddhist, were closed. Christians continued to meet secretly in homes. The Cultural Revolution is a deep scar on the history of China. Practically everyone we came to know had tales of horror and suffering that had occurred to them personally or to their immediate families. During that period everything old was deemed decadent and worthless. The schools and universities were closed. The youth were organized into "Red Guard" units who set about to deface, destroy, and root out everything and everyone they deemed reactionary, in an attempt to achieve a new socialist society. Many temples and other historic sites dating from China's cultural past were damaged. We encountered evidence of this frequently during the eighties.

For a time after the death of Mao, as his wife and three of her supporters, known as the "Gang of Four," sought ever greater power, ultra-leftism reached a peak. Only after their loss of power, trial, and imprisonment was there a more favorable climate for the open expression of religion. Christians sought permission to reopen churches for public worship, since the constitution guaranteed freedom of religion. The Three-Self Movement which had begun in 1951, emphasizing "self-government," "self-support," "self-propagation," and the principle of Love-Country—Love-Church, was revived. In the view of the government, missions and the churches which they had established were identified with foreign imperialism. The Three-Self Movement, being divorced from foreign influence and control, sought to overcome this notion. Gradually, then, churches began to reopen, beginning in Ningpo in 1979. Christians had come from many traditions—mainline Protestant denominations, small Faith missions, and indigenous sects. The Three-Self Movement was an umbrella under which all these began to merge and coalesce into one Christian community. Churches, where they have opened, now have Christians from varied traditions worshipping together. This has given rise to the term "post-denominational" to describe the church in China. There is no central church government, but rather the churches are organized locally, joining together in a loose countrywide movement. The churches focus on worship, propagation of the faith, and training of church workers.

In 1985, Dr. G. Thompson Brown (Tommy), executive secretary of the Division of International Mission (DIM), was in Shanghai studying, while seeking to establish contact with the Christian community and to learn how former Presbyterian mission institutions had fared. That spring, Dr. Paul Crane and his wife Sophie went to China as part of his orientation to the job in Health Ministries with the DIM. They visited Zhenjiang, where the Goldsby King Memorial Hospital had become Number One People's Hospital. There they met Dr. Zhang Zhiqing, former president of the Taizhou Hospital Board, who had retired as director of the Zhenjiang Hospital, but was still an active consultant. Dr. Zhang asked for news of his many missionary friends. He expressed a desire for a visiting physician, but did not know how that could be arranged. This was communicated to Dr. Brown, who knew that we were hoping for an opportunity to return to China. About this time, Amity Foundation was established, and when he visited Zhenjiang that summer, Dr. Brown put Dr. Zhang and the hospital in touch with this organization.

Amity Foundation

Amity Foundation was established to afford persons and institutions in China and abroad, a means of contributing to and promoting health, education, social service, and rural development in China. Amity is not directly connected to the Three-Self Movement, though the founders of Amity Foundation were leaders in that movement. Most of the support has come from Christians in China and abroad, although there are some non-Christians on the board of the foundation and some support has come from outside the church. Amity is the principal means whereby Christians in China can express their social concerns in ways not possible through the Three-Self Movement. It is supportive of the movement and has become a vehicle through which churches around the world can lend their support to the people of China. Amity offices are located in Nanjing; the foundation began its activities first in central China.

When the Zhenjiang hospital contacted Amity, the first group of teachers had been recruited to teach languages in some of the colleges and universities of central China, mostly English, but others, also, including German and Japanese. Most of these teachers were recruited and supported by churches abroad. Amity Foundation thus became the channel through which we would return to China as teachers. The first group began teaching in the fall of 1985. We had last returned from Zaïre in 1984, and I was working as an emergency physician. We expected to go to China in the spring of 1986, but it was decided to have us wait until the second group of teachers went out for the fall term. For the last six months in the U.S., I was working in a walk-in clinic in Knoxville one week, alternating with work as an emergency physician in a couple of Nashville hospitals the next week. This was strenuous, but allowed me to see Katrina, our oldest daughter, and her family, with whom I stayed in Nashville.

From the summer of 1986, the Presbyterian Church U.S. sponsored us under Amity. The church paid our travel to and from China and gave Amity a grant, which was funneled through the National Council of Churches. This grant allowed Amity to pay for our travel within China and to provide a small stipend to cover our living expenses. The recipient institution was required to provide adequate housing, according to standards set by Amity, and also to contribute to Amity's support. Friends at Second Presbyterian Church in Nashville, which had supported us as missionaries, heard that we were going back to China with Amity and once again contributed to our work.

Return to China

An orientation was held for Amity teachers from the U.S. and Canada at Stony Point, New York, in July. It was emphasized that we were not going as missionaries, certainly not as the term was formerly used. We would be going as teachers; however, this did not mean that we could not enter into the life of the church. We were also free to answer questions about Christianity, even in the classroom. We would have opportunities to witness through our personal lives, but should be careful to interfere in no way with the independence of the church from foreign domination.

We flew to Shanghai via San Francisco and Tokyo. Amity put us up in Shanghai, and the next day took us to visit the Three-Self headquarters. It was housed in the building which had been the Associated Mission Treasurers' office, formerly shared by several missions, including the Presbyterians. They showed us Bibles, New Testaments, and hymn books, printed in Shanghai, which they were preparing to ship for distribution. At this time, they were printing these on government presses. The demand was great, but they were only able to print small quantities due to lack of funds. As soon as one batch was distributed and sold, they printed more. Near the Three-Self offices, we noted that the church on the corner which we had seen in 1975, was no longer being used as a welding shop. I was told that it had been turned over to a Jewish congregation for use as a synagogue.

From Shanghai we were taken to Nanjing. Amity Foundation is located on the grounds of Nanjing Theological Seminary, near the center of the city. There we had another orientation meeting with the entire group of new teachers. Bishop K.H. Ting, the leader of the Three-Self Movement and the president of Amity, spoke to us. This was the first of many meetings we had with Bishop Ting. He gave us a report on the church in China, explaining that denominational lines based on the history and cultures of the sending missions had little meaning in the Chinese setting. The Three-Self Movement was built on "unity in diversity," welcoming all who believed in the saving grace of Jesus Christ. This included all those worshipping in the open churches, and also those who were worshipping in homes, where churches were not yet open. We also heard from Dr. Han Wenzao, the executive secretary of Amity. The government head of education spoke to us in Chinese with Dr. Philip Wickeri translating. Philip was serving as Amity's overseas coordinator, with offices in Hong Kong. Ting Yenren (Stephen), Bishop Ting's son, a professor at Nanjing University, worked tirelessly as Amity's education consultant. Directly involved with the care and oversight of Amity teachers, he gave us invaluable assistance, and we deeply appreciated his guidance, care, and concern. All members of the staff were extremely helpful. Many of them were voluntary workers; a few were salaried.

Amity's only medical programs at that time were a nutrition project in conjunction with the pediatric service at Gulou Hospital in Nanjing and a rehabilitation program for handicapped children. The latter program was not only for the rehabilitation of the handicapped, but also for training workers in this field.

Zhenjiang is about sixty miles from Nanjing. Following our orientation in Nanjing, the Zhenjiang hospital van came to get us. It was harvest time and the farmers were busy in the fields. On the way, at a number of places, they had spread stalks of grain on the road and were letting the traffic do the threshing.

Zhenjiang Number One People's Hospital

The Goldsby King Memorial Hospital (GKMH), now Number One People's Hospital, was located beside the old Grand Canal just west of the site of the city's old west gate. The city had expanded westward, so it was now almost at the center of the city. The canal was no longer in active use for transportation, as the Grand Canal had been greatly enlarged and relocated about ten miles east of the city. Zhenjiang is a port on the Yangzi and is the headquarters of a district which includes four counties. It is an industrial city, with many industries of different sizes, consequently there was much pollution, especially in winter.

The hospital had grown greatly. Both the old outpatient and inpatient buildings were still standing when we arrived. The former was being used for staff housing and the hospital day care center. A larger outpatient building had been added across the street. The inpatient building was in use, but was in poor repair. They were debating whether to renovate it, or tear it down and replace it. The old laboratory behind the main hospital building was there, as was the missionary doctor's residence. There were three large two-story inpatient buildings that had been built in the fifties during the Russian era, all with big red stars on the front. A smaller administration building was inside the front gate. Paralleling the canal, a much newer five-story building, with a

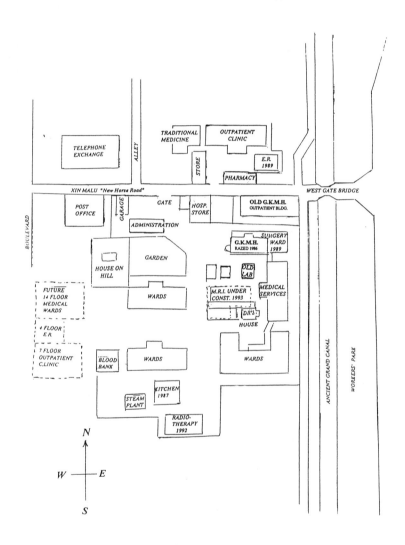

Zhenjiang
No. 1 People's Hospital
1986-1993

On left, Old Goldsby King Memorial Hospital being dismantled, Zhenjiang 1986; on right, medical services building beyond the site of old GKMH, Zhenjiang 1986.

large red cross on the front, housed the X-ray department on the first floor; the laboratories on the second floor; the central sterilizing service, library, and pathology labs on the third; operating suites on the fourth; and the old cadre wards on the fifth. The latter were the most comfortable patient rooms in the hospital, as this building was the only one with central heat. We observed that in all the hospitals we visited, the best patient facilities were always reserved for the elderly Communist leaders and veterans.

Hospital authorities had talked of housing us in a nearby hotel, so we were surprised that they arranged quarters for us inside the hospital compound, in the old missionary doctor's house. The ground floor was occupied by the hospital archives and older bound journals of their library. We were housed upstairs in two rooms on the south side of the house, with a bathroom connecting them. The southwest room was furnished as a bedroom, with a Chinese type bed made with tightly strung cord as the base, and a thin pad on top. In this room a heat pump window unit cooled in summer and heated in winter. The front room was furnished as a sitting room with a desk. The northwest room across the hall was set up as a kitchen and dining room. We were provided with a small refrigerator and a small two-burner gas stove. There was also a water heater. The only running water was cold, but we could carry hot water from the water heater to the bathroom for baths. Two other rooms on the upstairs floor were occupied during the day. The front room on the north side was used as an office for the hospital historian. An enclosed front porch was used as a studio by Ms. Ni Zhonghu, the hospital artist, whose main job was sign painting and keeping the bulletin board. Her surname, Ni, was the same as ours and is a rather uncommon Chinese surname. She was an accomplished portrait artist, painting with oils in Western style.

An older lady, Lao Xie, was assigned to help take care of the apartment and do the laundry. We had thought that we would arrange to eat with the staff, but the staff did not have a dining room. Most of them went to their apartments for meals. The residents got their food from the kitchen and took it to their rooms. Lao Xie brought ours to our room. We soon arranged to get only one meal a day from the hospital kitchen and to fix our own breakfast and supper.

Initially the hospital said they wanted me to help them modernize their emergency department. The concept of emergency medicine, as it developed in the U.S., did not fit the Chinese system. There was virtually no private practice, so the doctors were hospital based. Every hospital I visited had large outpatient clinics for primary care. The basic primary care services of surgery, internal medicine, pediatrics, and obstetrics and gynecology were kept staffed twenty-four hours a day to care for emergencies. Patients were sent directly to one of these services, rather than to the emergency ward. The hospitals were all overcrowded. Often outpatients who needed admission had to be held in the so-called emergency wards, waiting for a bed to become available. In some hospitals, this was as long as a week. In addition to being holding wards, full of acutely ill patients, the emergency rooms were used for giving intravenous or intramuscular medicines and intravenous treatment for dehydration to ambulatory outpatients.

After our arrival, it was thought that we could help best by teaching English to the staff. Our program consisted of several classes in English, with about twenty in a class. We tried to divide them into advanced and weaker sections. This was difficult, as some of the higher ranking staff members were weaker in English. Katie took the bulk of these classes and I taught a couple of classes dealing mainly with medical terms. Most of my teaching was done in a clinical setting. Every morning we attended morning report on one of the wards, rotating a week at a time, on general medicine, cardiology, surgery, pediatrics, and otolaryngology. After the nurses gave their report, the night duty physician would give his report in English. We would then discuss any problems and correct mistakes. I also made ward rounds once a week, again rotating through the services. Here we would have more detailed discussions and they would often ask for my suggestions. Dr. Yang Zhaosheng, the internist in charge of the general medical ward, often called on me at other times as well, for consultation with interesting cases. Once a month I gave a medical lecture in English to the entire staff. Doctors from the other hospitals in the city were also invited. I was required to write out the lecture completely and give it to them in advance to have it translated into Chinese. The English and Chinese versions were mimeographed and available to the staff when I gave the lecture. Dr. Zhang, whose English was excellent, would also interpret the lecture as I delivered it. Once a month we had a clinical conference where a case was chosen and written up by one of the departments. This was printed and distributed to the staff in advance. When we met, the case was presented and anyone who wished could discuss it and give their ideas about it. At the end, I was asked to summarize and give my opinion about the case. The X-ray department chairman asked me to come once a week and read films with them to help with their English. Our chief language difficulty related to the fact that the English spoken by the doctors who had studied Japanese and Russian was distorted by sounds from the other acquired languages, making it extremely difficult for us to understand and correct them. The chief of surgery asked me to attend his surgery outpatient clinic, where we saw patients together and I helped him with English as well. Thus, while I had no responsibility for primary care of patients, I was working in a clinical setting throughout our two years at Zhenjiang.

I was interested in the status of schistosomiasis, since I had been told in 1975 that it, along with sexually transmitted diseases (STD), had been eradicated from China. The doctors still claimed there was no longer any schistosomiasis. They said that canals had been drained and the snail, which is the intermediate host, had been eradicated; however, I noted that they always included it in the differential diagnosis in appropriate cases. During my stay at Zhenjiang, I saw a couple of affected patients, reportedly chronic cases. In 1968, *China Daily* reported that there was a resurgence of schistosomiasis in some areas south of the Yangzi. There were also reports of increasing occurrence of STD.

AIDS had not yet become a problem in China. A few cases had been reported in hemophiliacs, who received antihemophiliac blood products before AIDS was recognized. There were also several cases reported in foreigners. I was concerned because AIDS is transmitted by the same means as Hepatitis B, that is by blood and sexual contact. Hepatitis B is extremely prevalent in China. I suspected the mode of transmission was primarily by blood. Disposable one-use syringes and needles were not generally in use, and sterilization of syringes and needles was often suspect. In addition, acupuncture needles and dental instruments were not always kept sterile. I feared that once AIDS was present, it would rapidly become as prevalent as Hepatitis B, unless the danger was recognized and measures taken to prevent it.

About the time we arrived, there was an anesthetic death at the hospital. The hospital director was kept busy for months negotiating a settlement with the family. Partly as a result of this, they did not want me exposed to the liability of operating. I did visit the surgical suite to observe. They seemed to be doing an adequate job, as far as surgical technique was concerned. There were several breaches in operating room standards that would not be tolerated in the U.S. The most glaring was the fact that the operating rooms were not air-conditioned, so an electric fan was used, blowing dust around in the room. Another deficiency related to the fact that wall cabinets placed between operating rooms, for intravenous solutions and supplies, opened into both, thus allowing direct contact between the rooms.

In the laboratory, everything was done by hand. There was no automation of blood tests or blood chemistry examinations. In the administration building, they were still using the old Chinese typewriter which had trays of fonts containing thousands of characters. The typist had to know not only the character, but its position in the fonts. By striking the correct cross reference numbers, the typewriter would pick up the character, strike the page, and then replace it in the font. This was a very slow process, requiring prodigious memory on the part of the typist. Computers and electronic typewriters were available which could produce material in Chinese characters much more quickly, with easier means of calling up the characters, but the hospital had not yet purchased one of these. On the other hand, the X-ray department had computerized machines for doing gastrointestinal examinations. While we were at Zhenjiang, the hospital obtained a C .T. scanner from Germany, and sent one of the radiologists to Germany to learn how to use it.

Since departmental budgets depended, in part, on patient loads, there was no incentive to discharge patients as soon as possible. In fact, just the opposite occurred, resulting in much longer hospital stays for the same illness than in the States. This was one of the reasons for the overcrowding of the wards. Another result was that they were very reluctant to ask for consultations from another service and to transfer patients. Coupled with the fact that specialization occurred at an early stage in medical education, this often led to delays in getting the proper treatment for a patient. Doctors who lacked a broad basis for medical knowledge often failed to recognize conditions beyond their own special field.

Medical Education in China

In 1986 few physicians educated in China had the equivalent of an M.D. degree in the United States. There were several levels of medical education. The medical colleges gave three to four years of post-secondary education. Most medical universities had a six-year program. The last year of these programs was comparable to an internship. Eight-year programs comparable to U.S. programs, including university and medical school, were rare.

During the Cultural Revolution, the universities were closed for a time. When they reopened, admission was not by academic standing or competitive examination, but by recommendation from the work unit. Thus, for a period of time, many entered medical school because of their party standing, though poorly prepared academically. Many trained during that period had risen to positions as heads of departments or directors of institutions. The younger physicians under them were often better educated, which made for difficulties. China was in the process of phasing out the short medical college programs and upgrading them to five or six years.

During the last year of medical school, the students were assigned to hospitals for their year of clinical training. At Zhenjiang, we had physicians in training from three medical colleges: Nanjing, Zhenjiang, and the Shanghai Army Medical College. The ones from Shanghai seemed to have the best preparation.

When the graduates were assigned to a hospital, they could request a certain specialty. Whether or not they received their choice depended upon the needs of the institution and the openings on that service. For example, among our acquaintances was a young pediatrician who was overjoyed that he could fulfill his dream of caring for children. Another who was denied his first choice, adapted to working in a related specialty.

The duration of residency status seemed to be very indefinite. The most promising young physicians, after a few years as residents, were sent back to a medical university for a couple of years of study to earn a master's degree in their specialty. Official examinations were required for completion of residency and the achievement of staff status.

Zhenjiang

On arriving in Zhenjiang, I talked of buying a bicycle, but the streets were narrow and jammed with traffic: trucks, buses, tractors, and bicycles. The hospital vetoed that idea, as they were afraid I might be injured. Instead, I walked all over the city and rode the buses to get where I wanted to go. I had to go through the older sections of the city, just across the canal from the hospital, in order to reach one of the main shopping areas in the center of the city, and became quite familiar with the back streets.

Across the canal from the hospital was the Workers' Park. In the morning it was a favorite spot for *taiqi* exercises. There was a play area for children. Another section had some pavilions where old men played Chinese chess or gossiped in the afternoon. On Sunday mornings the "English corner" met there. This custom was prevalent in many cities, where those wanting to practice English would gather for an opportunity to converse. We did not attend this, as it conflicted with the church service. Also in the mornings and evenings, the park would be filled with the songs of birds, as the old men would bring their caged birds to the park and hang them in the trees. The most popular and best songbird was the *huamei*, a lark about the size of a mockingbird. A

Old gentleman taking birds to the park, Beijing 1989.

common sight in China was that of someone on the street carrying one or more cages of birds covered by cloth. A hill near the hospital had a running track on the summit that was another popular place to take birds.

Across the street from the Workers' Park was the Children's Palace. This was an enrichment center for gifted children, who were chosen from the various schools in town to come there after class for art, music, and science projects. We observed that the Chinese took special pride in their children. They loved to take them to their parks and have special occasions for them. China New Year celebration lasted a month and occurred in the early spring. The lantern festival that took place during this period was especially for children. In the evening, the streets were full of children with their parents, parading with their paper lanterns, which were often shaped like the animal representing the current year. Zhenjiang was famous for its lanterns. We once saw an exhibition of Zhenjiang lanterns in Beijing and another in Yangzhou, across the river from Zhenjiang.

At a small zoo in a park at the base of a hill west of the hospital, we discovered that there was also an entrance to an underground system of tunnels

鎮江古大運河
八七年九月二日
倪恩义画稿

Zhenjiang—Ancient Grand Canal
9-2-87—H. S. Nelson

built originally as air raid shelters when political relations with Russia were very tense. A portion of the tunnels had been turned into a children's arcade with electronic game machines, Ping-Pong tables, and activity rooms.

Soon after our arrival in Zhenjiang, a teacher from a former mission school came to see us. He was now the school historian. All the former mission institutions were in the process of gathering information to record their histories. He was seeking information about Pearl Buck. Her father, the Reverend A.D.D. Sydenstricker, was a Presbyterian missionary, and she had grown up in Zhenjiang. After going to the States for university, she had returned to Zhenjiang and taught at a mission school. We wrote home and obtained information for him. At one time, the Chinese were not pleased with some of her writings, but Zhenjiang seemed to be very proud of their famous author. We visited the school, which was on top of a hill near the new railroad station. They showed us the dormitory where she lived as a teacher. There were several other homes of missionary teachers still there. We also finally located three more of the Presbyterian homes on another ridge just west of the one with the school. One of these was the Sydenstricker home, where Pearl Buck had lived. They were included in the compound of an electronic parts factory and were occupied by some of their workers. We were not allowed to go up to see them, but viewed them from a distance.

A couple of Amity teachers were teaching at a college east of Zhenjiang. During a visit to them we all walked to the Grand Canal, which was just a short distance further east. This was the new location of the Grand Canal which was quite large and very active. The road passed over a bridge above a large lock, the operation of which was fascinating. The lock held about thirty or more canal boats at a time. Most of the boats were made of fibrocement; very few were wooden. They were all powered by one or two diesel motors like those used on tractors.

On a hill west of Zhenjiang there was an experimental station for silkworm culture. There we saw an exhibit showing the different species of silkworms and how the silk fiber is obtained from the cocoons. They showed us the rooms where silkworms feed on mulberry leaves, the cocoon spinning rooms, and sinks where the cocoons are dropped into boiling water and the fibers are caught and unwound. The buildings used for the experimental station were built by the Japanese as their military headquarters for the area. Interestingly, a Japanese teacher, now at the Shipbuilding Institute, had been stationed here as a soldier during the occupation.

On wooded hills south of the city, some temples were being restored. One weekend Ma Feng, Qian Wei, and Liu Wei, young doctors who were avid students of English, led us on a hike through the hills. We made a day of it, and they led us a merry chase. We started at one temple, climbed over the back wall, went over the top of a steep hill, came out by way of another temple, and then through some cultivated fields. In one of the farmer's yards, there was a water buffalo, a rather uncommon sight since tractors had become prevalent.

The hospital administration finally decided to tear down the old hospital building and replace it with a new surgical ward building. Shortly after we arrived in Zhenjiang, work on this began and continued night and day throughout our stay. When the old building was dismantled, the cornerstone was salvaged and placed in front of our house. The inscription, mostly in Chinese, included the English legend "Goldsby King Memorial Hospital 1922." We were told they planned to use it in the new building. The stone had a small cover sealed on the top. One night someone broke into it and stole the contents. The hospital officials were very upset over this and after several weeks finally recovered the contents. It had contained a Bible and some papers.

Zhenjiang is famous for three hills. The first, Jinshan (Gold Mountain) had a temple with a seven-story pagoda, the origins of which dated back to the fourth century. The main temple building burned in 1985. By the time we left, it was being rebuilt with fireproof construction. It was an active Buddhist temple, often visited by Japanese tourists. Reportedly, some of the funds for reconstruction had been raised in Japan. Jinshan featured in a legend involving it and the Bent Bridge in Hangzhou lake. We heard several versions of this *White Snake Legend*. All told of a business man from Zhenjiang who traveled to Hangzhou where he met a lovely maiden at the Bent Bridge. Unaware that she was really a white snake in disguise, he married her and brought her back to Zhenjiang. For some reason, the abbot at Jinshan disapproved of the marriage and managed to break it up. The White Snake Lady returned to Hangzhou by way of a cave, which can be seen to this day, located at the back of the Jinshan hill near the river.

The second hill, Beigushan, has an ancient palace on its summit which figured in stories of the battles among famous warlords. The bronze statue of an animal served as a seat for one of the lords while he plotted his tactics for battle. The bridal chamber of a young lady who featured in the story is maintained as a museum. The third hill, Jiaoshan, is on an island in the Yangzi River east of Zhenjiang. It has two peaks topped by pavilions. A grotto contains a seated statue of an ancient scholarly recluse who lived there. On the southern end of the island are remains of a fort which the British captured during the Opium Wars, leading to the fall of Nanjing. An ancient name of Zhenjiang was Jingkou, meaning the mouth or gate of the capital.

The most direct route to Jinshan followed an ancient street past a *dagoba*, a bottle-shaped monument like those often seen in India. The Zhenjiang *dagoba* was unusual in that the street passed directly under it. A short distance from the *dagoba* was a street named for Marco Polo, that ran toward the river. It formerly led to the ferry which crossed to Yangzhou. Legend says that he crossed the river there and came up this street. This may well be true, since he reportedly served as mayor of Yangzhou for a time.

Zhenjiang Churches

The old British consulate now houses a museum containing many interesting exhibits. Next door to the museum, the façade of the old Baptist church remains, with its inscribed cornerstone. The site of the old church building is now the schoolyard of a large secondary school. Before Liberation there were several Protestant churches in Zhenjiang. I was able to locate four former church buildings. One, several blocks west of the hospital, was occupied by an optical factory. I was never sure which mission had built it, possibly the China Inland Mission. I located two of the Presbyterian churches. The South Gate Church was being used as a machine shop. The other church was on a shopping street in the old city, a couple of blocks from the hospital. In 1986 it stood closed as a warehouse. When it was later remodeled, the cornerstone was exposed for a few days, enabling me to get a picture of it. The building now houses a furniture store. I was told that the Three-Self Church received some compensation that was used to restore the Sunday school building of the former Methodist church, now in active use. The former Catholic church was being used as a restaurant. No Catholic church was open in Zhenjiang. Catholics had to go to Nanjing or across the river to Yangzhou to attend a Catholic service. Some of them worshiped with Protestants in the Three-Self Church which we attended. This former Methodist church was located on one of the busiest shopping streets, about four blocks from the hospital, and it was always packed. The elderly pastor was present every Sunday, but was not able to preach. He always pronounced the benediction. His very presence was a source of encouragement. A somewhat younger Bible teacher, a woman from another province, shared the pastoral and preaching duties with two young Nanjing Seminary interns. Usually only one or two of them were present at the morning service on Sunday; the others held services at points in the surrounding county. They all usually held additional services in the afternoon. Toward the end of our time at Zhenjiang, Mr. Hu Shihui, a school director, retired and became pastor of the church. Pastors came from Nanjing, Yangzhou, Suzhou, and Wuxi for the ordination service.

Buddhists did not seem to be very active in Zhenjiang, but there was a large Muslim community. One day as we were walking through the back streets, a gentleman asked if we were looking for the church. I thought it might be one of the churches I had not found, so we followed his directions. In this way we found the mosque. The attendant welcomed us and showed us around. There was a large prayer hall. Instead of a minaret, there was a small Chinese style pavilion on the roof. The attendant showed us the ceremonial baths, which were equipped with heated water.

Taizhou

Our friend, Dr. Zhang Zhiqing, was anxious for us to see Taizhou, although foreigners, in 1986, were not yet allowed to spend the night there. He arranged for us to take a day trip, and accompanied us in the hospital van. It was a wonderful trip. About twenty of our former staff were on hand to greet us, including good friend and former head nurse, Chen Zi, and a couple of the other nurses. Tang Da, the skilled mechanic whose expertise had facilitated the reopening of the hospital in 1948, had died, but his

Dr. Huang Siren and Dr. Zhang Zhiqing, Zhenjiang 1988·

assistant was there. Sen Er, the O.R. orderly, and Xiao Gu, the chef, were among those who came to see us. Dr. Huang Siren was medical director, although he was nearing retirement. He preached regularly at the church, and before we left Zhenjiang in 1988, he retired and became pastor of the Taizhou church. The doctor in charge of the old city clinic, now Number Two People's Hospital, came to visit with us. That clinic had taken over the leprosy work after I left in 1951. Leprosy had been eradicated by some means. I was told that Number Two Hospital was the infectious disease hospital, but was becoming a general hospital.

Sarah Walkup Hospital, named for the mother of its donor, William Henry Belk, had become Taizhou Number One People's Hospital. The old mission hospital building was still standing, much to my surprise. It was being used as a staff dormitory, but was in very poor condition and they were planning to raze it. The T-shaped building, which I had used briefly prior to the Communist occupation in 1949, was still in use and in good shape. They had razed the nurses' dorm and, just south of its site, a large three-story surgical building had been constructed. East of the T-shaped building was a new four-story building for old cadres. The doctor's house was still there, the ground floor being used as storerooms for hospital supplies. Upstairs was the hospital laboratory, accessed by stairs added at the rear of the house. They had just equipped one room for the production of I.V. solutions. In front of the doctor's house and extending toward the west, a very large six-story building was under construction. This was to be the new outpatient department. When we made a second visit in the summer of 1987, this building was just completed and was ready for occupancy. A new kitchen with dining rooms had been constructed. The hospital officials served us a bountiful dinner there in a private dining room with some of the key staff members. We then went over to see the former Richardson house, which had been turned into apartments. The garden area was occupied by a large apartment building where more hospital staff were living. The primary school had become a school for rural medical workers. A dormitory occupied the schoolyard to house the students. All in all, we were very pleased to see the progress in development of medical services.

Taizhou had become an industrial city. From the hospital roof, we saw a tall television tower and many multistory buildings in the city. A wide boulevard had been constructed about a half-block west of the Richardson house. The road leading to the main gate of Number One Hospital, formerly the back gate, had been widened. Taizhou and the country north of the river had undergone a lot of changes. The Nanjing Bridge and paved roads made it

T-shaped ward building with new building for veteran cadres, Taizhou 1987.

much more accessible. Construction of a system of levees and dams maintained the water level in the canals in north Jiangsu. The canals were major transportation routes and provided water for irrigation. Trees lined the roads and formed windbreaks between the fields, where previously there had been a treeless countryside.

Nanjing

Nanjing was only an hour away from Zhenjiang by train, so we visited there often. The Jinling Hotel was in the center of town in the main shopping district. The room rate was too high for our budget, so we usually stayed at a little hotel around the corner and had some meals at the Jinling. The two churches we attended in Nanjing were both within walking distance. St. Paul's, formerly the Episcopal Church, was quite large and was always crowded. We often attended St. Paul's and enjoyed the excellent seminary choir. There were often foreign tour groups attending. We were surprised to be present on a couple of occasions when a visiting foreigner preached the sermon. Once a month, following the regular Chinese service, there was an English service in the church parlor, organized and led by some of the Amity teachers. The other church we frequented, the No Worry Church, was a little closer to the Jinling Hotel and also crowded. I thought this was a very appropriate name for a church; however, the "No Worry" came from the name of a legendary lady in an old Chinese tale and was the name of the street where the church was located. The majority of the congregation were older people, but when we sat in the balcony at this church, we were impressed by the number of young adults who were seated there. During the three years in China 1986-89, we observed that an increasing number of young people were attending church. At baptismal services, when members were taken into the church, most of the new Christians appeared to be between the ages of twenty and forty.

Nanjing with its long history is a fascinating city. Portions of the old city wall were preserved, including that part of the wall which was scaled at the time of the Taiping Rebellion, leading to the fall of the city. Some of the buildings used by the Taiping officials now house a museum of that period. Nanjing was also the last capital under the Guomindang (Kuomintang or Nationalist Government). Amity arranged for a tour of the courtyard and buildings where the Nationalists had their headquarters, which had been converted into a museum and government offices. We tried later to take our daughter Faye there, but as foreigners with no special permit, we were not allowed entry. We also visited the mausoleum of Sun Yatsen, who is revered by both Communists and Nationalists as the father of modern China.

The south gate of the city was a massive gate with barracks for the garrison. South of the gate, the road passed a hill with a monument to the victims of the Japanese "rape of Nanjing." A little farther to the south, the Amity Press was built. This project was begun during our stay at Zhenjiang. I was told that a Korean Christian, who visited China, was the first to suggest the project. It started with rather modest plans but quickly caught the interest of a number of Bible societies and churches around the world, with contributions totaling over six million dollars U.S. We visited the site in the early stages of construction, when it was ready for the installation of equipment, and then returned in December 1987, for the dedication and opening. Dignitaries from all over the world were there for the dedication.

The press accepts printing orders for secular jobs; however, it gives priority to printing Bibles and Christian literature. It has some of the most modern press equipment in China. The first Bibles were printed by offset and were photographic copies of the same Bible translation that we had used before Liberation, in old style characters. Since the Communists have simplified a large number of characters, many of the younger people have difficulty reading this edition. Amity has since reset the Bible, using the same translation, with the new simplified characters. This was completed and distribution began in 1993, several months ahead of schedule. Both editions are complete uncensored texts of the Bible. They are being printed and made available in sufficient quantities, so there is no justification for trying to smuggle Bibles into China. Such activity only serves to subject the Chinese church to charges of being under the influence of foreign subversives. According to the *Amity Newsletter Fall/Winter 1994*, over eleven million Bibles have been "printed and distributed in China since 1980" and Amity press is now printing Bibles for export.

Returning from Nanjing to Zhenjiang by train on one occasion, we were seated opposite a Chinese gentleman and a young lady. We entered into conversation and he generously complimented us on our Chinese. We told him that we had been in Taizhou before Liberation. At this point the young lady leaned over and whispered in his ear. The gentleman said she was asking if I had been known as the "doctor with the big shoes." I roared with laughter and asked how in the world she knew that, as she was not yet born at that time. She asked if I remembered her mother, whose name I did not recognize. She then told us that her mother had been among the cadres who had occupied Taizhou in 1949 and that I had operated on her. I immediately knew of whom she was speaking, the woman with the shortened heel cord, resulting from injury to the Achilles tendon. Apparently the story of the successful operation had often been repeated in her family. The gentleman, an official in Nanjing, asked us to contact him if we ever needed any assistance. We were amazed at this chance encounter. Coincidence, serendipity, providence?

Suzhou

Suzhou is one of the oldest cities in the Yangzi valley, with a history extending back around 3,000 years. Known as the "Venice of China" because of its numerous canals and bridges, it is located on the rail line about a third of the way from Shanghai to Nanjing. We had occasion to visit it numerous times. The most prominent landmark is Beisi Ta (North Temple Pagoda), said to be the largest pagoda south of the Yangzi River. It is nine stories tall and must be fifty or sixty feet in diameter at the base. The top two floors were closed, but Katie climbed as far as one is allowed to go. There are several other pagodas in the city. In the southeast sector, the twin pagodas are a beautiful pair surrounded by a small park. The first time we saw them, one was encased in scaffolding for renovation. Just north of the city, the famous Tiger Hill park contains the leaning pagoda, which is not as large as the leaning tower at Pisa, but leans at about the same angle.

The gardens of Suzhou are famous and numerous. They all have pavilions, ponds, and the weirdly eroded rocks from Taihu (Lake Tai), of which the Chinese are so fond. Our two favorite gardens were Wangshi "Master of Nets" and Yiyuan "Garden of Harmony." They are both small but quite lovely, with an individuality that sets them apart.

In 1987-88, Dick and Ann Harrison were Amity teachers in Hangzhou. At an earlier date, he had been our associate pastor at New Providence Presbyterian Church in Maryville. They once joined us in Suzhou for a weekend. We rode the city bus to Taihu, where we took a boat trip to visit a couple of islands in the lake. A cave on one of the islands contains many of the water-eroded rocks that are used in rock gardens all over China. I knew that they were referred to as Taihu rocks, but had always wondered how they could have been weathered in such a manner on a lake so near sea level. Perhaps currents in the caves are a partial explanation. It was a holiday, and when we returned from the boat trip, we found a mob waiting for the bus. When it arrived, the mob descended on it, fighting to get in, some even climbing in the windows. We could see that there was no way we were going to get back to Suzhou by the public bus. There were several tour buses parked nearby. Katie went to see if there were any chance we could catch a ride. The driver said, "No," but then members of the group began to talk to us. They were a group from a Shanghai factory, who were taking an excursion to Suzhou and Wuxi. They graciously invited us to join them. They stopped to see a couple of interesting temples on the way to Suzhou that we would not have had the opportunity to see, otherwise. Their kindness was typical of the many occasions when we were befriended by total strangers who graciously came to our aid.

We also took a canal boat from Liuyuan, a park northwest of Suzhou, to Tiger Hill. On a later visit, I took another canal tour from the railroad station to the south of the city. Both were very interesting. One has the opportunity to see a lot of the life of the city as one cruises along. The canals are solidly lined by homes, many with boat landings, balconies, and windows or doors open to the canal. People were washing vegetables or laundry in the canal. Waste water was often thrown in. The canal boat had horns that played a tune, so people were warned not to dump on us as we passed.

Of the six gates from the old city wall, only a couple have been preserved. Only the road portion of the west gate is preserved. In the southwestern corner of the city, the gate is complete, with one opening controlling entry into the city by canal and a second passage for entry by road. A canal encircles the old city just outside the site of the old city wall. It formerly served both as a moat and a transportation canal; part of it still forms a section of the Grand Canal. A large camelback bridge crosses this canal just outside the water gate. The opening of the bridge is only wide enough for one canal boat to pass at a time, so it is quite a bottleneck. The main canal traffic goes around the other side of the city, where the canal is wider.

In Suzhou we were privileged to visit with the family of our friend Dr. Ma Feng, whose father, brother, and sister-in-law were also physicians. The father, now deceased, was much loved and respected in the church and community. We were honored to be invited to the wedding dinner for Ma Feng and his lovely bride Ning Ning. It was held in a pavilion furnished with antiques in the beautiful Shizilin garden in the northeast corner of the city, overlooking the canal.

Xiamen

During each of our three years with Amity Foundation, conferences for the Amity teachers were held on the south China coast in Xiamen, called

Amoy when it was a treaty port. These meetings during the winter school breaks provided a welcome change from the bitter cold of central China, as Xiamen in Fujian Province has a semitropical climate. The conferences were very helpful, affording us an opportunity to compare notes and discuss what was and was not working in our teaching of English as a second language. The meetings and the orientation sessions were the only times we saw many of the other Amity teachers.

In addition to the meetings, we were given an opportunity to tour the city. There was a fort on the coast outside the city, where we looked across to Quemoy and Matsu islands, which remained in Nationalist hands. For a long time after the Nationalists moved to Taiwan in 1948-49, there was an exchange of shelling across the strait and Nationalist loudspeakers aimed propaganda messages toward the mainland. This activity had ceased. We visited the campus of Xiamen University which has a beautiful location on the coast. It received a lot of support from overseas Chinese. Xiamen had a number of condominiums and lovely homes of overseas Chinese, as it was a favorite retirement location. A large Buddhist temple was actively used for worship.

We took a ferry to Gulangyu, an island in the harbor, where all motor traffic is forbidden and the streets are narrow and steep. We walked to the summit of the island where a huge rock formation afforded an excellent view of the harbor. Trinity Church on the island is so named because this Three-Self church is made up of Christians from three different traditions—Methodist; an indigenous sect, the Little Flock; and Seventh Day Adventist. Worship services are held Saturday, Sunday morning, and Sunday afternoon. They told us that the former Seventh Day Adventists attended the Saturday services most of the time, and the Little Flock preferred the Sunday afternoon services, though this was breaking down, as work assignments did not always permit them to attend the service of their choice. The pastors of the three groups often swapped pulpits. One of the pastors was a very interesting elderly lady. She was still active the first time we visited, but was about to retire when we last saw her. She had fled to the interior during the Cultural Revolution and had continued to work in the underground church. She had some interesting tales to tell of her experiences. We also visited a beautiful small Catholic church on the island and met the priest. On a walk along the coast of the island, we passed by fishermen mending their nets. The coast was rocky and a large monument on a rocky prominence overlooked the harbor entrance. Back on the mainland we visited a church which, we were told, is the oldest Protestant congregation in China. It was closed, but the sexton opened it so we could go inside. It was one of the first churches to be reopened after the Cultural Revolution.

Hangzhou

Hangzhou, the capital of Zhejiang province, was not only one of our favorite cities in China, but has the same reputation among many Chinese.

They have a saying, "Above there is heaven, below there are Hangzhou and Suzhou." We had the opportunity to make several visits to Hangzhou. The first visit followed our first Amity conference at Xiamen. John and Betty Duley were Amity teachers at Zhejiang Medical College. They were visiting some other areas of China during the rest of the winter break and offered to let us stay in their apartment at the college. Mr. Liu, the foreign affairs officer of the college, was very helpful to us during this visit.

Hangzhou has many lovely and interesting places, most of them in or around the famed West Lake. There are three islands in the lake. The largest island is connected to the shore on one end by a causeway and the Bent Bridge of the *White Snake Legend,* and on the other end by another bridge. This island has a museum, several restaurants, and temples. Boats and ferries plied the lake, so the other two islands were readily accessible. They both had beautiful pavilions and gardens. Just south of the southernmost island, three stone structures with holes in the sides were mirrored in the lake. They were the basis for the name "Three Pools Mirroring the Moon" and are used as a symbol of Hangzhou. Even the low posts holding horizontal poles that mark bicycle lanes on the streets of Hangzhou were made to resemble them.

We walked or rode the city buses to many sites around the lake, and have visited most of them on one trip or another. "Precious Stone Hill" is north of the lake. On its north side, the "Yellow Dragon Fountain" was located in a Taoist temple, where the attendants were all dressed in traditional court costumes. Several groups played traditional Chinese musical instruments and Chinese opera was staged in one of the pavilions. West of this temple a path leads through a bamboo forest in which there are several caves.

During our first visit to Hangzhou we were treated to the sight of one of its rare snows, a wet snow that clung to the tree branches, making for beautiful scenes. We walked along the lake shore in two or three inches of snow, where the children were having snow fights and building snowmen. The snow melted fairly rapidly, and most of it was gone in a day.

Dr. Miriam Li and Sarah Pan, who had worked with me in Taizhou, were retired in Hangzhou. We contacted them and visited them several times. On one occasion they walked with us to the top of "Precious Stone Hill." A distinctive pagoda at the top of the hill is shaped like an inverted cone. It is surrounded by oddly shaped boulders, many of which have inscriptions carved on them. I think the Chinese must be the originators and masters of graffiti. Whereas this word usually denotes crudeness for us, the beauty and complex meaning of Chinese characters lends it elegance. Everywhere we went, there were characters carved on prominent landmarks. Dr. Li and Sarah pointed out to us a Bible verse carved on a stone, which escaped being defaced during the Cultural Revolution. They said that during the period when Bibles were confiscated and meetings were banned, the Christians took heart in this prominent visible portion of the Word of God.

We attended two churches in Hangzhou. Both were former Presbyterian churches, but had been reopened as Three-Self congregations. One was established by the Presbyterian Church (U.S.A.). It was not only open as a church, but also housed the Hangzhou Seminary. There was really not enough space for the seminary, and the students were living in very crowded conditions. The other church, named Gulou Church because it was located near the site of the old drum tower, was established by the Presbyterian Church in the U.S. The church building reminded me very much of the old Downtown Presbyterian Church (formerly First Presbyterian) in Nashville, Tennessee, where I had grown up. The church in Nashville was built in the style of an Egyptian temple, with decorated beams in a pattern of squares in the ceiling, and with pilasters painted in Egyptian designs around the walls. The Gulou Church had similar beams in the ceiling and pilasters around the wall, though they are painted in Chinese style, resembling some of the Chinese temples.

Mr. Liu was able to arrange visits to a couple of the hospitals in Hangzhou. The first was one of the teaching hospitals of the medical college, a former mission hospital. I visited the surgical section and was especially interested in the emergency ward. The latter, like several others I visited, had a large holding ward full of sick patients who were waiting for beds to become available. There were also a large number of patients receiving intravenous therapy, who would be discharged when the I.V. was completed. The emergency ward was being expanded and new treatment rooms and minor surgery rooms were almost ready for occupancy. I attended a lecture session on cardiopulmonary resuscitation, which was well done; however, I observed that many hospitals had no cardiac care units where patients could be cared for after resuscitation. Secondly, even though mannequins were available in a number of places, there was a reluctance to have sessions where the technique could be practiced. I questioned the practical value of lectures alone, under the circumstances.

During a later visit to Hangzhou, we visited the Children's Hospital where Project HOPE had set up and equipped an excellent training program for pediatric intensive care. This was one of several such programs that Project HOPE was directing. HOPE also funded some adult intensive care units in Beijing. Since HOPE received funds through USAID, they were required to use American equipment whenever possible. Initially, this made for smooth operation, but difficulty in obtaining replacement parts occasionally caused problems in maintenance of the equipment.

Jiaxing

While in Hangzhou in January 1987, we decided to visit Jiaxing (formerly spelled Kashing) where we had spent our first few months in China in 1947. At this time Jiaxing was still not completely open for foreigners, so we could not stay there overnight. We left Hangzhou at 7:00 A.M. for a two-hour train ride to Jiaxing. The station, located on the bank of the Grand Canal, appeared unchanged. After making return reservations on the afternoon train, we set out to find the hospital. A row of buildings now bordered the canal on a new vehicular road that paralleled the canal. We recognized the former mission school buildings close by, which guided us in the right direction.

The old mission hospital had become Number Two People's Hospital of Jiaxing. The two houses which were occupied by the Mason Youngs and George Hudsons in 1947 had been torn down. The street had been widened and turned, passing through the site where the houses had been. A three-story outpatient building now stood on the opposite side of the street. A new inpatient building was under construction between the new outpatient building and the old hospital building. At the gate we inquired of a young man who told us he was a graduate of Zhejiang Medical College, and he took us to meet the administrator, Dr. Yu Jimin. In spite of the fact that we had arrived unannounced, Dr. Yu was very cordial and brought us up to date on the hospital, which had grown from 108 beds to 360, with a staff of 450, serving patients from five counties. Like all hospitals in China, the outpatient department was very busy, with 380,000 visits a year. The hospital was one of three general hospitals in Jiaxing offering full services. There was also the former Catholic hospital, which had only internal medicine and pediatric services, and the Jiaxing Maternity Hospital.

Dr. Yu gave us a tour of the hospital. The surgeons were busy in the operating suite with one of the four thousand annual cases. The house that we had once been scheduled to occupy was being used as the X-ray department. Across the street from the north end of the hospital was a fairly new four-story dormitory for the three-year nursing school.

From the hospital, we went to look for the church. Finding ourselves on the main street, we asked at a couple of stores and none of the clerks knew where the church was located. One young woman suggested that we ask some of the older residents. We returned to where the Youngs' house had been and started back toward the school, using a different route. We went down an old street where I recognized a bridgelike passageway that connected the second stories of a couple of the houses. At the corner, Katie spoke to an old gentleman to ask about the church. He replied that he was a Christian and the church was right there in front of us. He pointed to the roof, but a store had been built in front of it, completely hiding the rest of the building and blocking the front entrance. He took us by way of a side street to the side door, which is now being used as the entrance. It was the only Protestant church open in Jiaxing, though there were five others in the surrounding area, all part of the Three-Self Movement. We went next door to meet a couple of the pastors. Pastor Zen Xingzhong, eighty-nine years old, had formerly served as chaplain at the hospital. He was still preaching every Sunday. Pastor Fan Zhizhong, eighty-six years old, had also been a Presbyterian minister. They were very encouraging about the vitality of the church in Jiaxing.

The mission school had become Number Two Middle School. We were there during winter break; none of the students were present. A teacher at the gate took us to see the principal. We were most cordially received. A number of the old school buildings were still in use, as well as several old dwellings, one of which I'm sure was where the Jack Vinsons had lived. We returned to Hangzhou on a fast train, feeling very satisfied with our visit and much encouraged by the contacts we had made.

Huzhou

While in Hangzhou, we wanted to visit my birthplace in Huzhou. Mr. Liu arranged for a car and contacted Huzhou for us. He warned us that the Methodist Hospital, where my father had worked, was now a People's Liberation Army Hospital, and we might not be able to get in to visit it.

An excellent highway led to Huzhou, with many tea farms along the route. As we approached the city, we observed a mountain ridge on our right topped by a pagoda. We checked in with the foreign affairs bureau of the city. Thanks to Mr. Liu, they were expecting us; they called the hospital and gave us directions. The hospital administrator and his assistant were at the gate to greet us. We were warmly welcomed. After the usual reception and tea, they took us on a tour of the hospital. As we approached the old building, I immediately recognized it from a photograph that had always hung in my father's office. It was built in 1922, the year before my birth. The old outpatient department had been converted to the hospital library. The former waiting room was now the reading room, one side occupied by movable stacks. As in all the major hospitals I visited in China, there was a very complete library of journals, with specialty journals from the U.S., Japan, England, Germany, and Russia. The former consultation rooms were being used as offices. The hospital was in spick-and-span order. The old operating suite was still in use; in fact, a procedure was going on at the time. The hospital was in better condition than any of the other old hospital buildings that I visited in China. They proudly showed us Dr. Manget's old office. Dr. Manget had been my father's colleague, and actually officiated at my delivery. In the laboratory, they showed us equipment and a refrigerator which had belonged to him as well. They took us out to see the cornerstone, which recorded that it was built by the Methodist Church. A number of the old missionary and staff houses were still being used. The nurses' dorm was closest to the hospital. Behind it was Dr. Manget's home, which is kept as a museum. All this in a People's Liberation Army Hospital was certainly unexpected. There were some newer buildings, including an outpatient building, ward building, and administrative building. Financial and medical records were all on computer, in a well-equipped computer room. They demonstrated to us how the Chinese characters were called up. The radiology department was also impressive. After the tour they invited us for dinner. The retired director, an elderly army officer, joined us for the meal. He had become a member of the staff as a young doctor in 1926, the year my father left China. The dinner was elegant, served with

Henry and Katie with administrative staff of People's Liberation Army Hospital, the former Methodist Hospital, Huzhou 1987.

excellent Chinese wine for the inevitable toasts. Nothing is too good for the army. Before we left, they presented us with a couple pieces of silk brocade, product of Huzhou, which is located in the center of China's silk industry.

On the way back to Hangzhou, we took a side trip westward to Moganshan, the mountain resort where my brother Charles was born. The road was steep but paved to the top, which was covered beautifully with a light snow. As a child, porters had carried me and the baggage, while my parents hiked up. The road passed through thick bamboo groves. I had been told that my parents' house on the mountain was no longer there. We saw a number of the old summer homes; a hotel, closed for the winter; and an interdenominational chapel. The chapel looked familiar to me. It may have been where I went for day care with the other English-speaking children, to get me ready for life in the States.

Taihu

Taihu (Lake Tai) is a large lake, with an area of over eight hundred square miles, located on the border between Zhejiang and Jiangsu Provinces. Wuxi and Suzhou are north of the lake; Jiaxing is southeast; and Huzhou is at the southwest corner. We crossed the lake twice by overnight ferry from Hangzhou to Wuxi. The first time was after our initial visit to Hangzhou. We left Hangzhou New Year's Eve, going first by canal to Huzhou, where the canal enters the lake. The evening was punctuated by fireworks all along the way. The cabin and bunks were comfortable and the passage smooth. Just before dawn, we drew close to the islands south of Wuxi. There, once again, the ferry has a short canal passage to get to the ferry terminal.

The second time we took the ferry, we had gone to Hangzhou for a weekend gathering of some of the Amity teachers who were teaching in the south Jiangsu-Zhejiang area. We were due back in Zhenjiang for afternoon classes on Monday and, since the ferry was scheduled to arrive at Wuxi shortly after dawn, we planned to catch an early morning train from Wuxi to Zhenjiang. We left Hangzhou on schedule and went to bed, while the ferry was still in the canal heading toward the lake. Much to our surprise, we awoke in the morning to find the ferry tied up to the canal bank at Huzhou. The ferry had very little freeboard. Due to a strong wind, the waves in the lake had been too high for the ferry to make the crossing safely. After the sun rose, the wind died down and the ferry resumed its journey. The lake was not too rough during the crossing and we arrived in Wuxi at midday. In Wuxi we caught the next available train, but missed our afternoon classes.

Wuxi

Wuxi is located on the rail line about halfway between Nanjing and Shanghai, a little over an hour east of Zhenjiang by train. It is a very old city with a history of about 3000 years. It was formerly named Youxi, meaning "has tin," for its tin mines. Tin, one of the components of bronze, made Youxi a prime object of conquest. The mines played out long before the time of Christ, so the name was changed to Wuxi meaning "no tin," to minimize its importance, so it would be a less tempting target for rival warlords.

Wuxi has three famous gardens. We stayed several times at Shuixiu Hotel adjacent to Liyuan Garden. About a third of the original garden is now reserved for the use of Shuixiu and Hubin Hotels, which stand side by side. The hotels and gardens border the canal leading from Lake Tai to the city. This is a very active canal with a constant flow of boat traffic. The garden has several large ponds with a number of lovely pavilions, covered walkways, and bridges. In the portion that belongs to the hotels, there were many trees which afforded interesting bird-watching opportunities. A lovely little pagoda stood on a breakwater at the canal bank.

We met a Chinese businessman from Hong Kong at the hotel, who was in charge of an amusement park that was just being completed. It was the joint venture of a Hong Kong business with a local group. Located beside another one of the gardens, Meiyuan, it was to open the day after we left to return to Zhenjiang. He invited us to go to the park with him, as they were going to have a dress rehearsal. They let us enjoy all of the rides. He invited us to lunch at a nice restaurant in the center of the park. He would not let us pay, as we were giving the staff a chance to practice. It was really weird, being the only guests in the park that day. We revisited it on a later trip to Wuxi when it was open to the public.

The first time we visited Meiyuan was in the dead of winter. There was little to see besides a couple of lovely pavilions on the hillside. Our next visit was with a group from Zhenjiang Hospital. A bus load of us made a daylong excursion to Wuxi and to a cave in a nearby town. It was springtime and the garden was lovely with flower beds, wisteria arbors, and plum trees in bloom. On this trip, one of the members fell and sprained a knee. There were a couple of traditional medicine doctors on the bus. One of them opened her purse and fished out a little tube where she kept her acupuncture needles. The top had come off and the needles had spilled into the purse. She gathered them up and proceeded to give an acupuncture treatment to the injured knee. She wiped the needle with an alcohol sponge, but it was not a sterile procedure.

Wuxi's third garden was on the tip of a peninsula, about half of which was a nature park with wooded hills and hiking paths. "Turtle Head Garden," at the end of the peninsula, had a number of ponds, bridges, and pavilions. A rocky formation jutting out into Lake Tai resembled, in silhouette, a turtle's head. On the "head" was a small lighthouse. We ferried from "Turtle Head" back across the canal to the amusement park and Meiyuan. From "Turtle Head" there was also a boat excursion out to Sanshan (Three Hills Isle) which the ferry from Hangzhou passes on its approach to Wuxi.

We went in search of a church in Wuxi. We finally found it, set back in a long courtyard off one of the main streets. It was a large brick church built in the style of a cathedral, with aisles outside of archways on both sides of the sanctuary. Tall windows above the arches rose to a vaulted ceiling. We stepped into the back of the church. A group of women were meeting at the front of the church. We turned to leave and one of the women leaders chased us down to talk to us. She introduced us to a couple of the pastors. They were having an anniversary celebration for an elderly woman, a Bible teacher in her nineties. They had prepared a luncheon in her honor and insisted that we join them. When they discovered that I had been born in Huzhou, one of the pastors exclaimed that he was also born in Huzhou at the Methodist Hospital the same year.

Faye's Visit

Faye, our youngest daughter, then twenty-one, planned to visit us during her summer vacation in 1987. She had developed her talent in art beginning at The American School Of Kinshasa (TASOK) in Zaïre, where she started with pen and ink and watercolors. While a student at Vanderbilt University, she had worked with acrylics. She expressed a desire to learn to paint with Chinese brush and ink while in China. Ms. Ni, the hospital artist, painted in Western style with oils. She said she was unable to teach Faye Chinese style painting, so she asked Dr. Yu Xingkun to contact the city foreign affairs bureau to see what could be arranged. Dr. Yu, being responsible for foreign affairs at the hospital, was our liaison officer. Never in our lives have we been so attentively cared for. He, in turn, went through the city bureau to contact Mr. Ding Guanjia, Director of the Zhenjiang Chinese Art Institute. Mr. Ding is one of China's one hundred nationally recognized artists. He has exhibited his art in China as well as in several foreign countries. He was often out of the city, but since he would be in Zhenjiang during Faye's visit, he decided to teach her himself. Mr. Ding had studied English as a high school student many years before, but was not conversant in English. Faye, of course, knew no Chinese. Shortly after Faye's arrival, Mr. Ding came to see us. His son, who was then in high school, had helped him write out his plan for her instruction in English. Our kitchen was converted into a studio. Mr. Ding came to the house and spent about eight hours a day teaching Faye for three weeks. I spent a great deal of time with them to translate, but it was amazing how well they communicated, in spite of the language barrier. Mr. Ding was most complimentary of Faye's talent. By the end of his instruction, she had quite a portfolio of paintings she had done under his tutelage. As a result of his teaching, I became interested in sketching again. I had been interested in art in high school, but had done nothing since. I began to sketch in Chinese style, using some Japanese pens that Mr. Ding gave me, which simulate Chinese brush pens. I continued sketching, not only during the rest of our touring in China, but also in the States and other countries we have visited. On weekends we took Faye to introduce her to some of the sights in Zhenjiang, Suzhou, Wuxi, Taizhou, and Yangzhou.

Yangzhou

Yangzhou is on the Grand Canal just north of the Yangzi River opposite Zhenjiang. Large ferries accommodating about thirty cars or trucks carried us across the river. It was always an interesting crossing, as there was a constant flow of river traffic: long strings of barges, small fishing boats, ocean freighters, and river passenger boats. A couple of times, as we crossed the river, we were privileged to catch glimpses of the endangered freshwater Yangzi River porpoises.

Yangzhou has a number of points of interest, the major one being Slender West Lake. This is a long serpentine lake with many interesting vistas, situated in a large park in the western section of the city. It is crossed at one point by a picturesque bridge which has a group of five pavilions in the center. There is also a large white *dagoba* modeled after the one in Beihai Park in Beijing. Some of our Amity friends were teaching in a college on the edge of the park. We had occasion to visit them and the park a couple of times. In warm weather, the lake was filled with visitors paddling about in rowboats or paddle wheel rafts.

On a hill north of the Slender West Lake, Fajing Buddhist Temple was often visited by Japanese tour groups. One of the very early Buddhist missionaries to Japan was sent from this temple. The Japanese contributed much of the fund for its restoration.

Two former staff members of Sarah Walkup Hospital in Taizhou lived in Yangzhou, Miss Tang, the pharmacist, and her older sister, the hospital seamstress. We visited them and met their nephew and his family. The church we attended with them was the former Baptist church. Only the sanctuary had been returned to the Three-Self congregation for worship. The Sunday school portion of the building was still occupied by a general store. We had a couple very happy visits with the Tang sisters. We were sorry to learn on our last visit to China in 1993 that the older sister had died and the younger was in failing health.

Beijing, Qufu, Taishan

As soon as the school year was over in July, we started touring with Faye. We first went to Beijing by train. China Travel made our hotel reservation using my Chinese name. We were met at the train by one of their representatives who was surprised to see that we were not Chinese. We were booked at one of the Overseas Chinese Hotels. It was adequate and in a convenient location; however, it was deliberately destroyed by implosion about six months later, to be replaced by a new four star hotel. We took Faye to see a number of Beijing's sights including the Great Wall, Summer Palace, Temple of Heaven, and Palace Museum (Forbidden City).

On leaving Beijing, we planned to visit Qufu and Taishan. Qufu, the ancestral home of Kong Fuzi (Confucius), is south of Taishan, but is not on the rail line. Knowing that it would be relatively easy to get train tickets to continue south from Tainan, the town at the base of Taishan mountain, we planned to visit Qufu first. We got off the train at Yanzhou, the station south of Tainan which serves Qufu, for the thirteen kilometer bus ride. Part of the Kong ancestral home was open as a hotel and the remainder was a museum. The large Confucian Temple and Memorial Hall were next door. It was an interesting experience, being housed in part of the home of the sage. There were some quaintly painted horse carts which offered transport for the two and a half kilometers up a slight rise to the Confucian Forest, the Kong family cemetery. Many in Qufu claimed to be descendants of Confucius. One of them who claims to be a seventy-third generation descendant was an old gentleman with a scraggly beard who sat at the entrance to the cemetery. He made a living by allowing tourists to take his picture for a price.

From Qufu we traveled north to Tainan by bus, arriving in the afternoon. Our hotel was at the base of the path leading up the mountain. Taishan, located in Shandong Province, is said to be the most revered of China's sacred mountains. It rises to 1545 meters (around 5000 ft.), which is not very high as mountains go, but it towers above the surrounding country. The ascent from the hotel was steep for a distance of seven kilometers (four and a half miles). There are stone steps all the way. Katie climbed up to the halfway point the afternoon of our arrival; I accompanied her part of the way. The next morning we took a taxi to the halfway point, where there was an

Qufu—Confucius Home
7-11-87—H. S. Nelson

option. Katie climbed the stairs leading to the summit. Faye and I opted to take the cable car for three valid reasons. We needed to get to the top ahead of the crowd in order to assure a place in the overnight lodge near the summit. We also wanted time to do sketching at the top. Thirdly, we did not want to tackle the steep ascent of the last section of stairs.

The ride in the cable car afforded spectacular views. The car carried about thirty passengers. The cables were over a mile long, swinging freely across a valley. We obtained the last rooms in the lodge. The accommodations were rather Spartan, the bedding damp from the fogs, and toilet facilities rudimentary. The scenery was unsurpassed! We watched the sunset and arose in the morning along with all the Chinese tourists to view the sunrise, the principal attraction. All available vantage points were occupied. Everyone was shivering and bundled up in the predawn chill. The three of us returned by cable car and took a taxi back to the hotel. We discovered that we could not get reserved space in a sleeper from Tainan, as there were no places reserved for Tainan passengers on the Beijing-Nanjing train. We had to gamble on getting moved to a sleeper by the trainmaster, and were prepared to sit up all night. Luckily we did manage to get moved to the soft sleeper after boarding the train.

Yangzi River Trip

The Bowers were teachers at Zhenjiang Shipbuilding Institute. Jim was from the States; Jytte was Danish. They had a teenage son, Eric, with Down's Syndrome. They had been told when he was a baby that he might not walk nor talk. He was a remarkable example of what loving care can do. He not only could talk, but won his way into the hearts of the Chinese and was a delightful traveling companion. He probably picked up more Chinese than most American adults in China. All of us were interested in making the trip through the Yangzi River gorges. We wanted to make the trip going up river, instead of down, as the passage was slower going against the current. Mr. Tian Wenxue, foreign affairs officer at the Shipbuilding Institute, arranged for our passage on one of the regular passenger boats. We boarded at Zhenjiang shortly after our return from the Beijing trip. The second- and third-class accommodations were well filled. We had three first-class cabins, which had two bunks to a cabin. Faye and Jytte shared one cabin, Katie and I, and Jim and Eric took the other cabins. The first-class lounge stretched across the front of the ship, serving both as a day room and dining room.

The changing scenery and variety of river traffic kept us constantly entertained. In some areas the land was flat and in others, hills would appear on one side or the other of the stream. Villages and towns appeared, some with pagodas, each one with its distinctive architecture. One of the most picturesque views was Xiaogushan, a Buddhist nunnery, built on an island that juts out of the river with steep cliffs on all sides. The steady pace of the boat made for constantly changing perspectives, which provided a challenge to sketchers as scenes slipped by.

泰山碧霞祠
八七年七月十三日
倪恩义画稿

Taishan
7-13-87—H. S. Nelson

Mr. Tian had only been able to get our reservations as far as Wuhan. The passenger boats on the lower Yangzi are too large to go through the locks in the dam just above Wuhan. One must transfer to smaller boats for the passage on up through the gorges to Chongqing. We expected to have to stay in Wuhan until we could get passage for the remainder of the trip. A Chinese lady, Mrs. Huang, boarded the boat in Nanjing. She had just returned from the U.S. and was on her way home to Wuhan. When she heard our plans, she said that she knew the captain of the boat. She offered to ask him to radio ahead for reservations on the connecting boat. When we arrived at Wuhan, the other boat was waiting. The captain had the purser take us off the ship first and accompany us to the other boat. We gratefully accepted the favor.

The boat for the upper reaches of the Yangzi was a slightly smaller version of the boat we had just left. We had similar accommodations. The passage through the locks was fascinating, as the ship rose sixty feet in ten minutes. The river was at flood stage and we learned later that our boat was one of the last to go through the locks before they were damaged by the high water. Traffic through the locks was then halted for over a month while repairs were being made.

The gorges lived up to their billing. The steep hills rise about a thousand feet on either side, dwarfing the ship. On the cliff sides we saw the old tow-paths where teams of coolies formerly towed the boats up against the current. At Fengdu we stopped behind a line of five or six passenger boats. Here the boat remained for twenty-four hours, waiting for the flood waters to recede. When we continued upstream, we could see where the water level had dropped twenty feet or more at some of the towns. Another unusual and interesting scene was Shibaozai (Stone Treasure Stronghold). A monastery was built there on a small plateau with vertical cliffs on all sides. A pagoda built against the side of the cliff provided access to the monastery.

Chongqing, the Nationalist wartime capital, is built on a steep and narrow hill between the Yangzi and the Jialing Rivers, which join at this point. When the flood receded, it left a thick carpet of mud over the street and lower floors of stores that were thirty feet above the boat landing. Our hotel was on top of the hill. Shortly after we registered, a tour group arrived. They had been on one of the tour boats going down the river. They had gone through a couple of the gorges when the lock was damaged, then had to debark and travel back to Chongqing by bus. They had been on the bus for over twelve hours. They only had about four or five hours rest at the hotel before they left by air to resume their itinerary schedule. It made us realize how lucky we were to get through the locks when we did.

In Chongqing we parted company with the Bowers. A short distance from the hotel, a cable car descended the hill to the railway station. We were able to get soft sleeper tickets to go south to Guilin the next day. We bought tickets all the way to Guilin, but were required to get seat assignments for the soft seat coach when we changed trains at Liuzhou. As we were having trouble finding where to go, an army officer kindly responded to our questions and directed us through the mob to the foreign passenger service

Xiaogushan

7-18-87—H. S. Nelson

window. We found that an army officer was frequently the best person to ask for assistance. Finally on our way to Guilin, the train passed through countryside with steep hills, many of them terraced for cultivation.

Guilin

The principal attraction of Guilin was our trip on the Li River. The river boats were shallow draft and carried about fifty people. The lower level had seats, but the deck above allowed a better view of the scenery as the boat drifted down the stream. The limestone hills in the region have weird shapes, with almost perpendicular sides as they jut up out of the fields. These hills have inspired artists for generations, for scenes from Li River are common in Chinese paintings. Along the banks we saw occasional herds of water buffalo. Fishermen on rafts of bamboo were a common feature of the river. Some of the fishermen used cormorants. A ring around the bird's neck permitted it to swallow only the smaller fish. When it caught a fish too large to pass the ring, the fisherman retrieved it from the bird's throat. The sketches I did on the boat trip had to be done rapidly and were not finished due to the ever changing perspective as the boat drifted along. Lunch was served on the boat. Buses met the boat at Yangshuo, a small town at the end of the cruise, for the return trip to Guilin.

The road back to Guilin passed through intensely cultivated fields interspersed with vertical hills. We were told that many of the hills were honeycombed with caves. The soft limestone dissolves and when the caves collapse, the weird shaped hills result. One rainy day we visited a cave on the outskirts of Guilin. On the way we sat in the rear of the city bus with a young tourist couple. The cave site was at the end of the line, so everyone had to get off the bus. We five foreigners were last to get off. Before we could descend from the bus, a crowd of Chinese started fighting to get on. I had to physically force my way off and block the door to allow the others to get off. A tour group arrived about the same time. The tour guide noted our difficulty and integrated us into her group. It was a wet cave, with a lot of stalactites and stalagmites which were well-lighted to show off the formations. The tour bus had space available, so they graciously gave us a ride back into town, stopping on the way at one of the city parks.

From Guilin we flew to Hangzhou to show Faye some of the sights that we had enjoyed there. On leaving Hangzhou, we traveled by bus eight hours westward to Huangshan (Yellow Mountain) in Anhui Province.

Huangshan

Huangshan is a group of peaks in south Anhui province that rise out of the fertile Yangzi plain. They are a little more than 6000 feet in elevation. The

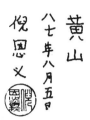

八月五日
黄山
八七年
倪恩义

Huangshan
8-5-87—H. S. Nelson

summits are frequently above the clouds which blanket the surrounding low countryside. After spending the night at the base of the mountain in the only hotel open to foreigners, we went up the next morning by cable car. We obtained a room in the Beihai Hotel. It was one of the worst accommodations we have ever encountered. The bedding was dirty and damp. The toilet facilities were communal and filthy, with water on the floor, and were kept locked part of the time. By evening the beds were all rented, and people were bedded down on the floor in the lobbies and halls. A group occupied the hall outside our room and played cards all night. The attraction of Huangshan is the scenery which is celebrated in Chinese poetry and is the subject of a great many Chinese paintings. I was out sketching when a Chinese man approached me. He was an artist, living on the mountain for the summer in order to paint. He invited himself to our room to show us some of his work. Of course, we were obligated to buy one of his paintings, but he also gave us one. We rose before daybreak along with everyone else to view the sunrise. The Chinese delight in giving colorful names to natural formations. One of those at the summit is a rock that in profile looks like a sitting monkey. It is named "Monkey Contemplating the Sea," referring to the sea of clouds that often cover the lands below. As we hiked down the mountain, we viewed a large granite boulder balanced on a narrow base, entitled "The Rock that Flew from Afar." It was very familiar to us, as a picture of it was used as the opening scene for a television series of the ancient novel, *Dream of Red Mansions*. The next morning, after a good night's rest, we caught the bus to Nanjing for another eight-hour ride.

Faye's visit was over all too soon. We accompanied her on the plane from Nanjing to Hong Kong, then spent a couple of days with her, enjoying the sights and shopping before she boarded the plane for the States. We then returned to the People's Republic of China.

Zhenjiang Number One People's Hospital 1987-88

On returning to Zhenjiang we began once again our teaching schedule. In addition, I was called upon by a couple of the staff to edit articles they had written in English. One of these was the orthopedist. He had designed an external fixation device that he was using for the treatment of a variety of fractures. One of the local factories had produced them to his specifications. I saw a number of the patients on whom he had used the device, including one with a fractured pelvis. The internist, Dr. Yang Zhaosheng, was another avid student and writer. He did the endoscopic examinations and had quite a series of cases on whom he had detected cancer of the stomach at a very early stage.

An orthopedic surgeon from Shanghai came for a visit and gave a couple of lectures to the staff. He had formerly worked at Zhenjiang. He was reportedly world famous for his work in reattaching severed limbs. The main impediment to this type of surgery in most areas in China was the lack of trained emergency medical technicians and ambulance personnel who knew how to take proper care to preserve the severed part and transport the patient to a facility in time to perform such procedures. A Shanghai kidney transplant specialist came to help with the first kidney transplant to be done at Zhenjiang. When we heard that he was scheduled to come, we asked how they could know in advance that a kidney would be available. We were told that a major source of donor organs in China was from persons executed for the death penalty. In this case, the date of execution for the donor was set.

Annular Eclipse

During our second year at Zhenjiang, we were invited to teach a class for the professors at Zhenjiang Medical College. Katie taught the English professors, who primarily needed help in pronunciation and oral skills. My class was mostly basic science teachers. The first day we went for class coincided with the occurrence of an annular eclipse. We were fortunate that Zhenjiang was in its direct path. Since it was annular, it did not get as dark as the total eclipse we had seen in Zaïre. We prepared to demonstrate the eclipse by projecting the image through a pinhole onto a piece of paper. Our classroom was on the second floor and there was a balcony where we all went to observe the eclipse. Looking down on the ground, we could also see the annular images beneath the trees wherever the sun filtered through the leaves.

Visitors

During our two years at Zhenjiang we had a number of visitors from the States. Among them was a team from DIM. Dr. G. Thompson Brown, executive secretary; Insik Kim, area secretary for the Far East; Dr. Brown Dennis, board physician; and Dr. Paul Crane, medial consultant. As a result of their visit, some needed endoscopic equipment was provided for Dr. Yang. They also promised to provide a scholarship for one of the doctors. The doctor chosen by the hospital for the scholarship was Dr. Zhang Guohui, one of the internal medicine residents. The hospital wanted him to be trained in some of the new cardiovascular techniques. We worked with him to improve his language skills. It took a couple of years to work out the details and to cut through all the red tape. He finally did make it to the States in 1989 after the Tiananmen incident. The cardiologists at St. Thomas Hospital in Nashville undertook to instruct him. The board had agreed to underwrite his initial expenses. Dr. Marshall Crenshaw, whose father had been born in Zhenjiang, was on the staff at St. Thomas and enabled him to extend his period of study.

Doris Caldwell had studied Chinese with us at Yale and Beijing. She was a Presbyterian missionary who, after she had to leave the mainland, served for many years in Hong Kong. She retired and was visiting old friends in Hong Kong and the mainland and included us on her itinerary.

Dr. Joe Wilkerson and his wife Estelle were also in language school with us in Beijing. Joe was assigned to take over from Dr. Young at Jiaxing. He was under house arrest during the last year he was there and was finally allowed to leave after the Richardsons and I left in 1951. He and Estelle were reassigned to Taiwan. We visited them in Taiwan in 1974. At that time their son Douglas showed us around Morrison Academy in Taizhong where he was in high school. In 1987, Douglas was in Nanjing working on his dissertation for his Ph.D. from Yale, writing on an aspect of Chinese opera. We contacted him and visited him in Nanjing; he then came and spent a weekend with us at Zhenjiang. He later became professor of Chinese at the University of Tennessee in Knoxville and has stayed in our home in Maryville several times while we were overseas on short assignments.

We also had some of the Amity teachers visit us at Zhenjiang and enjoyed showing them the sights of the city. Ting Yenren, the Amity educational consultant; Dr. Philip Wickeri, international coordinator; and other Amity representatives came to check on us and the other Amity teachers in Zhenjiang. All Amity personnel were unfailingly considerate and responsive to our concerns and needs.

The largest group of friends who visited us had grown up in Huaiyin. They were Aurie Montgomery Miller, Sophie Montgomery Crane, Virginia Montgomery McCall, Jim Montgomery with his wife Marge, Bob Montgomery, Betty Yates White, and Virginia Yates Miller with her husband Charles. We had a delightful visit with them. Yang Jingfang, a retired nurse, who was a childhood friend from Huaiyin, brought them Chinese dumplings.

Huaiyin, Huaian

Katie and I had been to Huaiyin to celebrate the New Year in 1988, at the invitation of Gene and Lucy King, Amity teachers who were working there. A system of dikes and locks that parallel the Yangzi had raised and maintained the water level in the canals in north Jiangsu. The bus took a road that ran beside the Grand Canal much of the way. Grand Canal certainly fulfills its name in that section, as it was a broad waterway teeming with barges and launches.

It was bitterly cold; the Kings' apartment had terrazzo floors and was not as well-heated as our upstairs quarters in Zhenjiang. As a result, Lucy suffered from frostbite. The church building in Huaiyin had not been returned to the congregation, but was occupied by a hardware store. On Sunday, we worshiped in a former missionary residence. Every room was packed, upstairs and down, the service being carried throughout the building by a speaker system. The old Presbyterian Hospital was now occupied as a Traditional Medicine Hospital. A number of the former missionary residences were still there. A new building was under construction adjacent to the former residence of Dr. Nelson Bell. The house was due to be torn down, but was preserved temporarily in anticipation of a visit by Dr. Billy Graham, whose wife, Ruth Bell Graham, grew up there.

We took a side trip to nearby Huaian. This was the hometown of Chou Enlai, whose home is maintained as a national shrine. Although not elaborate, it has been beautifully restored and is charming in its simplicity. He is much revered and loved by the Chinese, in some ways more than Chairman Mao, these days.

Media Coverage

We were interested in the media coverage given to foreign teachers in China. On one occasion, we were interviewed by the local television station. On National Nurses' Day, Katie was invited to attend the ceremonies and pictures of her were prominent in the local television news. There was also a speaking contest that received media coverage for which Katie and other foreign teachers were asked to judge. The most interesting interview was by a reporter for the national magazine, *Beijing Review*, which is distributed widely and is issued in several languages. She wrote a very sympathetic article on Amity Foundation and included interviews with a couple of Amity teachers. She was especially interested in our Christian motivation for serving in China.

National Day

National Day is one of the big holidays and the Foreign Affairs Bureau took the occasion to arrange a tour for the foreign teachers. Our first year, the local bureau took us on a day trip south of Zhenjiang to visit a Taoist (*Daojiao*) temple, in an area of traditionally strong Taoist influence. There was evidence of a resurgence of Taoism in that area, as mobs of pilgrims climbed the long hill to visit the temple. The floor plan of the temple was much like the Buddhist temples. The major difference was the absence of statues of Buddha and the presence of many of the Taoist statues. On this trip they also took us to see a silk rug weaving factory. The workers at the looms were all women; they explained that men couldn't stand the tedium of sitting for the long shifts.

Our second year, we were included in the tour that was given by the Nanjing bureau. We met the Nanjing group in Wuxi and were taken by bus to spend the night in a rural farming commune north of the city. The amount of space the farm families have was quite a contrast to the cramped quarters of professionals living in the cities. Rural electrification had also markedly changed the farmers' lives. We witnessed the installation of a newly married couple in their apartment. There was a long procession bringing all the wedding gifts. These included bed, cupboards, tables, chairs, lamps, refrigerator, electric sewing machine, radio, a number of small electrical appliances, linens, and comforts, to list a few of the items. The apartment was in a group of row houses. The stairs to the second floor were narrow, so the large items of furniture for the upstairs rooms were hauled up with ropes to a balcony and taken into the room through French doors. The irrigation system on the farm used electric pumps. They also had a historical display of two of the old methods of pumping water into the fields. One was a wooden treadmill that turned a continuous band with cups that scooped up water and dumped it into a trough carrying water to the field. The second method was operated by a water buffalo going round and round a turnstile. These were the methods in use when we first went to China, but are rarely seen in modern China, as electric and diesel pumps have replaced them.

We next ferried the river to Nantong, an industrial town on the north bank of the Yangzi. Most of the industry was new, as joint ventures with foreign interests were being encouraged. In fact, the hotel in which we stayed was a new joint venture between some farming communes and a Hong Kong firm. A small hill at Nantong had interesting temples on the summit, from which we had a good view of the river and the country north of it. We were told of plans to build a bridge there similar to the one at Nanjing, with railroad on the lower deck and a road above. The railroad is to link Wuxi with Nantong and continue to Taizhou and the northeastern part of Jiangsu Province. North Jiangsu was already starting to develop industries and this promises to speed the development tremendously. The tour ended by Yangzi river boat. We were dropped off at Zhenjiang, with the rest of the group returning to Nanjing.

Harbin

Vacation at China New Year lasts about a month. Following the Amity meeting in Xiamen in January 1988, we decided to go see the ice carvings at Harbin, the capital of Heilongjiang Province. Harbin is well north of Korea, and endures sub-zero weather most of the winter. Each year they have an ice carving contest in January. Many of the larger, more elaborate carvings have lights in them, so are called ice lanterns. Mr. Tian, our friend from the Shipbuilding Institute in Zhenjiang, had transferred back to Harbin, his home town. We wrote to him and asked him to make hotel reservations for us. He met us at the railroad station and escorted us to the hotel. The temperature hovered around minus twenty centigrade (-4 Fahrenheit) for the entire time we were in Harbin. The buildings, however, were overheated.

The ice carvings formed a fantastic display. We went to see them first during the day and returned again at night when they were lighted. It was the year of the dragon, so there was a large carving of a dragon at the entrance to the park. Some of the carvings displayed were very large, constructed of many blocks of ice. Several were shaped like temples, one of which was three stories tall. The Songhua River was frozen solid. On the river bank, there was an ice slide down which children were sliding. We rode on the river in a one horse open sleigh! A swimming pool was carved in the ice. On TV we had seen some swimmers taking a plunge in the icy water, but no one attempted it while we were there. We could not bear the cold more than an hour at a time before returning to the warmth of the hotel.

Mr. Tian proudly showed us around the city and took us to the home of his parents for dinner. Harbin was at one time the largest Russian city outside the USSR. Much of the architecture strongly reflects Russian influence. The Three-Self church, which we attended on Sunday, resembled a Russian Orthodox church. It was overcrowded, with standing room only.

There was an extensive underground city. Tunnels, built for air raid shelters at a time when they feared a Russian attack, had been converted to stores. I found them to be very poorly ventilated. Mr. Tian took us to see an industrial exhibition and a Chinese opera. Ordinarily we had difficulty following Chinese opera, but he was able to explain the plot and tell us what was going on, which made it interesting. The only trouble was that the auditorium had very little heat. At the end of our visit, Mr. Tian came in a car to take us to the train. He really made our visit a memorable one.

Transition 1988

Since we were to complete our Amity assignment at Zhenjiang in July 1988, Amity officials encouraged Katie to accept an invitation to serve as a nursing consultant with Project HOPE, relative to their Faculty Preparation Program at Beijing Medical University (BMU). This three-phase program was designed to facilitate the upgrading of nursing faculty for China's new Bachelor of Science in Nursing programs. I was invited to continue with Amity at BMU, teaching graduate students, with a focus on oral and scientific English.

At the close of the school year, we shipped our belongings to Beijing for storage, and prepared to join a group of my family for a two-week tour of China. We planned to spend a few weeks in the States before returning to Beijing in September.

Nelson Family Tour

The family group included our son Sperry, my brother Charles, his wife Betty, his daughter Melissa, Betty's sister Wilma, my cousin Robert Kearley, his wife Marlene, Dr. Terry Bingham with his wife Kathy, their daughters Brandi and Wendy, and their teenage son Jared, which brought the total to fourteen. We joined the group in Suzhou, went to Hangzhou by train and back to Shanghai, then flew to Beijing. Most of the sights of interest we had visited before, but it was fun to see them again with the family. We were taken to a few places that were new to us, mostly visits to factories and a tea plantation. We also persuaded the guide to take the group to see the ancient observatory at Jianguomen and let us climb to the top of Coal Hill for a panoramic view of the Forbidden City. In Beijing, Robert and Marlene met some relatives of their son-in-law.

Xian

From Beijing we flew to Xian. The visit with the Nelson tour group was actually our second visit there and Katie was to return later for sessions at Xian Medical University. Our first visit was in the dead of winter. We took advantage of a Christmas special at the Golden Flower Hotel, a Swedish joint venture. The warmth, Christmas decorations, carols, and holiday food were a welcome break from the cold Yangzi valley. We had our introduction to some of the Xian sights at that time.

Xian has a long and illustrious history extending back some 6000 years to Neolithic times. Over a period of 3000 years, Xian was the capital of numerous Chinese dynasties including the Qin, Han, Sui, and Tang. It is one of the few Chinese cities that has preserved its city wall. The wall was impressive, though not quite as massive as the Beijing wall, before it was torn down. There was much to see in Xian. Most impressive were the terra-cotta warriors that were still being excavated near the tomb of Qin Shihuangdi, the first emperor of a unified China. A very large hangarlike building had been constructed over the site. Row on row of the life-sized army of statues were exposed and restored. On the way to see the warriors, we stopped to see the interesting ruins of the Neolithic Banpo village which is estimated to be 6000 years old. On the same road was Huaqing Pool, an ancient spa, famous as the site where Chiang Kaishek was captured in 1936 and finally released.

In the center of town, the Bell Tower and nearby Drum Tower date from the Qing Dynasty. Such structures were built in many cities of that period and were used to signal the time of opening and closing of the city gates. Near the Drum Tower, we saw the Great Mosque of Xian. We climbed the Big Goose Pagoda, outside the city wall and Little Goose Pagoda inside the city. The provincial museum contained the "forest of steles," huge stone tablets containing many ancient writings. Of major interest to us was the Nestorian tablet engraved in 781 A.D. to mark the opening of a Nestorian church. The Nestorians were a Syrian Christian sect which eventually was suppressed.

One day was spent on a bus tour to the imperial tombs. The tomb of the third Tang emperor was eighty-five kilometers from the city. The tomb, like most of the imperial tombs around Xian, was a huge mound of dirt and had a large avenue of stone animal statues leading to it. Most of the imperial tombs had not been excavated. The tomb of Princess Yongtai was an exception. It contained beautiful frescoes which were losing their color, showing evidence of damage, perhaps due to moisture and to pollution resulting from the visits of many tourists. From Xian we flew to Guilin, where we took the Li River trip with the family group and then went on to Hong Kong.

Hong Kong

We have visited Hong Kong on several occasions, on our way to or from China. The Nelson tour group spent a day there. On Hong Kong Island we went to the peak, where one has a magnificent view of the harbor. A trip to the floating city on the back side of the island was fascinating. The harbor was packed with junks of all sizes, seeking refuge as a typhoon was due to hit the island that evening. Part of the day was given over to shopping. In the evening, Sperry went with us to a Chinese restaurant several blocks from our hotel. During the meal the typhoon struck. We came out to a torrential downpour and a high wind. The streets were several inches deep with water. We stood in line under a shelter waiting for a taxi. When a taxi drove up, a man ran out to get ahead of the line instead of waiting his turn. The wind caught his umbrella and pulled him down. When he fell, he broke his leg and couldn't get up, as the wind dragged him along the ground. Someone had to go and help him to shelter, until an ambulance could be summoned. We were sorry about his leg, but heard many murmurs to the effect that he "got what he asked for."

Twice, following Amity meetings at Xiamen, we traveled to Hong Kong on overnight ferries which had Chinese names. The second time, when we boarded the ferry, it seemed very familiar. It was not until we went to the dining room that we discovered the reason. Outside the dining room was a play area which we immediately recognized as one where Sperry's children, John and Anne, had played when we were on a family trip to Scandinavia. The ferry had been the *King Olaf V* on which we sailed from Oslo to Copenhagen in 1983. It had been sold to the Chinese, and we sailed on it again five years later, on the other side of the globe.

In Hong Kong, we have usually stayed at the YMCA on Kowloon peninsula, since it is very conveniently located near the main shopping street, subway, and Star Ferry. The ferry across to Hong Kong Island is very cheap and affords a fantastic view of the harbor. The island is lined with skyscrapers and the harbor is busy with ships and boats of all descriptions, going in every direction. On one visit we took a trip by ferry to one of the smaller islands in the territory, to see a fishing village and an old temple.

The office of the Overseas Coordinator for Amity, Dr. Philip Wickeri, is located in Hong Kong at the International Church, conveniently near a subway stop. We have worshiped there while in Hong Kong on Sunday, and the Amity office has been a regular stop. Philip and Janice Wickeri and the Amity staff serve wonderfully well the needs of wayfaring Amity teachers.

Macao

Nearby Macao can be reached by way of several different kinds of ferries. The main difference among them is the speed and time that it takes to make the trip. We chose to go by the hydrofoil, which is the second fastest. Most people went to Macao for gambling, which was unlawful in Hong Kong. That didn't interest us, but there were other things that did. Robert Morrison, who translated the Bible into Chinese, was buried there along with his wife and son who continued his work. We visited their graves. Dr. Sun Yatsen also lived and practiced there for a while and his house is preserved as a museum. The façade of an old cathedral remains high on a hill, outlined starkly against the sky, all that is left following destruction by a typhoon. Its picture is used as a symbol of Macao. We cut our visit short as a typhoon was due to hit and we were afraid that ferry service would be disrupted.

Beijing Medical University 1988-89

On July 20, 1988, following our trip in China with the family group, we returned to the States for a few weeks before going back to Beijing. Since Project Hope receives funds from USAID, its consultants are required to travel via U.S. flag carriers whenever possible. Katie was booked on Northwest Airlines from San Francisco to Tokyo. I was sent by the Presbyterian Church to work with Amity, so had to fly the most economical way. We flew together to the west coast, then parted company, as Katie's flight was not until the following day. Actually, it was further delayed in leaving the States, so she had a very close connection in Tokyo. Her baggage did not make the transfer and came on a later flight, resulting in the loss of one trunk. Unfortunately it contained, among other things, some of our medicines. It took six months and numerous trips to the airport before we finally received some compensation for the lost piece of luggage. Sperry had to send more medicines to us. Fortunately a nurse from Knoxville was coming to Beijing for a conference and delivered the package to us.

Beijing Medical University (BMU) was located in the northwest section of Beijing on Daxuelu (University Avenue), where there were a number of specialized universities. In China, specialization begins at the university level, rather than at the graduate level, in many fields of study. The Telecommunications University was south of BMU. The Aeronautical University was across the street. Iron and Steel University was just north, with the Geographical University across the street from it. Farther out the avenue were the Mining University and Foreign Language University. BMU should not be confused with Peking Union Medical College and its Capital Hospital, which were located downtown in the old city, just a few blocks east of the Forbidden City. BMU had a number of schools, including the under-graduate program for physicians, nursing, hospital administration, phar-macy, and public health, and a graduate school for preparing basic science teachers. My English classes included graduate students and doctors from all over China, who came for continuing education. In addition, during the sec-ond half of the year, I had a drill session with a group of about fifteen stu-dents who came to BMU for an intensive course in English, mostly from hos-pitals in north China. Among them were a couple from Tibet and a couple from Inner Mongolia. Several were hospital administrators. They were all Communist Party members and leaders in their respective communities. I was also asked to give lectures in English to the junior and senior classes of medical students, to give them an opportunity to hear English spoken.

Selling Bibles at Chongwenmen Church, Beijing 1990.

Katie was involved in preparations for the second phase of the Faculty Preparation Program at BMU, but went to Xian Medical University for a month to teach their nursing faculty. While Katie was at Xian, I went to visit her one weekend. A young couple teaching English there were sponsored by one of the groups who go to China with the avowed intention of evangelizing. They were very critical of, and did not cooperate with the Three-Self Movement. When we invited them to go to church with us, they suggested that the Three-Self churches did not preach the full Gospel, used a censored Bible, and restricted Bible sales. We told them that we had attended many services in widely scattered churches and had heard the Gospel preached, including salvation through Jesus Christ. We also knew that the Bible was the same version that we had used prior to 1949, having been printed by a photo-offset process. We prevailed upon them to go with us. When we arrived, the church was overflowing and the courtyard was filled with chairs. One of the pastors was in the courtyard selling Bibles and Christian literature from a table loaded with Bibles. We asked the price of the Bibles and found them to be very reasonable, since they are partially subsidized. We next asked the pastor if he had difficulty getting Bibles to sell. He beamed and replied that since the Amity Press had opened, he was able to get his stock of Bibles replenished as fast as he could sell them.

Beijing Churches

While living in Beijing in 1988-89, my experience with the Protestant churches there was limited, since we usually attended Chongwenmen Church. Once in the fall of the year, I attended Xisi Church, located just south of the intersection where Xisi Pilou (West Four Memorial Arches) formerly stood. The church was just off the street behind some stores. The large rectangular hall holds about eight hundred and was crowded, which is typical of all the churches we attended in China.

Chongwenmen Church was accessible for us by taking a bus from our campus to the subway. The church is on an alley close by the subway stop of the same name. It was formerly a Methodist church, and there was a former Methodist mission station and school next door. The latter is now a government school. When we first attended Chongwenmen, they were attempting to locate former graduates of the mission school, as they were planning a reunion. While we were in Beijing, the gate of the mission station was restored, and the doors painted bright red. Plaster was removed from the lintel that had hidden the name, "Methodist Mission." Former President George Bush had attended this church when he lived in Beijing and represented the U.S. presence there. He also attended later, when he visited Beijing in 1989. On that occasion, the church held a special early morning service for him, to which attendance was restricted. We were not invited to attend, but saw his convoy of cars leaving the service before we entered for the regular service.

The sanctuary is a large octagonal room. The choir sits on the right of the pulpit. Behind the choir, a partition can be raised to open a large Sunday school room where overflow crowds are seated. As is the custom in many churches, most of the congregation gathered a half-hour early. At this time a song leader directed the practice of the hymns to be used in the service. Many of the people did not have hymnals, so at this time they learned the words and melodies of the hymns. There were often two or three tour groups present on Sunday at Chongwenmen Church. They were usually seated in the rear or in the Sunday school addition. They often stayed through the worship portion of the service and left just before the sermon. This was understandable, since most tourists do not know Chinese and the sermons often lasted about an hour. Some of the churches we attended insisted upon seating foreign guests in the front. It was somewhat disruptive to have a large group get up and leave just before the sermon, but it did not seem to bother the Chinese worshippers.

The International Church met in the International Club downtown. English services there were attended by a number of the international students as well as business and embassy personnel. The International Church sponsored an annual Easter sunrise service in English on the Great Wall at Badaling. We attended this service in 1989 and 1990; there were several hundred in attendance in the chill predawn each time. Proclaiming the risen Christ at such a place and in company with Chinese friends and visitors from all over the world was a rare privilege.

The Great Wall

The Great Wall snakes over rugged mountains and guards passes for some 5000 kilometers (3000 miles) from Shanhaiguan on the east coast to

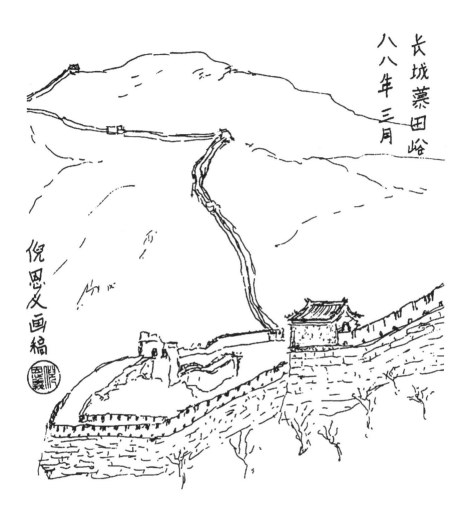

长城慕田峪
八八年 三月

倪恩义画稿

Great Wall—Mutianyu
3-88—H. S. Nelson

Jiayuguan in the Gobi Desert. Badaling was the closest and most accessible site on the wall for tour groups in Beijing. Most foreign tour groups combined a visit to it with the Ming tombs and the Summer Palace. We saw the Great Wall at Shanhaiguan, where it dips into the sea, as we passed by on the train en route to Harbin. Three other points were being developed for tourism, in an effort to relieve the pressure of tremendous crowds at Badaling; these were frequented more often by Chinese tour groups. The first time we visited the wall at Mutianyu was just before it was officially opened. A cable car up to the wall was operating and we rode up and walked about a mile along a section of the wall that had been restored, then walked down the mountain on well-paved paths and stairs. There were only a couple of other persons there at that time. We returned later with a group of Katie's students. It was beginning to be commercialized, and there were a number of Chinese tourists, but it still was not nearly as crowded as Badaling, which was closer to Beijing.

Jinshan Pass was scheduled to be developed. At the time we visited it in 1990, there was road access, but no commercialization. It was a minor pass and the wall ascended steeply on either side, dotted with the usual guard and signal towers. A unique site on the wall was at Simatai Pass, above which we could see the wall snaking along the crest of long jagged ridges. A dam has created a lake that fills the pass. We rode a boat on the lake through the pass to a hot spring. The wall rose steeply out of the water on either side of the narrow lake. This site was farther from Beijing than the others we had visited, except for Shanhaiguan. No other tourists were there at the time. I enjoyed sketching scenes at all these places.

Beijing Sights and Sounds

Living in Beijing for a year afforded the opportunity to visit many of the sights that are not included in the usual two or three day tour. I bought a bicycle which I often used to visit some of the closer ones. Most places could be reached by public transportation. The Bell and Drum Towers were both mounted by means of long steep internal stairs. There were reproductions of the great drums in the Drum Tower and an enormous bell in the Bell Tower. The bell was rung by a huge log swinging on chains that struck the outside of the bell. There was a marketplace between the two towers, which were surrounded by old one-story gray brick houses with gray tile roofs. The houses were built in a series of crowded courtyards, separated by narrow *hutongs* (alleyways).

The Great Bell Temple had a collection of old temple bells. It also had a very interesting exhibit showing a couple of methods that were used to cast the bells. The Confucian Temple, where genealogical records were kept, was near the Lama Temple, and the street in front of it still had beautiful memorial arches. In 1988 after a couple of tries, we finally found the Five-Pagoda Temple. When we first saw it in 1948, it was outside the city, surrounded by fields. We now located it behind the zoo, in a densely built-up neighborhood, accessible by an unpaved street. A small park surrounded it, in which a number of steles and stone animals, resembling those that formerly lined the road out to the Summer Palace, had been collected.

On one of the BMU English Department's Saturday outings, we went to see Luguoqiao, better known as the Marco Polo Bridge, so-called because he admired it. This was the site of an incident on July 7, 1937, which Japan used as its excuse for attacking and capturing Beijing, marking the start of the Sino-Japanese War. It seems that fighting between Chinese and Japanese troops was precipitated by illegal occupation of a railway junction near the bridge, outside the town of Wanping. This little town, with its wall intact, stands at the Beijing end of the bridge. The wall is not as massive as the Xian wall, but it encircles the town, giving a good idea of what the old cities were like. We made the circuit of the town, on top of the wall, looking down on the surrounding houses and streets. Returning to BMU, we stopped to see the oldest pagoda in the Beijing area, a very well-preserved pagoda dating from the Sung Dynasty. A park was under construction around it, which has since been completed.

At the entrance of Beihai Park, northeast of the Forbidden City, stood the Round City, Kublai Khan's palace. In the audience room was a white jade Buddha standing a meter and a half tall. It was almost flesh-colored. A lake in the Beihai Park was filled with paddle boats in warm weather. On an island in the lake, a small hill was topped by a large white *dagoba*, one of two in Beijing. A number of restaurants stood on the north side of the island. The nine-dragon screen, a wall covered with dragons depicted in tile, was located on the north side of the lake.

Before moving to Beijing in 1988, we had enjoyed the TV series of the classical Chinese novel, *A Dream of Red Mansions*, which was written in the mid-eighteenth century, during the reign of Emperor Qian Long (1736-95). The sets for many of the scenes were built in the southwest section of Beijing, and had been turned into a park. Some of the costumes were also on display there.

Zhao Li, son of our friend Mr. Ding, the Zhenjiang artist, was studying at the National Art Institute. His father had told him of our transfer to Beijing. He graciously invited us to attend a Chinese opera with him. He gave an excellent explanation of the plot. Much of the meaning is imparted through the elaborate costumes and stylized gestures. The singing in falsetto and high strained voices, accompanied by much loud clashing of cymbals and gongs, required some adaptation on the part of our unaccustomed ears.

In contrast, we were amazed and delighted at the superb renditions of European classical music by Chinese vocalists and instrumentalists. Many of the tourist hotels featured live music in the lobbies. Often it was a pianist or a chamber orchestra. Every Sunday morning, we would hurry from church to the Jianguo Hotel, where the Beijing Opera Orchestra gave a free concert in the lobby from eleven to one. The first hour was given to instrumental numbers and during the second hour, the orchestra featured vocalists. *Ave Maria* and other selections with religious connotations were oft repeated favorites. We went regularly, so we got to know the conductors and several of the performers.

The Beijing Concert Hall was closed for renovation during the latter part of our stay in Beijing. We attended several concerts before it closed. One of these was Beethoven's *Ninth*. The hall was packed, with standing room filled. A large chorus accompanied by the orchestra totaled some one hundred fifty musicians. The technically expert presentation in Chinese was powerful indeed. On another occasion, the People's Liberation Army Opera Group presented Puccini's *Tosca*. The stage setting of an elaborate baroque church was quite convincing, and the performance was excellent.

Prodemocracy Demonstrations 1989

What started in April as memorial services for Hu Yaobang, soon turned into demonstrations for reform. The movement began and was spearheaded by students at Beijing University and soon swelled to include essentially all the universities in Beijing, with students occupying Tiananmen Square. Groups of students marched daily down University Avenue (Daxuelu) to the square, carrying the flag and singing the *Internationale*. They demanded to be heard and called for reform within the Party, not for overthrow of the system. The movement gathered momentum. Students from universities in other parts of the country came riding free on the trains to join them. The general populace and workers in Beijing showed sympathy, in some cases demonstrated, and became increasingly involved. China had scheduled a reconciliation with Russia, which was to be cemented with a state visit by Mikhail Gorbachev. Media reporters from all over the world came to cover the event, which was completely overshadowed by the student demonstrations. Normally, visiting foreign dignitaries were welcomed by a televised red carpet reception in front of the Great Hall of the People. Because of the occupation of the square by the students, Gorbachev had to be welcomed at the airport. When he was brought to the Great Hall, he was, reportedly, slipped in by the backdoor. This constituted a great loss of face for all the authorities. On returning to Russia, Gorbachev was quoted as saying that it seemed as if the Chinese leaders were losing control. This seemed to seal the fate of the students, but by this time, workers and the population at large supported them. Local troops balked at moving against the students. Troops were mobilized from all over the country. The bus and subway workers went on strike and the populace began blocking all the intersections to prevent the troops from coming into the center of the city.

The students at BMU had entered into the demonstrations later than some of the other universities. They were mainly involved in manning the Red Cross tents in the square. A boycott of classes was partially observed. My classes with the graduate students continued. Teachers were required to meet classes as long as one student showed up. My lectures to the undergraduates continued to be fairly well attended. The students of the Faculty Preparation Program cut classes one day to march to the square. As the situation tightened, by increasing the number of class hours per day, that program was completed one week ahead of schedule. The students who came from nursing schools in other parts of the country went back to their homes.

On Saturday, June 3, we went to the station to board the early morning train, en route to visit friends in Tianjin. I was surprised to see that the soldiers who had been guarding the railway station had been withdrawn. We were waiting at the gate of the platform, when a very agitated young man rushed up and inquired in English if he could ask a question. We were glad to listen. He was so excited that he couldn't find words to express himself. We encouraged him to speak in Chinese, hoping that we could understand. He then began to tell of an attempted attack on the students in the square. He spoke so rapidly and excitedly that we didn't get it all. This really didn't matter, because he was just using us as a forum to inform the crowd that gathered around us. We proceeded to Tianjin on schedule, toured the city, and spent a quiet, enjoyable day. We arrived back in Beijing after 6 P.M. There was an eerie quiet at the train station. No taxis were available. We walked a couple of blocks to the International Hotel on Changan Road. This boulevard passes in front of Tiananmen at the north end of the square. The hotel was located three long blocks east of the square and a block west of Jianguomen, which is on the ring road that follows the route of the old city wall. No vehicular traffic was moving. Many people were milling about on Changan Road, and when we looked toward Jianguomen, we saw the street blocked by several trucks and buses. We went up to the recently opened revolving restaurant on top of the International Hotel for dinner. A huge telescope was mounted on a tripod pointing toward Tiananmen Square, where we could barely see the Goddess of Democracy, surrounded by a mass of humanity. Looking in the other direction, the reason for the vehicles blocking the road became apparent. A convoy of about twenty army trucks was attempting to turn onto Changan Road from the ring road. The intersection was blocked by a mob of at least a thousand, as well as by the vehicles.

About 8:30 P.M., we finished dinner and went down to look for a taxi. Nothing was moving on Changan Road, so we decided to walk over to the Palace Hotel. This was a new hotel located a couple blocks north of Changan Road between the International Hotel and the Palace Museum (Imperial Palace, Forbidden City). We walked over by way of some of the back alleys. People were streaming into town on their bicycles, many with children riding on little seats in front of their parents. Katie commented that it didn't look as if they were expecting trouble, since they had brought the children along. At the Palace Hotel, a notice was posted that the taxis would stop running at 10 P.M. We asked for a taxi, but were told none were available. Just then a taxi arrived and discharged a passenger. Katie immediately got in and persuaded the driver to take us to BMU.

The taxi driver had to use back streets as the ring road was blocked. As we drove behind the Palace Museum, I noted that there were a number of tour buses parked there. This was strange; the Palace Museum had been closed to tourists because of the demonstrations. It was almost 10 P.M., so in any case, it should not have been open at that hour. Major intersections were blocked all over the city by the people, who would not let army vehicles pass. The tour buses have tinted windows, making it difficult to see who is inside. The buses were being allowed to pass the roadblocks, so there was speculation that they had been used to transport troops. Our driver encountered traffic jams caused by the obstructed intersections and had to try several routes before he was finally able to deliver us to BMU in the northwest corner of the city.

Tiananmen Incident

Sunday morning, June 4, VOA and BBC were continually broadcasting news of the massacre in Tiananmen. We stayed glued to the radio, as news reports were being constantly updated. We were living in the international student dormitory, which was located at the back of the BMU campus. A new avenue had recently been completed, between our campus and the Iron and Steel University. At midmorning, I heard the sound of gunfire coming from the street behind the dormitory. Our second-floor rooms were on the front side of the building, but there was a communal kitchen on the back. I went to the kitchen window where I could see over the back wall of the campus. A convoy of army trucks was trying to pass down the road, in spite of efforts to block it with steel drums and telephone poles that were not yet installed. The soldiers in the trucks were firing into the air and forcing their way ahead. They passed our dorm, but the last three trucks were stopped at the next intersection, left by the soldiers, and finally overturned and burned.

The head of the English Department came to warn us not to leave the dormitory. The university canceled classes and closed for the year. All the hospitals in the city were taking care of wounded. I offered my assistance, but it was not accepted.

Most of our students had already left the campus, returning to their homes all over the country. Our Chinese faculty colleagues were urging us to leave as soon as possible. We already had a reservation to leave in two weeks on United Airlines, the only U.S. passenger carrier that flew into Beijing at that time. On Monday morning we called to see if we could get the departure date moved up, and were told that they could give us a place in one week, but that we would have to come to the office to get our tickets reissued. The United office was on Changan Road just a block from Jianguomen, where chaos still prevailed, so this was no help. One of the other English teachers had managed to get a private telephone line. She allowed us to use this and to give the number to our children. Katrina in Nashville and Sperry in Knoxville called us a number of times, so we were in touch with one or the other several times a day. They both made calls to the State Department, United Airlines headquarters, and to Senator Al Gore. They received a much more helpful response from Gore's office than from any other.

On Tuesday, June 6, I ventured out on University Avenue on my bicycle. The avenue was littered with debris and partially blocked by barricades. I rode out to the Foreign Language University, where the branch bank that kept the foreigners' accounts was located. I stood in line among a group of the language students, waiting to close our accounts. The young man next to me had been in Tiananmen Square when the soldiers attacked. He reported that the Chinese student next to him had been killed and he had helped another wounded student to safety.

All the universities on University Avenue had black crepe ribbons on the gates and black crepe flowers pinned on the shrubbery. At BMU, a memorial room was set up with pictures of the BMU students who had been killed. Funeral music was played all day on Tuesday. We went to express our concern and signed the register. We were told that some of the students had been crushed as vehicles had rolled across the Red Cross tents where they were on duty. We recalled that, during the preceding weeks, these same students, carrying their national flag with pride, and singing the *Internationale* with fervor, were simply pleading for peaceful reform. Everyone was in shock and disbelief at what had happened.

Finally on Wednesday morning, June 7, Sperry called to say that Senator Gore's office had notified him that it was now possible for United Airlines to issue tickets at the airport. United was also putting on two special charter flights. I went to the Foreign Affairs Office of the university to see if we could get a university car to take us to the airport. The director regretted that none of the university drivers were willing to drive on the streets. He said he was sorry that he could not drive, or he would take us. I went to check my mailbox and saw a group of students. Much of the news was being carried by word of mouth, so I stopped to ask if there were anything new. It was feared that there might be civil war between the local troops and those that had been brought in to attack the students in the square. One of my graduate students was there. He thought the situation was serious and advised me to leave. I told him that I was unable to get a taxi and the university cars were not available. He said he thought he could help me. I went back to the room to help Katie finish packing, as there were a number of last minute chores needing to be done. Katie had already stored the notes and materials for her courses at the nursing department on Tuesday. Shortly my friend came to say he had located a small minivan. The driver was committed to take someone else to the airport, but would come back and get us. The round trip to the airport took over an hour, so that gave us a little more time. The price charged for taking us was about ten times the normal taxi fee, but we didn't quibble about that.

A convoy of army trucks was parked beside the road to the airport, at the intersection with the outer ring road. These troops were not interfering with traffic to the airport, so gave no difficulty. The terminal was packed with people trying to leave. The United extra flights had already come and gone. I went to see if we could get on a Japan Airlines (JAL) flight to Tokyo. Several hundred people were in line waiting to get into the JAL office. It stretched around a couple of corners of the corridor. I next tried the China Air (CAAC) window. While I was standing in line, a woman came up and posted a notice that Cathay Pacific, the main Hong Kong airline, was putting on a special flight. I went to their office and found that they were taking people on a first come, first serve basis, giving preference only to those that already had Cathay Pacific tickets. I signed up and then had to return to the CAAC window to purchase the tickets. After a couple hours of waiting, we were on our way. As the fully loaded plane lifted off the airstrip, there was a chorus of grateful expressions of relief. We were glad to be heading for home, but heartsick at the grief and despair of beloved friends and esteemed colleagues, with whom we had labored together for the development of their great nation and the well-being of its people.

On arrival in Hong Kong, we found all the motor vehicles flagged with black streamers, and a pervasive atmosphere of grief and shock. The United desk was about to close, but they were able to put us on a flight that left the next morning. We obtained a place in a nearby hotel for the night. In Tokyo, the terminal was packed with people who had come from Beijing, seeking ongoing flights. Having been booked through from Hong Kong, we had no problem, and thankfully proceeded on our way home.

5. Subsequent Glimpses: 1990-93

Beijing 1990

The third phase of the Faculty Preparation Program at Beijing Medical University was scheduled for the spring of 1990. When we arrived back in the States in June 1989, we received a request to go to Malawi to work with Dr. Kenneth McGill in the expanding medical program at Embangweni Hospital. He had transferred to Malawi after his last term at Bulapé. Having known the McGills in Zaïre, we viewed this opportunity as a high privilege, and agreed to go for five months, October 1989 through February 1990. Katie was already committed to return to China in March. This was our third time to circle the globe. Leaving Malawi the end of February by way of Nairobi, we went to Hong Kong to obtain the necessary visa for China.

In Beijing we stayed once again in the international student dormitory. Katie was busy with preparation and teaching for the Faculty Preparation Program. Dr. Marcia Petrini, then coordinator of HOPE's nursing programs in China, was also involved with the course. I received a request from the English Department to teach a group in the Public Health Department. They were preparing for a research study in cooperation with a team of doctors who were scheduled to come from Atlanta, and they wanted to improve their English skills. During our first meeting, I asked each one to give me some details of their personal history. It was an interesting and diverse group of students. The vice-chairman of the department had been trained as an army medical worker. A number of the young doctors had advanced degrees. Some of the secretaries, who would be operating the computers, also joined the class.

The mood in Beijing was very subdued. No one was talking about the events of Tiananmen. Even our close friends avoided the subject. I frequently rode to town on the bus and subway. Previously there was always a lot of conversation, especially on the subway. Often someone would engage me in conversation. At this time, however, I was aware of the dead silence. No one was talking. One could have heard a pin drop.

Chengde

Chengde, northeast of Beijing, was an eighteenth century imperial resort. Katie, Dr. Petrini, and their colleague Guo Guifang went there to visit a nursing school and to give some lectures. We had visited Chengde briefly before, during our first year in Beijing. The imperial park, a large part of which was forested, was surrounded by a six-mile wall. It contained a lake, many paths, a number of picturesque bridges, and a large pagoda. In the vicinity of the park, there were a number of temples; most were built in the eighteenth century to celebrate the sixtieth birthday of Emperor Qian Long and the eightieth birthday of his mother. Putuozongsheng, a Lamaist temple, was built in the style of the Potala in Lhasa for the Dalai Lama. The sixth Panchen Lama visited in 1781 and Xumifushou was built in his honor. Across the river from the park, a round temple resembled the Temple of Heaven in Beijing. A tall mountain towered over the city with "Hammer Rock" on the summit, which in profile looked like a hammer standing on its head, with the handle sticking up in the air. We rode a chairlift two miles to the crest of the hill in order to climb up to the rock. There was enough room for fifteen or twenty people to stand on the head of the hammer. The handle was a rock about fifty feet tall, balanced on its end. On the walk down the mountain, we passed several other rock formations that have been given picturesque names, such as "Toad Rock" and "Monk's Hat Hill."

The nursing school at Chengde was emphasizing English. They were primarily interested in preparing the students to work abroad. Apparently the government's main concern was to earn foreign exchange, as the salaries would go largely to the government, rather than to the nurses. Katie questioned whether there was a risk of losing the nurses to emigration. This was an acknowledged problem if they were going to the U.S. or Canada. Most of them would go, however, to some of the Arab countries where they are not allowed to stay.

Luoyang

Luoyang, in Henan Province, dates back to 1200 B.C. It was the ancient capital for ten dynasties. Each spring a peony festival is held there. In 1990, we visited Luoyang with Marcia, the weekend following that festival. The peonies were past their peak, but still lovely. The profusion and variety of blossoms was amazing. When Buddhism was introduced from India, Luoyang became the center of that religion in China. The first Buddhist temple constructed in China is said to be the White Horse Temple. Reportedly, the first Buddhist missionary came riding a white horse, so a white stone statue of the horse in the temple yard commemorates this event. At a nearby pagoda, rides on white horses were offered to tourists. The famous Longmen Caves are to be found sixteen kilometers south of the city. Rock cliffs stretch for a mile along the bank of Yi River where thousands of statues of Buddha are carved in natural or man-made grottoes. Many of the statues have been mutilated. Some have been carted away to museums; others were defaced during the Cultural Revolution, but many survived.

Inner Mongolia

On one of the brief holidays, Marcia joined us for a visit to Inner Mongolia. The train took us to Huhehaote. This is the Mongolian name that the Chinese use. On many maps it is shortened to Hohhot, or Hohhehot. The Five-Pagoda Temple in the city was very similar to the one in Beijing. Islam was strong in this locale, as was Tibetan Buddhism We visited the Great Mosque, where a service was just concluding. The congregation, of course, was all male. They were very cordial to us. We did not enter the mosque, but looked in from the courtyard.

Our main interest was to visit the Mongolian grassland steppes. About thirty miles out on the grasslands, we reached the small village of Silanmuren. The grasslands were an impressive treeless sea of grass on rolling plains as far as the eye could see. The small village boasted a Lamaist temple which had been recently restored. We had dinner in a local restaurant, where Mongolian hot pot was served, accompanied by Mongolian songs and strong *maotai*, a potent and popular distillate of grain, reportedly named for its village of origin. Herds of sheep and cattle were the basis of the local economy. They also had a few camels which were available for short rides.

The wind blew constantly and was quite cold, especially at night. We spent the night in a yurt with double felt walls. There was a small stove in the center which burned "chips" (dried animal dung), a highly satisfactory fuel and surprisingly odorless. We slept on thick pads spread on the floor, and passed an amazingly comfortable night. On the way back to the city, we visited a high point in the plain on which was a cairn. We were told this was raised to honor local gods to insure their protection of the grass. Everyone who visits is expected to add a rock to the cairn.

From the grasslands, we returned to Beijing, where plans were made for Katie to return in 1991 for some nursing seminars. These were to be conducted by Project HOPE in cooperation with China Nurses' Association. During our stay in Malawi, my legs had begun to give difficulty and this became worse while I was in China. After returning to the States, I soon reached the state where I could not walk a quarter of a mile, nor stand more than a half-hour before my legs became numb and weak. Our daughter Faye's wedding to Bill Maynard was set for June. I was concerned that I might not be able to escort her down the aisle, but managed it without difficulty. Dr. William S. Reid, a neurosurgeon at University of Tennessee Medical Center in Knoxville, diagnosed my problem as spinal stenosis and performed an extensive laminectomy in September 1990. This resulted in immediate and

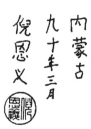

Inner Mongolia
3-90—H. S. Nelson

complete relief of the problem. There was the slight complication of a gastric hemorrhage. Fortunately, I had banked two units of my own blood before the operation, so only had to have an autologous transfusion.

Beijing 1991

In October 1991, we found the general mood in Beijing much improved since our previous visit in 1990. People seemed much freer to express their opinions. Katie's first workshop was at Beijing Nursing School, which was not located in the city of Beijing, but in Tongzhou, a small town in Tongxian (Tong County) east of Beijing. Tongzhou was the northern terminus of the Grand Canal. A park at the canal's end had a couple attractive pagodas. The nursing school occupied buildings that had been North China American School for the children of U.S. personnel in Beijing before 1949. Katie was very impressed with the staff and the cooperation she received during her course. The grounds were beautifully kept and the garden contained a striking statue of Florence Nightingale.

After Tongzhou, there was another workshop in Beijing. During these weeks when Katie was fully occupied, I took the opportunity to visit my friends in the Yangzi valley.

Amity Headquarters in Nanjing

The soft sleeper on the overnight train was a very comfortable way to make the journey from Beijing to Nanjing. After arrival, I visited the Amity offices, where I met Dr. Philip Wickeri, who happened to be in town. He invited me to have lunch with him, Bishop K.H. Ting, and Ting Yenren. I learned that Amity had expanded its efforts to aid in rural developments. One of the projects was a training program for rural health workers from the poorer western provinces. At that time, they were bringing groups of midwives to Nanjing for a refresher course. Amity financed the course, which was taught at Nanjing Medical College by the obstetric professors. I visited a

Amity Foundation, loading Bibles for shipment, 1991.

class comprised of the second group of midwives who had come to Nanjing for this program. The Amity Press was still printing Bibles in the old characters, but was well on the way toward the resetting of the Bible in the new simplified characters used on the mainland.

Zhenjiang

Original cornerstone of Goldsby King Memorial Hospital displayed in front of new surgical wards, Zhenjiang 1991.

From Nanjing, I took the train to Zhenjiang. At Number One Hospital, Dr. Zheng Guoqiang, hospital director, and Dr. Yu Xingkun, foreign affairs officer, welcomed me and took me on a tour of the new surgical ward building that had just been completed. The cornerstone of the old Goldsby King Memorial Hospital was prominently displayed in front of the building with the added inscription that the hospital had been founded as a Christian hospital. Construction had begun for a new radiotherapy building.

It was a pleasure to see many of our old friends. Dr. Zhang Zhiqing seemed to be in good health and was his usual cheerful self. The hospital invited me for lunch with him and several other of the senior administrative staff. Dr. Zhang Guohui was back in Zhenjiang, having completed his training in the States. He was a bit frustrated at not having all the equipment and ancillary services that were available in Nashville. He proudly showed me some of the cardiac angiograms that he had done since his return.

Fenyang

Marcia and Katie's last workshop, in November 1991, was in Fenyang, which is located in Shanxi Province, in an area that was officially closed to foreign tourists. The China Nurses' Association was able to get special permission for us to go there. We went by train to Taiyuan, where we spent the night in the fairly new Grand Hotel. The car from the school came to get us the next morning. Our departure was delayed for a while, until last minute clearance could be completed for us to proceed to Fenyang. The area is rich in coal and iron. The industry of the region produces an acrid smog and pollution that was the worst we have experienced. The road trip took a couple of hours. We were housed in a hotel which had been part of a Catholic school. Across the courtyard from our rooms and just outside the wall of the compound, we could see the Catholic church. We arrived on Saturday and the opening sessions of the seminar at the nursing school were scheduled for Sunday. While Katie and Marcia were occupied with the seminar on Sunday morning, I walked around the block to the Catholic church. The exterior was rather drab, but it was open, so I went in. The early morning mass was over. There were a couple of people lighting candles or praying. The interior of the church was beautifully restored. I talked to a priest and asked him if he could tell me where to find a Protestant church. He gave me general directions. From what he said, it was not too far away. I set out to see if I could find it. I ended up on the main street and walked several blocks, stopping at several stores, but no one seemed to know where it was. On the way back to the hotel, I stopped at a group of pedicabs and asked if they could help. One man said he knew where it was, and agreed to take me there. I had missed the street by one block.

When we arrived at the church, it appeared to be closed. The upper windows were blocked up and I found the door locked. I was standing in the street in front of the church taking a photograph, when a soldier and another gentleman came out of the house next door. I asked the gentleman if the church was open for services. He thought so. His soldier friend was leaving, so he invited me into his home. It turned out that he was an off-duty officer in the People's Liberation Army. He offered me tea and introduced me to his teenage son, who was the same age as our second grandson. He left me to talk to his son and soon returned with an old lady. She was a Christian and informed me that the church was not yet open, as there were several Christian groups and the government had not decided which one to allow to have the building. She said a church service was being held in a village about fifteen kilometers away on that Sunday. She also said that there was a home church service that would be held in about an hour and asked if I would like to attend. I replied in the affirmative. She left to see if that would be all right. I continued visiting with the officer and his son for about an hour. When the lady did not return, I decided that they probably felt it was not a good idea to have a foreigner attend the house service, so I returned to the hotel.

I was concerned that there was some reaction to my wanderings. Fenyang was a sensitive area, normally closed to tourists. I was assigned a guide, to let me know that I was not to wander about the city unaccompanied. For the rest of the time we were there, he kept me company. He took me on a tour of the city, and covered much of the same ground that I had done by myself. He showed me a remnant of the old city wall that was preserved as a monument to the Liberation martyrs. A small park nearby contained a memorial hall with the names of the martyrs inscribed in stone. I discovered why I had trouble finding the church. There was a large secondary school between the church and the main street. It was the former mission school, and several of the old buildings are still there. There are also some newer buildings that blocked the view of the church. The former mission hospital was nearby. The original buildings were in excellent repair and still in use. They were built with Chinese style roofs and decorated eaves. I did not tour the hospital, but we did step inside, and I was impressed with the cleanliness. No one could tell me

*Abbot of Xuan Zhong Shi
preaching to a group of
tourists, Shanxi 1991.*

what church had established the mission. We searched for a cornerstone or plaque that might tell us. If there is one, it is plastered over. Some of Katie's students told her that Fenyang had been a Methodist mission station. I was told that one of the American ambassadors had grown up there as a child, but I was unable to determine to whom they were referring.

One day a trip was arranged to take me to Xuan Zhong Monastery. We went halfway back to Taiyuan and then turned off on a new road. I was told that the road had been built by the Japanese, as this temple had sent some early Buddhist missionaries to Japan. The recently restored temple was built in tiers up the steep side of a mountain. Old paintings represent it as being above the clouds; the name seems to imply that it is shrouded in mystery. While we were there, a group of young Chinese tourists arrived. The abbot gave them a lecture extolling the teachings of Buddhism and the religion's significance in Chinese history and culture.

The nursing faculty workshop in Fenyang was highly successful, one which Katie and Marcia thoroughly enjoyed. They were somewhat annoyed, however, that while they worked day and night, I was being privileged to special guided tours, in spite of my unauthorized wandering.

Revisiting Friends 1993

In the spring of 1992, I had a total replacement of my right knee with excellent results, thanks to Dr. William Youmans. While we were at home 1992-93, our good friend, Dr. Huang Siren, wrote from Taizhou that the congregation had received permission to build a church and they hoped to complete it in December 1993. Having been invited to return to Zaïre for three months in the fall of 1993, we planned to continue on around the world to China, hoping to be there for the dedication of the church. While in Zaïre, we received word that the building of the church had been delayed, because there were still people living on part of the site; we decided, however, to continue with our plans and obtained visas in Hong Kong within twenty-four hours.

Amity

Arriving in China from Hong Kong, Nanjing was our first stop.We stayed at the new Central China Hotel, which is conveniently near Nanjing Theological Seminary, where the Amity office is located. We learned that the Amity program for training rural health workers had been moved to the western provinces, to avoid bringing students to Nanjing. Amity had also translated David Werner's book *Where There Is No Doctor* into Chinese. We had used the French version of this in Africa. Amity was using it for the rural health workers and was also distributing it to evangelists through the evangelistic schools.

I had written to Stephen Ting to tell him of our plans to visit. Amity then had several teachers in Zhenjiang. Stephen had conveniently arranged to visit them at a time coinciding with our visit. We expected to go to Zhenjiang by train, but he offered to take us by car. Miss Tsau, who works with the educational division of Amity, also accompanied us. The road to Zhenjiang was greatly improved. It is part of the new toll road that was then under construction between Nanjing and Shanghai, some sections of which are divided highway.

Zhenjiang

Zhenjiang had changed greatly since my last visit in 1991. A number of the main streets had been widened, so many of the old buildings had been torn down or given new façades. Several new high-rise office buildings had been completed. One of the Amity teachers was teaching at the Shipbuilding Institute. We arrived there in time to have Chinese breakfast with her. Stephen Ting arranged for us to stay at the guest house of the institute, which was much cheaper and more conveniently located than the Jinshan Tourist Hotel.

The hospital welcomed us with open arms. Dr. Zheng, the director, came himself to get us. He invited us for the inevitable luncheon. Dr. Zhang Zhiqing came over in great spirits. He had arranged for Andrew Sure to go to Taizhou with us. Dr. Zhang Guohui was not there, as he was in Shanghai for additional study. The hospital now had six hundred beds. We toured the new surgical ward building. The radiotherapy center was completed and Dr. Shang Wei, one of our most competent former students, was in charge. He proudly showed us the Siemens X-ray therapy machine, the Chinese-made cobalt therapy machine, and the Chinese-made simulator. The blood bank had been moved over to Zhenjiang Medical College and its old site was now occupied by a radioimmunology diagnostic laboratory (also known as nuclear medicine laboratory). A four-story magnetic resonance imaging (MRI) building was under construction, partially encircling the old doctor's house. We were told the MRI would cost around one million dollars and was scheduled for completion in 1994. The house where we had stayed was being preserved as a historical site, as the house of Zhenjiang's first foreign doctor. Our old rooms were occupied by some administrative offices. We were shown plans to expand the hospital westward to a new boulevard. A new entrance to the hospital would be created there with a large building having a fourteen-floor tower on one end for medical wards. The other end would have a seven-floor outpatient department. The two towers would be connected by a four-floor emergency department. The cost of this project was estimated at ten million dollars.

In 1992, Zhenjiang celebrated the centennial of Pearl Buck's birth. One of the missionary homes in which she had lived was turned into a museum. This was one of the homes that we had located earlier, but to which we had been denied entrance. Now it was open to the public. The walls are covered with pictures from her life, and they have a collection of her books that have been translated into Chinese.

Several of our former students heard that we were in town and came to see us, including Dr. Ma Feng and his family from Suzhou. We were overjoyed to see them and to learn of their advancement in their specialties.

Taizhou

The Zhenjiang hospital car took us to Taizhou on a Saturday morning, accompanied by Dr. Zhang's young friend, Andrew Sure. The road to Taizhou was now much improved, being a dual toll highway part of the way. Traffic, however, was terrible, especially as we passed through the outskirts of Yangzhou. The increase in private vehicles made traffic problems everywhere. The main difficulty, though, was due to the grand mixture of all sorts of conveyances, with different speeds, using the same road. I made a note of the different modes of transportation that I saw on the short stretch through Yangzhou. They included pedestrians, pushcarts, bicycles, pedicabs, bicycle carts, horse and donkey carts, motorbikes, motorcycles of all sizes (some with sidecars), two-wheeled tractors towing carts of all descriptions, four-wheeled tractors, passenger cars of several sizes, small and large buses, trucks, cranes, vans, crew cab pickups, tractor trailers, a tank truck, and the typical north Jiangsu wheelbarrows.

In Taizhou, Dr. Huang had arranged for us to stay at the Qiaoyuan Bingfang (Lofty Garden Guest House). This is a new hotel a short distance from the hospital. It takes its name from a Ming Dynasty garden which is now part of the hotel grounds. I had not known about this garden during the time I lived in Taizhou, as it was a private garden then. It contains a couple of lovely pavilions and a lot of the usual, oddly shaped Taihu rocks.

Changes had taken place at the hospital. The outpatient building was in full operation with around 1,500 clinic visits daily. The largest number of visits in a single day was 2,300. Taizhou serves an area with a population of around 3,000,000. The oldest hospital building had been razed and replaced by a glistening white tile-surfaced five-story building which contained the chemistry laboratories and facilities for the production of intravenous solutions. The T-shaped brick building had been stuccoed. A new wing had been added to the surgical ward building. They told us that the old doctor's residence had been condemned and was scheduled to be torn down.

Dr. Yang, retired surgeon from Number Two Hospital, invited us to visit there. When he was a young man, I had assisted him with medical school. The Number Two Hospital was located south of the old city in a new section of town. It was formerly the infectious disease hospital, but had become a multi-service hospital. Most of the buildings were single-story pavilions surrounded by parklike gardens. A new two-story tile-surfaced building contained the radiotherapy cobalt machine. Oncology was one of the special services that this hospital provided for the Taizhou district. We were really touched by the warm welcome. They made us feel that we were honoring them by our visit. In Taizhou, I am still always referred to as *Yuanzhang* (Hospital Director).

Taizhou had grown rapidly. Air conditioners were the most widely known product of Taizhou industries. There were a number of other small industries, including the manufacture of motorbikes. Much more expansion is expected when the rail and car bridge is built across the Yangzi north of Wuxi. They were preparing for this by widening the major streets, including the one in front of the hospital. Already under construction, at the site of the south gate, was a television tower with a revolving restaurant that will be similar to the one in Seattle. The four supporting legs of the tower will straddle a major intersection of the main street and the ring road where an old city gate once stood.

Taizhou church was reopened in 1979 with thirty members. It has grown to over one thousand members, with new members joining at the rate of one hundred each year. Services were being held in the missionary home known as the Lancaster house, located across the street from the entrance to the hospital outpatient building. Every room was packed, including the sun porch and the front porch. We were encouraged to see that although there were many senior citizens, about half the congregation appeared to be middle-aged adults, young people, and children. Following the service, a group of women stayed to eat lunch on the back porch which they called the canteen. These were members who had come from a distance and cooperatively prepared a meal, so that they could stay for the afternoon women's prayer meeting. The service was preceded by the usual hymn practice session. Dr. Huang's son-in-law preached the sermon. His theme was the divinity of Christ and salvation through Him alone.

We were shown plans for the church to be built on the lot where the Lancaster house stands. The design takes an L shape in order to preserve a large tree in the yard that is said to be the oldest tree in the district. It is to seat one thousand and will have a twenty meter tower topped by a cross. The plan was drawn by a Christian architect whose services were largely donated. In December 1993, construction had been delayed because some employees of the hospital were still living on the back part of the lot. The director of the hospital came over to assure us that they would be out by the end of the year.

The Richardsons' house, Morningside, had burned several months before our visit. We were saddened to see that only blackened walls remain. Dr. Huang lives in the yard in a hospital apartment house. The fire had apparently been caused by electrical wiring. I have many pleasant memories of my association with the Richardsons there.

Beijing

Since the shift to a market economy, the Chinese have more freedom to travel, making it difficult to obtain train reservations. Dr. Yu, however, was able to arrange for soft sleeper tickets for us from Zhenjiang to Beijing. In the capital, joint ventures were thriving, and the city was swarming with business persons from all over the world. The streets of Beijing were crowded with vehicles, many of which were taxis operated by private companies. There were still a lot of restrictions, but the mood was much freer than on our previous visit in 1991.

Katie was primarily interested in seeing some of the nurses with whom she had been associated. She went out to Beijing Medical University one morning for a visit with the nursing faculty. A delegation from the Beijing Nursing School in Tongzhou came to invite her to return there to teach.

There was an interesting article in the *South China Post* on December 8, 1993, telling about the crackdown and fining of one of the Christian groups in Anhui Province, who persisted in holding secret meetings. The police were also searching for one of the underground Christian preachers; others had been jailed and were being sent to reform farms. The government continued to be very sensitive to, and suspicious of, any clandestine activity. On the other hand, the open churches were attracting more and more young people, and for the most part were unhindered. New rules were published the end of January 1994, barring foreigners from religious activities and from setting up schools.

On a Sunday in December, 1993, we were warmly welcomed back at the door of Chongwenmen Church, which was packed as usual. The church was decorated for the Christmas Season, and we enjoyed the excellent choir. The sermon was from the first chapter of John; the text, "The Word became flesh and made his dwelling among us . . . " was very apt, as we felt His presence in worship, and saw Him in action in the lives of Chinese Christians from day to day.

Reunion of China Missionaries

At the initiative of Bishop K.H. Ting and the invitation of Columbia Theological Seminary, a reunion of former Presbyterian missionaries to China and missionary children with China ties was held in Decatur, Georgia in October 1994. One hundred sixty attended and we had the opportunity to renew many friendships. Bishop Ting and his son, Professor Ting Yenren, now Amity's secretary for education, came to establish contact with the missionaries who had served in China.

The highlight of the meeting was Bishop Ting's address. He said that the Chinese church was "occupied for a number of years with the task of the development and preservation of its Chinese Christian selfhood." He explained that "The church in China must not be a replica of something western, but have a Chinese selfhood in order to gain the right to be heard by our fellow Chinese. Hence our Three-Self Movement, a movement to achieve self-government, self-support and self-propagation. After working at it for three decades, we are now in a preliminary way self-governing, self-supporting and doing the work of propagating the Christian faith ourselves."

He pointed out that, "Early in the fifties, there was in China an accusation movement which was anti-western and anti-foreign. It was a deviation under the influence of ultra-leftism. . . . To condemn all missionaries as imperialists is a good example of ultra-leftism. For years now I have not met Christians who hold to that view of missionaries. I want to apologize to former China missionaries and their families on behalf of Chinese Christians for all the suffering wrongly imposed on them forty years ago. I will be glad if you take my presence here as a token of healing and reconciliation in Christ after the wrong you have suffered from. I assure you we do make a difference between colonialism and imperialism which exploited the missionary movement on the one hand, and the missionaries themselves who were inspired by Christian faith and sacrificed themselves for their love of the Chinese people on the other hand."

In reporting on the status of the church, he said, "Since the end of the Cultural Revolution and with the overall criticism of ultra-leftism, there has been a return to the principle of religious freedom. Protestant churches are reopening or newly built at the rate of three every two days for the last fourteen years. In addition, there are tens of thousands of groups of Christians meeting in homes . . . For a church of several million members, there are only some 1,200 ordained ministers, most of whom joined the rank of the clergy in the 1940s . . . As a result of the nation-wide criticism of ultra-leftism after the downfall of the Gang of Four who controlled the Cultural Revolution, the intellectual climate for Christianity has entered a new stage. There has arisen an unprecedented appreciation for Christianity and the Bible."

Bishop Ting summarized two aspects of the church in China saying, "Within the church, we emphasize the seeking of a Chinese Christian selfhood, the guarding of our post-denominational unity through mutual respect in matters of faith and worship, the doing of a good job in building up the spirituality and corporate life of the church, the education of ourselves on the universality of the church, the training of the laity and the broadening of our unity through service and through reconciliation so as to embrace all in China who honor Jesus Christ as Lord. Towards the outside world, we try our best to guard against ultra-leftism in our political life, to elevate the image of Christianity as a Chinese religion, to witness to Christ, especially in response to the openness of the intellectual community today, and to carry on the

on-going discussion with the state with a view to safeguarding the principle of religious freedom."

For all of us, especially for those who had not been privileged to return
to China since 1949, the occasion was a powerful experience of reconciliation and a cause for joy and thanksgiving. We are indebted not only to
Bishop Ting, but also to Dr. G. Thompson Brown, and to our hosts,
President Douglas W. Oldenberg and all his Seminary staff.

As we ponder Bishop Ting's apology for the ultra-leftists, we are
reminded that we have often felt the need to apologize for the ultra-right-
ists in our own society, who refuse to acknowledge the virtues of
Christianity in China today. Perhaps it is only in seeking centrality in Christ
that we can overcome the "ultras."

Part II
Africa

Africa

6. New Horizons: 1951-52

Reassignment to Africa

Our missionary career began in China in 1947. Katie left in December 1948 with Sperry, who was nineteen months old. Our second son, Lee, was born in January 1949. I returned to the States the first of February 1951, so did not see Lee until after his second birthday. Since I had been in the Naval Reserve program for the last two years of medical school, I was obligated to stay in the Naval Reserve and to keep the Navy apprised of my whereabouts. The mission board reassigned us to Africa, in what was then the Belgian Congo. I sent two letters to the Navy in the same envelope. One reported my return to the States, the other requested permission to leave in order to go as a missionary to the Congo. The Navy complied with my request.

The Belgian government required that physicians practicing in the Congo first take a course in tropical medicine. There were only a few schools that were recognized as meeting this requirement. Tulane and Harvard in the U.S., London School of Tropical Medicine, and the Institute of Tropical Medicine in Antwerp were among those approved. One year residence in Belgium was also required, so the obvious plan of action was to take the course in Belgium. Missionary teachers and school directors were required to take an education course at the Colonial Institute. The government had organized a French course which began in September, to facilitate preliminary language study.

Since we needed to study French in order to take the tropical medicine course, we wanted to take advantage of this French class. This meant that I only had a little more than six months in the States, between the time I left China and then went on to Belgium. It was a busy time, visiting family and supporting churches. Katie's father was a mechanic and had a lot of contacts. He was able to locate the car that we wanted to take with us, a light blue 1951 Ford sedan. We also had to reequip and order the supplies necessary for our term in the Congo.

We sailed from New York in August on the Cunard liner, the *Mauretania*. After boarding, while we were getting settled and exploring the ship, Sperry became separated from us when he tried to go back to the cabin. He went down the wrong hallway and ended up in someone else's cabin. They held him there to keep him from getting more confused. We had a few anxious moments searching for him before we finally located him. The Halverstadts—Jim, Charline, and their son Hugh—were also on the ship. They had been commissioned in 1946 at the same time that we were commissioned to go to China. Jim had completed one term in Congo as the mission treasurer and Charline as a school director. Under new regulations, it was necessary for her to take the colonial course in Belgium. We both had our cars on board. The ship arrived at Le Havre. We claimed our cars and drove together to Paris. We spent two days there seeing some of the sights: Versailles, the Eiffel Tower, Notre Dame Cathedral, the Arc de Triomphe, and the Louvre. It was very rushed, but we needed to arrive in Belgium to get settled before the course began.

Belgium

The Belgian Protestant Bureau helped missionaries find lodging and obtain tutors during their stay in Belgium. Most of the missionaries lived with French-speaking Belgian families in boardinghouses, known in Europe as *pensions*. A number of the Congo missionaries were just finishing a year in Belgium. We were able to move into a *pension* with the Jugnon family, where Ted and Elaine Stixrud and the Alex McCutchen family had been. The Jugnons lived in the old city of Brussels, below the hill on which stood the Palais de Justice, only a couple of blocks from Grand Place and within walking distance of the commercial center. The apartment was over a butcher shop. This could be unpleasant when the butcher made sausage, but otherwise was very satisfactory. The Jugnon family belonged to the Salvation Army Church which was just around the corner. The church had a kindergarten which fulfilled our boys' need.

Brief Visit to England and Scotland

After settling in, we found that we had a little over a week before classes began. The Halverstadts joined us for a short visit to England. Since I had the proper insurance and papers for my car, we all piled in and drove to Ostend, crossing the channel on the ferry. We visited London and drove up to the lake country in northwest England, then on to Edinburgh and down the east side of England through York. It was a hurried trip but we enjoyed it. Driving on the left side of the road in an American car was quite harrowing, especially since most of the roads were narrow and there were often huge trucks on them. Jim sat in the right front and would direct me when to pass, as I could not see until I pulled out into the right-hand lane. We saw many points of interest in a short time, among them the Tower of London, changing of the palace guards, the Houses of Parliament, Windsor Castle, Stratford-on-Avon, the castle in Edinburgh, John Knox's church, and Hadrian's Wall.

Brussels

On returning to Belgium, we plunged into French study. In addition to taking the French course at the Colonial Institute where we were in the weak beginners' section, we engaged a tutor who came to our *pension* three times a week, and we used a tape recorder to help us in our study. We also enrolled in the Brussels night school, which was a couple of blocks away, near the Palais de Justice. This met a couple nights a week and helped us advance more rapidly.

The area where we lived in Brussels was pretty rough. The police always went in pairs. The Communist Party headquarters was just half a block down the street. One night we were awakened by an explosion. Someone had set off a bomb in front of the headquarters. Luckily no one was injured, but a lot of windows were blown out across the street. We occasionally were awakened by noisy drunks fighting or singing in the street. One night there was a fusillade of gunshots as the police chased some thieves. In spite of this, we found it to be a convenient location. We were within walking distance of the opera house, Théâtre de la Monnaie, where we attended regularly. Opera in Brussels was accessible to everyone for a very reasonable fee. We were once privileged to hear Sylvia Stahlman from Nashville when she performed under her Italian stage name, Giulia Bardi, in the title role of *Lucia di Lammermoor*, Donizetti's tragic opera. Her lithe figure was a striking contrast to that of the usual buxom diva. She was an instant favorite.

Weekend outings were frequently arranged for the missionaries who were there studying, so we had an opportunity to visit many of the interesting sites and cities in Belgium. We were fortunate to be there for the light and sound extravaganza of the *Legend of Holy Blood* in Brugge, which was held in the city square. It was quite impressive. Legend says that Joseph of Arimathea collected some of Christ's blood, which is contained in a vial, among the treasured relics of the cathedral at Brugge. It is believed that at a certain time each year, the blood becomes liquefied. Another evening, we attended Shakespeare's *Macbeth* performed in the old Château de Beersel on the outskirts of Brussels. A little farther south, Waterloo with its panorama was also an interesting visit.

We always took advantage of the holidays. One big holiday in Europe is All Saints' Day. John Pritchard joined us for the long weekend. We drove to Cologne, which was just beginning to rebuild from the devastation of World War II. The trees were in their fall colors, so the drive down the Rhine as far as Heidelberg was spectacular. The river was full of boat traffic and there seemed to be a castle on every prominent hill.

Christmas in Italy

In Belgium, both St. Nicholas Day and Christmas are celebrated. On his day, December 6, St. Nicholas was dressed in ecclesiastical robes with miter. They also staged a parade before Christmas, featuring Santa Claus with his sleigh and reindeer. During the Christmas vacation, we made a trip to Italy. The Halverstadts drove down through France. We took the route through Switzerland. We planned to meet in Florence for Christmas. The Bolton family accompanied us, so our car had eight occupants, Katie and me, our two boys, Ruth and Eric Bolton, and their two children. We left Brussels and got as far as the Swiss-French border. There we encountered a dense fog that enveloped all of western Europe. Fortunately when it caught us, we had just passed a hotel. We groped back to it and were able to get the last two rooms. There were not enough beds to go around, but we piled in for the night. The next morning the fog lifted enough for us to continue. We spent little time in Switzerland and put the car on a train to go through the St. Gotthard Tunnel. In Italy we again encountered dense fog. As we entered Milan, I was able to get into town by following a trolley. We stayed close behind it, as we could barely see the curb of the road. We stopped at a corner and asked a man for directions to the hotel where we were booked. We had just passed it, on the other side of the street. The fog was so dense though that I had to get a bell-hop to come and lead us to it. We didn't see much of the city, but did get to see Leonardo da Vinci's mural of *The Last Supper*, which had escaped the destruction of the hall where it was located, now rebuilt. The next day we went on to Florence where we had expected to meet the Halverstadts for Christmas Eve dinner. They had encountered the same fog and spent the night in a train station, so were late getting to Florence. They joined us for a Christmas celebration the next morning.

From Florence,we drove down to Rome for a couple of days. Eric was interested in the cathedrals of Rome as he had studied engineering and architecture. I think he had written a paper on the dome of St. Peter's. Katie and Ruth gave up after a number of the churches, but Eric and I saw many of the titular cathedrals in the city. We also visited the Forum, Colosseum, and the Catacombs.

From Rome, we drove on to Naples and Pompeii, then took a ferry over to the Isle of Capri. Here we had one of our hair-raising adventures. It was a windy day and the waves were high. We hoped to visit the Blue Grotto. When we arrived at the island we were told that the waves were too high, but they hoped that they would subside enough to go after lunch. After a visit to a sculpture garden and lunch, they were ready to attempt the trip to the grotto. We boarded a launch with about thirty or forty people to go around to the other side of the island. Here we were met by a fleet of rowboats. In the confusion, Katie got into one boat with Lee and I got into another with Sperry. The boatman then approached the vertical cliff, and we could see what was in store. There was an opening to a cave, at the right of which was a ledge where a man was standing beside a little shrine. To the left of the opening, attached to the cliff wall, was a chain that ran into the cave. The waves were coming at an angle and were high enough that every now and then, one would completely cover the mouth of the cave. We had to lie down in the boat covered with a canvas in order to enter the tiny opening. A boat would maneuver up to the cliff wall. The boatman would grab the chain and time it so that he could pull the boat through the cave mouth in the trough of a wave. Katie's boat was just of ahead me. Her boatman was a bit hesitant and missed his opportunity to enter, so backed off. My boat went ahead. I had several anxious moments waiting for Katie's boat to come in, as several other boats came in behind mine before she appeared. The cave opening was only about four or five feet high in a calm sea, but it extended down in a deep cleft below the level of the water. Light filtered into the cave through the water, giving both water and cave a beautiful azure glow. Whenever a wave completely covered the cave mouth, it caused a momentary rise in the air pressure inside the cave, causing one's ears to pop. Getting out was another story. It was impossible to see the waves coming because of the angle they made with the cave mouth. The function of the man on the ledge then became apparent. He watched the waves and judged when it was safe for a boat to come out. The boatman had to put his faith in the judgment of the man on the outside and pull the boat out by the chain on command. Fortunately all the boats made it in and out without mishap.

When we returned to Belgium, we chose the route through France. We had another close call on the northwest coast of Italy, where the road ran along the coast. A cliff dropped off sharply to the sea on our left. On our right was a railroad embankment. As we descended a hill, the road ahead made a sharp turn through an underpass. A truck loaded with oxygen cylinders came through the underpass and started up the hill toward us. Just before it reached us the rear axle broke. The truck tilted toward us and the cylinders started cascading into the road. I slammed on the brakes and stopped just short of the truck. The cylinders were bouncing toward us, so I had to put the car into reverse and back out of the way quickly. The road was completely blocked. I got out of the car and helped the driver close the valves on some of the cylinders that had begun to leak. It took almost an hour to clear the road. A long line of cars grew in both directions. The Halverstadts joined the line about ten or fifteen cars behind us.

Outside of Paris it began to snow. The road became icy and we slid off into a ditch on the left side of the road. I had chains and was in the process of putting them on when the Halverstadts caught up with us again. After applying the chains, we continued to Brussels without further difficulty.

Antwerp

In January 1952 we moved to Antwerp, having found an apartment on Avenue d'Amérique, just a block from the Institute of Tropical Medicine. The boys were enrolled in a Flemish kindergarten just around the corner, where they were exposed to yet another language. After we had been in Antwerp for several weeks, we asked Lee to say the blessing at table; we were startled to hear him burst forth in Flemish. Belgium being a bilingual country, the move from Brussels to Antwerp gave rise to many valuable learning experiences. In Brussels, we lived among French speakers. While in Antwerp, we were surrounded by a Flemish-speaking population. Our struggle to learn French continued, since that was the principal official language in the Belgian Congo. In Antwerp, however, we found that the local merchants, who easily identified us as Americans, often ignored our efforts at French and responded in English. In this setting, we were fortunate to find a Parisian tutor who greatly assisted with our pursuit of her language.

While we were in Antwerp, Easter vacation gave us the opportunity for a trip to Netherlands. A South African doctor, Pamela Garsides, her husband John, and Carolyn Saltenberger, a nurse, went with us. Pamela spoke Afrikaans, a dialect of Dutch, and acted as our interpreter. We visited the polder district. In Alkmaar a local university student saw us in the street and took the opportunity to speak English with us. He helped us find lodging and offered to take us the next morning to see Edam cheese being made. We had to get up very early, but we watched this interesting process without regret, and we remember the visit with great pleasure. We spent Easter at Zeist, with friends whom we had met aboard the *Mauretania* during our Atlantic crossing in August 1951. In this Moravian community, the architecture of the church and brothers' and sisters' houses reminded us of Salem in North Carolina. The Easter sunrise service was all in Dutch, of course, but we could follow it with ease, as it was the same liturgy used in the Moravian Church in the States. Just as in Bethania, Katie's home church near Winston-Salem, brass bands played familiar chorales as we went from the service at the church to the graveyard for the concluding liturgy.

Katie's older brother, Ed Wolff, had been on the crew of a B-17 during World War II and had been shot down over Belgium. We had the opportunity to meet several of the people who had helped him escape capture. We went to Aublain, a small village near the border with France, to visit the Gerboux family who were the first ones with whom Ed had come in contact. They had put him into the hands of the underground resistance. In Brussels we met Mlle. Yvonne Bienfait, a nurse in the underground, who had taken care of him during the time he was hiding in that city before beginning his journey across France to Spain.

Institute of Tropical Medicine

Before leaving the States, I had been in touch with Dr. Eugene R. Kellersberger, whom I had met in China in 1947. He was then President of American Leprosy Missions. I had corresponded with him about getting medicine to start treating leprosy patients at Taizhou. He had formerly been the missionary doctor at Bibanga in the Belgian Congo and had a very large leprosy camp there. He had given me a letter of introduction to Dr. Albert

Dubois, who was an old friend from his Congo days. Dr. Dubois was director of the Institute of Tropical Medicine in Antwerp and author of the textbook that we used for the course. Before moving to Antwerp, I went there to meet Dr. Dubois and present him with the letter and greetings from Dr. Kellersberger. The course in Antwerp was given in two sections, one in French and the other in Flemish. Most of the Protestant missionaries were, of course, in the French section. Most of those in the Flemish section were Belgians, men who were being trained to go out as *agents sanitaires* for the government, and Catholic sisters who were going as nurses to work in the government hospitals.

The course was a series of lectures in French and laboratory sessions, in which we were taught to diagnose the various tropical parasites in blood and stools. I found that I was greatly helped by several circumstances. First, at Vanderbilt we had a public health course which incorporated a very good laboratory section that had exposed me to most of the tropical diseases. Most of my classmates had thought the course a chore and of little use. I had been planning all along to work overseas, so had paid special attention to this course. Secondly, my experience in China had included cases in all the groups of tropical parasites. The distribution and prevalence differed in China and Africa; nevertheless, there were examples of related species in both areas. The third help was the excellent textbook in French that Dr. Dubois had written. We were taught by several different professors, but many of the lectures followed the textbook closely.

During one of the early quizzes, we were given an unknown slide to diagnose. It was supposed to be a slide of sleeping sickness. By mistake I was given a malarial slide. When the professor came to check and saw my response, he immediately said that it was wrong. I was sure that I was right and insisted that he look at the slide. When he looked at the slide, he had to agree with me. Again on the final lab test, I was given a slide, to diagnose the species of sleeping sickness. To make the diagnosis, one needed to examine the slide under the highest power with oil immersion. When I tried to set up the slide for examination, I found that the preparation was so thick that one could not focus with oil immersion. I went to the professor to try to get another slide. He would not listen and would only say, "Make your diagnosis." I went back and made the best guess I could under plain high power. When he came to check and looked under the microscope he said, "You can't make the diagnosis under high power." I agreed and repeated that the preparation would not allow oil immersion. He tried himself and found that I was right. Thus for the second time, it seems that I had inadvertently committed the unpardonable sin in Belgium of putting a professor on the spot. I was still blissfully unaware of his feeling toward me. For whatever reasons, when the results were announced, I found that I was among those who had not graduated. We were not given individual grades in the various courses, so I did not know which course I had failed. Repeat examinations were scheduled for the fall. One was required to retake the examinations in all subjects, not just the subject failed.

After the results of the first examination, I entertained the possibility of going to the London School of Tropical Medicine, where proficiency in French would not be a factor. Dr. Helen Roseveare had been in the course with us and invited me to visit her home in London. Her father, Sir Martin Roseveare, had held an important government post during World War II, as designer and administrator of the ration system. I met him briefly while there. Years later, I was to have several contacts with the Roseveare family. After visiting the London School of Tropical Medicine, it was apparent that the most expeditious way to complete the requirements was to review and retake the exams in Antwerp.

Katie was pregnant and expecting our third child in August 1952. We moved back to Brussels in June, this time to a *pension* with Mme. Marie DeGueldre in the Uccle section of Brussels. Mme. DeGueldre was the widow of a physician, a wonderful landlady and a staunch friend. The house was close to Edith Cavell Hospital, where Katie was to have her delivery. There was a primary school and kindergarten next door which we arranged for the boys to attend. I engaged my old tutor and set to work trying to improve my French and review for the reexaminations.

In the fall I went to Antwerp at the scheduled time. The examinations were all oral. I thought I was doing fine until I met the lab professor. Even though I thought I answered his questions satisfactorily, he let me know that he had no intention of passing me. I was devastated. As I left the room and started down the stairs, I met a Belgian doctor who had been in the course with me. He was about to leave for the Congo and came to pay his respects to Dr. Dubois. He asked me how I was, and I told him the situation. He at once advised me to continue with the rest of the examinations and to go and tell my story to Dr. Dubois. I took his advice. Dr. Dubois also encouraged me to continue with the remaining exams. When the exams were over, the results were delayed for hours while the professors discussed them. I passed. This incident was beneficial in that it sensitized me to the extreme importance of cross-cultural communication. It also provided an opportunity to study French a few months longer and forced me to go over the medical material in French more thoroughly. This helped me later in teaching at the various levels in Congo.

My mother came to Belgium in the summer to be present when Katie delivered. In late June, Mother, our two boys, Dr. Arden Almquist, his wife, and I went on a trip to Sweden. Katie didn't attempt the trip as she was getting close to term. Arden was Swedish-American and spoke a little Swedish, which came in handy, as we didn't find many people who could speak English. The main purpose in going was to see some of my father's Swedish relatives. Dad's sister, Ruth Nelson, had once visited Sweden and made contact with a number of them. We drove up through Denmark and spent the night in Copenhagen. While there we saw a production of Shakespeare's *Hamlet* in the castle that was said to be the original setting for the play. We ferried over to Sweden and made contact with my Grandpa Nelson's older sister, Aunt Elvira, who at the time was over a hundred years old. We drove on up to Stockholm and met several of my second cousins and their families. These were cousins of my Grandma Nelson, whose maiden name was Wahlström. Eric Wahlström was in the medical supply business. He gave me a ring cutter that he had invented, which proved useful to me several times in Africa. Another cousin was an orthopedic surgeon who arranged a visit to the local hospital.

Katie gave birth to our third child on August 16 at Edith Cavell Hospital in Brussels. The Belgian doctor not only allowed the fathers to be present, but required them to be there, so this time I was privileged to be with Katie during the entire labor and delivery. We named her Kathryn Faith for Katie and my sister Faith. Mme. DeGueldre always called her "Katrine," which soon became Katrina. The latter stuck with her until her college years, when it was shortened to Kat.

While we were in Belgium, Franklin Watt, one of the Congo missionaries, came through Brussels. When I was in grade school, the Watts' children had suffered from polio and the family had been in the States for several years of treatment. They had lived in Nashville and attended First Presbyterian Church, so I knew him well. When he heard that I intended to drive up to the Kasai from Léopoldville, the capital, now called Kinshasa, he was able to give me some valuable information. There was no published road map available at that time. He and the Reverend Earl King, Sr. had made the trip up and had drawn a map of the route. They had indicated on the map the mission stations along the route and places where gasoline and lodging were available. He gave me a copy of his map which I kept for reference.

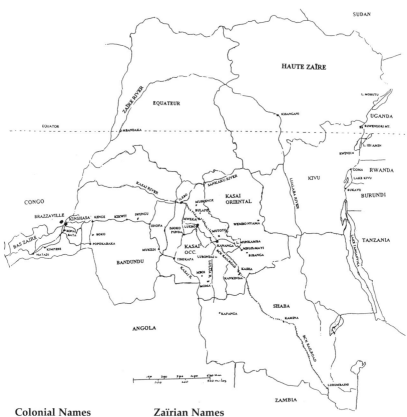

Colonial Names	Zaïrian Names
Belgian Congo	Zaïre
Congo River	Zaïre River
Léopoldville	Kinshasa
Port Francqui	Ilébo
Charlesville	Djoko Punda
Luluabourg	Kananga
Bakwanga	Mbuji-Mayi
Élisabethville	Lubumbashi
Stanleyville	Kisangani
Katanga Province	Shaba
Kasai Province	Kasai Oriental & Kasai Occidental

Zaïre

7. Final Years of
Colonial Period: 1952-60

On to Congo

We were finally ready to travel on to Congo by November 1952. We boarded a Belgian vessel, the *Léopoldville*, a mixed passenger and cargo ship with excellent accommodations. Because of our experience of losing one of the boys on the *Mauretania*, we put tags on them to be sure they would get to the right rooms. When we crossed the equator there was quite a ceremony. King Neptune "came aboard," and all the "pollywogs," those who were crossing the equator for the first time, were inducted into the royal order of "shellbacks." The Belgians took delight in castigating us for treating our boys like baggage. The food on the *Léopoldville* was excellent and we enjoyed the two-week voyage immensely.

The ship called first at Pointe Noire, French Equatorial Africa and then at Luanda, Angola before finally arriving at Matadi, the Belgian Congo's only port, located at the head of navigation for oceangoing vessels. Just above Matadi is the lowest of the Congo River cataracts. The series of cataracts extends all the way to Léopoldville, the capital city.

We claimed our car without difficulty, and drove one hundred fifty miles to Thysville, where we spent the night in a hotel surrounded by a lush tropical garden. We had stopped briefly by Kimpese, where a Protestant medical center was to be developed. The next day we continued to Sona Bata. Doctors coming to the Congo were required to spend one month in a *stage*, a training period to acquaint them with the medical system in the colony. Normally this was done in a designated government hospital. At that time the Baptist Mission at Sona Bata had the only Protestant hospital in the colony with an accredited nursing school. It was also the only mission hospital designated for the *stage*. Leaving Katie and the three children at Sona Bata, I went to the ministry of health in Léopoldville and received permission to return there for my *stage*.

The *stage* lasted the entire month of December. I enjoyed very much getting to know Dr. Glen Tuttle, who had been in Congo for many years. I also

Stanley's survey marker,
Léopoldville 1953.

enjoyed working with Dr. Carrie Sprague and Dr. Walker. I rotated through the various departments of the hospital and was privileged to attend the graduation of the last class of nurses to complete their studies at Sona Bata. The school moved the next year to Kimpese and became a union school of the Baptists in cooperation with several other missions in the Lower Congo area.

On completion of the *stage* we drove to Léopoldville. As we approached the city, we passed over a hill where we saw the column erected by Henry M. Stanley that he used as the zero point when he surveyed the area and founded the city in 1887. The hill overlooked the broad expanse of Stanley Pool where the Congo River widens before rushing down the cataracts to the sea. We could look down on the shipbuilding area where the riverboats and barges are assembled to be used on some twenty-one thousand miles of navigable river above this point. We stayed in the Union Mission House, a big two-story building with large verandas on all sides both upstairs and down. Katie and the children flew up to what was then Luluabourg, now Kananga. A mission school teacher from Bibanga was in Léopoldville. He agreed to accompany me to the American Presbyterian Congo Mission (APCM) area in the Kasai Region.

Léopoldville to Kasai by Road

My first trip into the interior by road was quite an experience. I went back to Sona Bata, then on south almost to the Angola border before turning back north. There were a total of thirteen ferry crossings on the trip. The largest rivers were the Kwango at Popokabaka, the Kwilu at Kikwit, and the Kasai at Port Francqui. The car gave me trouble all along the way and I got my initiation in automobile mechanics. My first mishap occurred when I got stuck in the sand when trying to ease by a Catholic priest's truck on a narrow stretch of the road. The starter wouldn't function, so the priest and his workers helped dig me out and pushed me off. I crossed the ferry at Popokabaka and drove on to the Baptist Mission station at Boko. I tried to find the trouble with the starter which was only working intermittently. Changing the spark plugs seemed to help. The next day I arrived in Kikwit in midafternoon.

There I met Mr. Yost, a Mennonite missionary who was a skilled mechanic. He looked at the car and cleaned the battery cables, but couldn't locate the trouble. There was time to cross the ferry before it stopped running at sundown, so he invited me to go a little further down the road to his station at Iwungu for the night. A short way beyond Kikwit the road went down a long hill. What began as a small rut in the middle of the road became bigger and bigger until it was a large gully. It became so large that the wheels of the car could not straddle it. When one wheel dropped into the gully, something snapped. I found that the steering wheel no longer controlled the front wheels. Mr. Yost was following in his pickup and shortly came down the road. He helped me find the trouble. The bolts holding the end of the steering wheel to the chassis had snapped. Luckily he had some tools and a few bolts in his pickup. He was able to effect a repair right there, though the replacement bolts he had to use were iron and not steel. Iwungu was just a few kilometers away. I drove on gingerly and spent the night there. The next morning before I finished breakfast, he had gotten up and replaced the bolts with steel ones to make it possible for us to continue on our way. The next day, because of frequent ferries and getting stuck once again in a sand pit during a rainstorm, I was able to make only ninety-two miles to Mukedi, another Mennonite post. Here Dr. Merle Schwartz had a Ford service manual. Together we removed the starter and found that the starter drive was sticking. Cleaning this with kerosene left an oily film which cured the problem. I continued on, crossing the last ferry at Port Francqui late in the afternoon. The Kasai River is very wide at this point and the motor ferry does not run after dark. The landings are not opposite one another. In fact, one is about a quarter of a mile downstream from the other.

My destination was Bulapé. I had been given instructions about a short-cut, so I did not have to go all the way to Mweka on the main road. It was after dark when I arrived on the station. I was not sure where I was until I met Garland Goodrum on his way to the work shed where the radio was installed. He was hoping to contact the Mennonite Mission to see if they had any news of my whereabouts. A station supper to welcome our family was in progress. I arrived just in time to join Katie and the children for this happy occasion.

Bulapé 1953

Bulapé station has an interesting history. It is located about fifteen miles north of the rail station of Mweka and about sixty miles north of the oldest of our mission stations, Luebo. Bulapé is in the kingdom of the Bakuba, but the local village is inhabited by the Bakete, formerly a subject tribe. The Kuba capital, Mushenge, is located about twenty miles northwest of Bulapé. When the American Presbyterian Congo Mission (APCM) first tried to reach the Bakuba, the effort to establish a station in their territory was resisted. The first attempt in 1897 was made at Ibanche, which is in the southern part of the Kuba kingdom about ten miles southwest of Mweka. This mission station

Shashenge Matshikana, Bulapé 1984.

was attacked and destroyed by the Bakuba in 1904. Fortunately, the missionaries had enough warning to flee and none were killed. In 1915, the government granted a concession for Bulapé station. Bulapé was given the Kuba name of one of the early Afro-American missionaries, Mrs. Annie Taylor Rochester, who died at Mutoto. Bulapé was also, reportedly, the name of the first member of the royal family who became a Christian. In 1919 during epidemics of dysentery and influenza, the Bakuba called upon the mission for help. One of the early missionaries, the Reverend Hezekiah Washburn, went to Mushenge and brought the sick to an isolation camp near Bulapé until the epidemic was controlled.

Shortly after we arrived at Bulapé, there was a visit from the then current *Nyimi*, Bopé Mabintshi. *Nyimi* is the king's title in the Kuba language, Bushongo; *Lukenga* is the term used for him by neighboring Luba peoples. Bopé Mabintshi suggested that they give me his name; however, the church session preferred to name me for Kueta Mabintshi, the paralytic king who was a great friend of the mission. Katie was given the name, Tshiekueta, which had been the name given Mr. Washburn's wife, Lillie. Thus we acquired African names in addition to our English and Chinese names.

Bopé Mabintshi was an imposing character. He was quite overweight and always dressed in the traditional garb of a gathered raffia skirt and little conical Kuba hat. We visited him in Mushenge, the capital. This was quite an establishment, with the royal compound surrounded by a high fence of woven palm leaves. To get to his quarters we were led through a labyrinth. It was said that every time one entered, a different route was used. There was a large harem, as each subject village was required to furnish the king with a wife. Reputedly there were over two hundred women in the harem. Usually a young girl was sent and was not replaced until she died, so the "wives" were of all ages, young girls to very elderly women. In effect, they were really hostages. Only about eight were in constant attendance to the king. Traditionally at the death of the king, those wives in close attendance were buried with him. This assured that they would be very solicitous of his health and welfare. Some years after we left Bulapé, we had a visit from Dr. Frank W. Price. He had been the last of our missionaries to leave China. His last few months in China were spent under house arrest. He had finally been permitted to leave in December 1951, eleven months after I left. During his trip to Africa we took him to Mushenge to visit the king.

Bopé Mabintshi was really the last of the kings that reigned in the traditional style. He lived to see Independence, dying a few years thereafter. Unfortunately we were in the States at the time of his death and did not get to attend the funeral. We visited Mushenge after we returned to Africa the following year and went to see his grave, which was sheltered under a thatched shed with a couple of carved elephant tusks implanted as grave markers. As was the custom, the royal village had been moved a short distance from the former one. The new *Nyimi* was Kueta Bokashanga. In the Kuba matrilineal society, the kingship does not pass down from father to son. Instead, the son of a sister of the king becomes the ruler. So with the names of the kings, the second name is the name of his mother. In the case of Kueta Bokashanga, he was not the one who was originally expected to become the king. Kueta Bokashanga was very active politically and so was named king, having political clout as well as being in the legitimate line of succession. When we visited him at Mushenge, his audience room was a thatched shed, but it had a rug on the floor and several overstuffed chairs. An audio system was playing with a small generator furnishing current. He did not continue to maintain the traditional harem, although he is polygamous. More recently, he has spent most of his time in Kinshasa, the national capital, allowing the royal establishment at Mushenge to deteriorate.

Bulapé station was built on a ridge with the mission houses down the two sides and a grassy open area down the middle. Lapsley Memorial Hospital was at the north end, with the airstrip beyond it. On the other side of the airstrip was the sleeping sickness lazaret, said to be the only one in the Belgian Congo. There were usually around one hundred fifty patients under treatment there at any one time. In the center of the station, on the west side, were the large church and the school. The girls' boarding home was on the side opposite the church. The boys' home and evangelistic school were at the opposite end from the hospital. In the center of the station, there was a large tree under which the village elders often held their meetings.

The village elders dressed in their traditional skirts made of *madiba*, raffia cloth, and wore conical hats. The hat of the *diulu*, "sergeant at arms," sported pompons and frequently had a couple of feathers stuck in it. The conical hats were held in place with a hatpin, often made from a bicycle spoke. The women at Bulapé often went bare to below the waist. Their abdomens had beautiful geometric designs made by scarification, sometimes tattooed by rubbing ashes into the cuts. When operating on these

Elder weaving raffia cloth, Bulapé 1973.

women we tried to be careful to match up the designs when their wounds were sutured. It was not uncommon for keloids to form in the scars. Sometimes these overgrown scars would become so large that I had to perform plastic procedures to remove them. This was especially true when keloids formed in the scars resulting from piercing the ear lobes. I have seen keloids in this site larger than a softball.

Bulapé, a relatively isolated post in the southern edge of the equatorial forest, had neither a central light plant nor a central water supply. Instead, there were large cisterns that collected water during the nine months of rain, which would last through the three months of dry season, if guarded carefully. Each house had a cistern and collected water off the galvanized roof. Several of the missionaries had their own individual light plants. A couple of these were 110 volt systems, but the first house we stayed in was where Lena Reynolds, the nurse, usually lived. She was on furlough and her electric system was 12 volt DC. The generator furnished lights and charged a battery, which powered the lights when the motor was not running.

Bill and Jean Mulcay lived next door. Garland Goodrum, one of the two industrial missionaries on the station, was building a new residence into which the Mulcay family was to move in July. We were to move into the house the Mulcays had been occupying, to vacate Lena's house for her return. Later in the year, Lawrence DeLand, the senior industrial missionary at Bulapé, started construction on another residence.

Mr. DeLand was a builder and maintenance man. He was quite an individualist and a very enterprising character. There was no stone available in the vicinity. All the newer buildings at Bulapé were built of brick which he made. The kilns were down by a stream in the forest, where he had quite a plantation of bananas and plantains. He made his own vinegar from bananas. He was also the watch repairman for the mission. Their house had originally been the station warehouse that he had converted to a home. He often brought orchids that he found in the forest and placed them in the hedge in front of his house or on old stumps in the yard. He kept a string of donkeys which he used as pack animals and also had a mare. One day our boys, Sperry and Lee, came home to tell us that they had been watching Mr. DeLand deliver his mare of a foal. For them, growing up at Bulapé under Mr. DeLand's tutelage was highly instructive.

Dr. Mark Poole was the senior doctor on the station. He was also a pilot and had the first airplane on the mission. His first plane had been a Piper Cub. When we arrived, this had been replaced with a four-place Cessna. He had built an airstrip at Bulapé, which ran east and west across the ridge. The ends of the strip had been built up with dirt fill. Even then the strip barely met the government's minimal length requirement, and it dropped off sharply at both ends. It was like landing on an aircraft carrier. Mark visited three rural dispensaries, Bambuyi, Mbelu, and Batua, each of which had an airstrip. Bambuyi dispensary was out on a plain and the road served for the airstrip. Mbelu was at the ferry on the Lubudi River. The third dispensary was in the forest on the east side of that river, built to serve the Batua, the

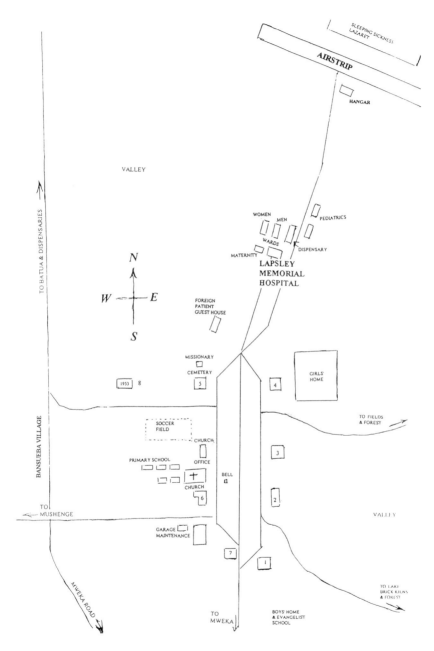

SLEEPING SICKNESS
LAZARET

AIRSTRIP

HANGAR

VALLEY

WOMEN
MEN
PEDIATRICS

WARDS
DISPENSARY

MATERNITY

LAPSLEY
MEMORIAL
HOSPITAL

N

W ── E

S

FOREIGN
PATIENT
GUEST HOUSE

MISSIONARY
CEMETERY

TO BATUA & DISPENSARIES

1953 8

5

4

GIRLS'
HOME

BANSUEBA VILLAGE

SOCCER
FIELD

CHURCH

TO FIELDS
& FOREST

PRIMARY SCHOOL

OFFICE

3

CHURCH

6

BELL

2

TO
MUSHENGE

VALLEY

GARAGE
MAINTENANCE

7

MWEKA ROAD

1

TO
MWEKA

BOYS' HOME
& EVANGELIST
SCHOOL

TO LAKE
BRICK KILNS
& FOREST

Bulapé
1953
Missionary homes are numbered.

original inhabitants of this area. Mark loved to tell how the airstrip there and the one at Bulapé were compacted by the women locking arms, dancing, and stamping the dirt until it was packed hard.

Our first and principal job was to learn Tshiluba. This was the language spoken throughout the Kasai Region, being the language of the Baluba and Bena Lulua tribes. At Bulapé, the native tongue of Bansueba, the local village, was Tshikete and the language of the Bakuba was Bushongo. There was little literature in either of these. In any case, Tshiluba was much more widely used. Bulapé was not the best place to study Tshiluba, since we didn't hear it spoken all the time. A new program of language study was being developed, however, by Virginia Pruitt and Winnie Vass. The early version of this was available in mimeograph form. We found a Tshiluba-speaking schoolteacher for an informant. Eleanor Goodrum directed our study. Ruth Worth, whom we had known in China, had also been reassigned to Congo and was at Bulapé. The three of us studied Tshiluba together. In addition to the Tshiluba study, I filled in for Dr. Poole when he was off the station. His two girls were then attending Central School for missionary children at Lubondai. He occasionally flew down there and was also away for dispensary visits or to make trips to Luluabourg or Léopoldville on hospital business.

In China I became known as the "doctor with the big shoes" because of the box-like ski boots that I wore in winter. In Zaïre I soon deserved the reputation as the "doctor with the big hands." I was the only doctor on the mission who wore size 8 1/2 or 9 surgical gloves. I soon learned to carry some gloves with me, as none of the hospitals stocked my size. On short terms during later years of our service in Africa, I took a half footlocker of gloves with me each time. I had a similar problem in the States and always had to be sure the surgery and emergency rooms were notified in sufficient time to stock gloves for me.

Once when Mr. and Mrs. DeLand had to go to South Africa for a medical problem, I was asked to take over his work crew. One of the projects that I undertook at this time was to remodel the hospital boiler room which furnished steam for the autoclave. A government inspection had required that the boiler be removed from the building. I supervised filling in the floor to bring it up to the level of the other rooms. Openings had to be made in the brick walls for a new window and a new door. I strained my back using a crowbar when I became too involved. This marked the beginning of my back problems.

New missionaries were encouraged to visit all the APCM stations, to get an overview of the work of the mission. Our first opportunity to visit another station came when we were asked to transport a couple of visitors to Mutoto. Dr. Tinsley Smith showed us the hospital. I was also privileged to go with the Reverend Plumer Smith to a village where he performed a wedding ceremony. Our next opportunity came when we made a trip to see Dr. Sandy Marks, our dentist, who was stationed at Lubondai. We went on to Moma, a station that the mission had taken over from the Foursquare Gospel Mission. It served the area of the Basala Mpasu, a cannibal tribe, who dressed very scantily and filed their teeth to sharp points. We also visited Kasha and

Kankinda. Our friends the Boltons were at Kasha near the railway, where Eric was starting an industrial school. Nearby Kankinda was a fairly new station built for the expanded normal and Bible schools. It was situated below a plateau and was unique in that its water supply came from a spring above the station. The water flowed by gravity without the need of pumps.

Continuing our tour of the mission, we headed on to Bibanga. The road went by way of Bakwanga, now Mbuji-Mayi. The battery in our Ford sedan was mounted under the hood just inside the right fender. On a rough, rocky section of the road, it broke loose and fell into the fan, bending the blades so that they cut into the radiator. This caused us to lose our cooling fluid. I was able to put the battery back in place. The only thing I could get to staunch the flow of the water from the radiator was beeswax. I stopped up the holes and begged water from a village to refill the radiator. We drove slowly until the radiator got hot enough to melt the wax and it leaked again. We went through this process several times until we finally limped into Bakwanga. Bakwanga was the big diamond mine site and was officially off limits, but they were very gracious. It was just before quitting time and the head mechanic, who had known Dr. Kellersberger, said they would work on it in the morning. In the meantime they put us up in the guest house. The next day he took the radiator off and repaired it, closing off the badly damaged pipes and soldering the others, so that we could continue on our way.

Bibanga sits on the edge of a plateau. It overlooks Bakwanga and the Lubilashi River valley. Dr. Kellersberger's large leprosy camp was about eight or ten kilometers from the station. He had planted groves of chaulmoogra trees and made chaulmoogra oil to be used in leprosy treatment. Bibanga also had one of the two hydroelectric plants on the mission. This plant made use of a small stream that came out of the side of the plateau. There was a small dam to redirect the flow into a raceway, but the grade was so steep that it did not form a lake.

The only APCM station we didn't visit during the first year was Mboi. Luebo was the closest station to Bulapé and we had the opportunity to run down there a couple of times, so gained a pretty good picture of the entire mission. Driving on the rough roads took its toll, as I began to have trouble with a pilonidal cyst, which finally required surgery. The wound broke down twice before it finally healed, putting me to bed off and on during the latter part of the year. During one of the times when I was confined to bed, Bulapé had an episode involving elephants. A small herd wandered up to within a quarter of a mile of the station, laying waste to the fields nearby. The villagers went wild and attacked them with their muzzleloading guns, killing a mother elephant and her young. In the melee, they wounded another one of the elephants. In the wounded animal's rampage, it gored Nurse Kangombe, one of the operating room assistants, whose death was a sad loss.

While at Bulapé I had my introduction to amateur radio. The mission stations kept in regular contact by radio on a daily net. In addition, Mark Poole had a ham set. He and Garland Goodrum both had Congo amateur radio licenses. I applied for and received a license with the call letters OQ5FV. Mark was primarily interested in talking to his family in the States on a regular weekly schedule. He generously let Garland and me use his set at other times to make DX contacts with other ham stations. I was able to talk with our families as well as to amateur operators elsewhere in the world.

When we arrived in the Congo, each of the five major APCM hospitals, Bulapé, Luebo, Mutoto, Lubondai, and Bibanga, had schools for *aides-infirmiers* (nurse aides). The students were all men and most of them had only finished five years of elementary school before spending three years in the hospital program. Actually they served more as medical assistants, not only caring for the patients, but also seeing outpatients. They treated patients with minor complaints, performed triage, and referred to the doctors those who needed surgery or who had diseases the aides could not diagnose or treat. I was still recovering from surgery when mission meeting was held in the fall of 1953. Katie attended the meeting that was held at Lake Munkamba, while I stayed at Bulapé with our children. At that meeting, it was decided to start a school for *infirmiers* at Lubondai. This was the next level of preparation for nurses, which led to a diploma. Dr. William Rule and Dr. John Miller were charged with initiating the program. Dr. George Cousar was then at Lubondai, so he changed places with Dr. Rule, who had been at Bibanga. Dr. Miller was moved from Luebo to Lubondai, and we were moved from Bulapé to Luebo, to replace the Millers there. The school was to start after the beginning of the new year. I went down to Luebo in December to consult with John and arrange to take over the hospital.

The nursing school at Lubondai was named Institut Médical Chrétien du Kasai, usually referred to as IMCK. When first established, it had only the nursing section. Later a dental section was added and functioned until Independence in 1960. I served on the first board of the school. One of the tasks in which I participated, in consultation with a number of interested parties, was the drafting of a constitution for the institution. The Mennonites wanted to join with us and it was hoped that we could interest the Methodists as well. We wanted it to be an ecumenical project. The initial board had representatives from the Presbyterians, Mennonites, government, and one member from the Methodists. Unfortunately, although the Methodists held a place on the board for a number of years, they never became a supporting body and, after a number of years, they were dropped from the board.

Luebo 1954-56

Luebo was the first Presbyterian mission post in the Belgian Congo. In fact, when the missionaries arrived in 1891 there was only a small trading post on the south bank of the river. This was the first Protestant mission in the Kasai Region and antedated the Catholic mission by a year. William Sheppard and Samuel Lapsley had come up the Congo River to the Kasai River and then continued up its tributary, the Lulua River. Just above the

Luebo ferry 1955.

entry of the small Luebo River from the south, there were rapids in the Lulua that were impassable for the river boat. Here at the head of navigation, the river flowed in a deep narrow valley between two plateaus. Sheppard and Lapsley chose to place the station on the north side of the river opposite the trading post. Luebo station was situated where the plateau already began to slope off toward the river. The mission concession had a slope of five to ten percent, and the drop from the edge of the station was then very steep. Two hundred feet below, a narrow strip of land formed the riverbank. The river was about 150 yards wide at that point.

When we moved to Luebo, one still had to cross the river on a ferry, constructed of three large metal boats lashed together, with a platform across the top. The approaches on each side were fairly steep and large planks were wrestled into place between the shore and the ferry for boarding. Cars and trucks had to be guided onto the ferry, which held about four cars or two trucks at a time. The ferry was connected to a pulley that ran on a cable stretched across the river, and was angled so that the current pushed it across, like wind pushing a sail. It always required a lot of poling to get the ferry properly positioned on each bank, and usually took thirty to forty minutes to cross the river, once the loading of the ferry was completed. There was often a line of cars and trucks waiting to cross.Although cars were given priority over trucks, it usually took an hour or more just to cross one way. If we had business on the other side, we would frequently go down in a car, then cross in a pirogue. The pirogues, hollowed from huge logs, were often large enough to accommodate five or six passengers. The boatman stood upright to paddle the dugout across the river. Since we had to cross the river to get onto the road to Luluabourg (now Kananga), if a trip was pending, we would get up before daybreak and go down to the river to get across on the first ferry, as it only operated during daylight hours.

Because of the time and trouble that it took to get across the river, we often heard the talking drums passing messages back and forth at night. The talking drum or *tshiondo* is a two-toned drum made from a hollowed log with a slit through which it has been hollowed out. The two sides of the slit are carved to different thicknesses so that there is a high and low note when each is struck in turn. Since Tshiluba is a tonal language, by striking the *tshiondo* with the rhythm and tones of words, the drum actually approximates the

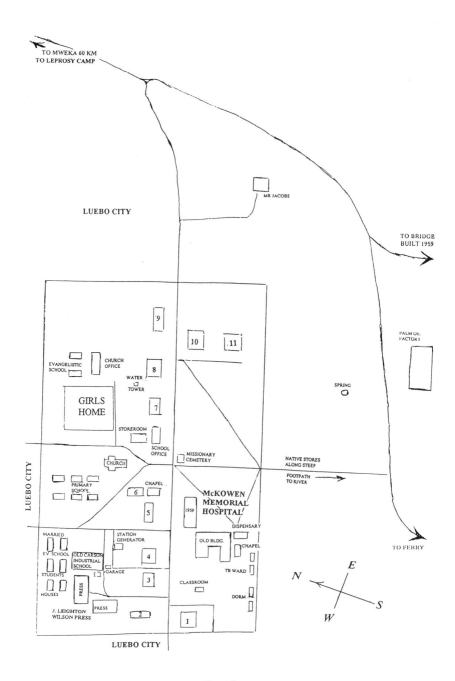

Luebo

1954-1961

Residences are numbered.

sound of those words. The leprosy camp had a *tshiondo*. When I arrived for visits they would call the patients with it. I could hear the drum saying, "The doctor has come, the doctor has come. Come, come, come."

In 1954 Luebo station was surrounded by a large *centre extracoutumier*. This term was used for a town occupied by a large population living outside their traditional tribal areas. Luebo had grown as people came to settle close to the mission. Some had originally been slaves, or were descendants of slaves, who had been redeemed by earlier missionaries. The north bank of the river was the southern edge of the territory of the Bakete. Across the river was the territory of the Bena Lulua. The native city around the mission station numbered around forty thousand people. There was one other foreigner, Mr. Jacobs, who lived near the station and operated a palm oil factory located on the riverbank. The south bank had the docks and warehouses for river transport, a flour mill, and then a series of stores on the road ascending the hill. The Catholic Mission was located there, along with Luebo District offices, the District Hospital, and an army camp. There was an airstrip and a native city of about ten thousand. In addition to the road leading southeast to Luluabourg, another road crossed the Luebo River on a bridge going west to Charlesville (Zaïrian name, Djoko Punda) on the Kasai River, where the Mennonites had a station.

The large church, with its four-faced clock tower, occupied the center of our Luebo station. Other institutions on the station were the church offices of Luebo Presbytery, the evangelistic school, a large primary school, the girls' home, the J. Leighton Wilson Press, and the McKowen Memorial Hospital. The former Carson Industrial School was used as a carpenter shop. Most of the eleven missionary residences faced a road which ran the length of the station.

During the two terms we lived at Luebo, there was a large turnover of mission personnel due to furloughs. There were usually three or four evangelistic couples, one or two units for the school, one or more nurses, a builder and maintenance man, the director of the press, Dr. Gladys Smithwick, and, until he retired, the dentist, Dr. Hugh Wilds.

We were assigned the house numbered "4" on the station map, known as the Georgia Home, since funds for its construction had been generously provided by the Women of the Church in the state of Georgia. Located near the hospital, it had long been the residence of the missionary doctor. It was a big house with a large verandah on three sides. On the fourth side, the verandah had been enclosed to make a bathroom and a sewing room. Katie used the latter as a classroom for the children. The verandah provided ample space for large gatherings, meetings, picnic suppers, and celebrations of all kinds, especially during the rainy season. Georgia Home was built high off the ground with a crawl space that varied from four to six feet in height. The crawl space was a favorite birthing place for the village sheep. To be awakened by the bleating of a ewe in labor was a fairly common occurrence. It was one of the few houses on the mission with wooden floors.

For us the house had another very attractive feature. In the early mission residences, many of the bathtubs were made of concrete. In the old Washburn house at Bulapé the tub had a rather rough bottom. Hence five-year-old Sperry's elation when, after circling through the new home on a tour of inspection, he came running back to Katie saying, "Oh, Mom, do come look at the slippery tub!" A real bathtub was cause for thanksgiving.

The children of missionaries went to boarding school for fourth grade through high school at Central School (CS) at Lubondai. The first three grades were usually taught by the mothers at home using the Calvert School home instruction course, ordered from Baltimore, Maryland. At Luebo there were several children the ages of Sperry and Lee, so Katie was able to cooperate with other mothers in teaching them. This helped a great deal, as she also carried a full load at the hospital.

McKowen Memorial Hospital was a U-shaped building. In 1954, the north wing, which had contained the original operating room, now housed the administrative office, laboratory, and X-ray room. In the past, this wing had been damaged by fire, which was started when someone was filling a kerosene refrigerator. With the attached north-south section, containing four wards, it formed the oldest part of the hospital. In the early fifties, there was already talk that the roof and framing needed to be replaced. The south wing was of newer construction and contained the operating room, sterilizing room, surgical storeroom, delivery room, a six-bed ward and four two-bed rooms for maternity patients. The dispensary building, downhill from the main hospital, contained the outpatient waiting room, doctors' consultation room, treatment room, and pharmacy. Behind this was a chapel shed where the day's activities began with morning prayers, and where regular clinics for well children under five were held. Small buildings farther west were used for tuberculosis patients and for student dormitories. An old garage had been converted to a classroom, to help accommodate the increasing number of students.

I was fortunate while at Luebo to have the collaboration of a number of excellent missionary nurses; in addition to Katie, Jean Shive, wife of Alexander M. Shive (Aleck), was there until they retired in 1960, just before Independence. Margaret McMurry's administrative skills greatly facilitated the surgical program. Mary, the Reverend John Morrison's wife, was involved in the very busy outpatient department. During our first term at

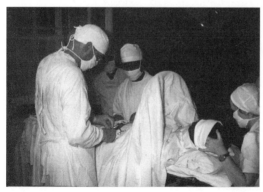

Operating room at Luebo, author operating, Katie monitoring patient, 1955.

Luebo, Dr. Gladys Smithwick came to join us and to fill in for our furlough. Gladys had been in China before the war, but had to leave the field because of illness, and had become an anesthesiologist. After a number of years, she was reappointed to Congo. She took over the medical and pediatric patients and I concentrated on surgery, obstetrics, and gynecology. She was truly expert in her specialty and a real wizard at adapting to local limitations. She demonstrated her teaching ability by working with Katie, passing on knowledge and skills that made it possible for us to function in the absence of a fully qualified anesthetist. We rejoice that anesthetics are now administered by Zaïrian nurses with graduate preparation.

I have mentioned two China connections, Ruth Worth and Gladys Smithwick. There were several others at Luebo and on the mission. Aurie Montgomery Miller grew up in China as did Betty Yates White, Dr. Carleton White's wife. The Whites had been at Luebo and left shortly before we went there. The Reverend Charles McKee, one of the evangelistic missionaries at Luebo, had served in China on the Burma Road during World War II. Bill Worth, Ruth's brother and the son of Dr. George Worth, also grew up in China. Bill took over the press when John Vass left for furlough. Ruth Romig Bolton, who was in Belgium with us, was the daughter of Presbyterian missionaries to China; the Boltons were stationed at Kasha and later at Bibanga. Dr. Hugh Farrior, whose parents Stacy and Kitty we had known in China, came to Congo during our second term. After covering for Dr. Tinsley Smith's furlough at Mutoto for one year, he moved to Bibanga and then later to the IMCK.

In some ways I found administering a hospital in Congo to be more difficult than in China. I did not have as many skilled persons to whom I could delegate jobs, so I had to perform many nonmedical tasks myself. We had a standby generator at the hospital which I had to learn to repair. Not having any experienced foremen, I had to be more directly involved in assigning jobs to the hospital workers. There was no one who could do the bookkeeping or type letters until I trained someone for these tasks. Preparing the budget, mission reports, and especially the government statistical reports at the end of the year took a tremendous amount of time. Equally time-consuming was the preparation of orders for hospital supplies. We were allowed to order limited amounts of drugs from the central government pharmacy in Léopoldville. Delivery usually took up to six months. One could never be sure how much of the order would be filled. Our mission appropriations were used mainly to order drugs and equipment from the States. These took even longer to arrive, often up to a year. Linen supplies came for the most part from the Women of the Church through the "White Cross" program. The lead time on these orders was usually over a year, but they were invaluable, as there was absolutely no source of such supplies within the country.

We attempted always to upgrade the level of teaching for our students. From the start, it was apparent to all that a handful of expatriate doctors and nurses could not begin to meet the demands for health services, hence the emphasis on educating local personnel. Soon after we moved to Luebo, we sought to increase the requirement for entrance to the *aide-infirmier* program, with admission based on examination results. I taught anatomy, physiology, and tropical diseases, while the nurses taught pharmacology and the nursing subjects. A couple of the best students, who were qualified, transferred to the nursing school at Lubondai. I was named to the district examining board that met at the government hospital across the river. We examined students from the District Hospital, Bulapé, and the Mennonite Hospital at Charlesville, in addition to our own students. I was usually pleased with our students' results. They consistently had a relatively high level of success. We were fortunate to follow Dr. John Miller at Luebo. His knowledge of French and Tshiluba had facilitated a tradition of quality education.

Normal deliveries were usually capably handled by older Congolese women who had received practical training in midwifery. Congolese patients preferred this to delivery by a male doctor, and active prenatal clinics helped us to identify high risk patients. I was called whenever there was difficulty in resuscitating a newborn, when there were obstetrical complications, or when a C-section was necessary. The normal deliveries that I attended were nearly all missionary wives and a few other expatriate women. At Luebo the single delivery room was very small, so we set up the X-ray room for use as a second delivery room when needed. Katie was pregnant when we moved to Luebo. Elizabeth was born there on April 4, 1954. I had the pleasure of delivering her with the help of Jean Shive and Mary Morrison. I almost missed Elizabeth's delivery as Katie was having a slow time. I went around to the operating suite to get some more supplies and got back just in time. I was able to send our families news of Elizabeth's birth through amateur radio contacts in the States.

In a large workroom at the back of our house, I had installed a small ham radio transmitter purchased from Dave McLean. Carroll Stegall, then retired in Black Mountain, North Carolina, had built the house. When I contacted him on the radio, he told me that, in 1924, he was the first amateur radio operator to transmit from the Congo. He operated his radio from that very room with a small generator that was powered by a boy pedaling a stationary bicycle.

All our APCM hospitals had leprosy camps. While we were at Bulapé, Dr. Poole had asked me to oversee the one there, which had only about sixty patients. The camp at Luebo had about two hundred and fifty patients. In 1954 the American Leprosy Missions sent Dr. Robert Cochran to hold a leprosy conference at Lubondai for all the missionary physicians. He gave a very helpful and thorough course in the diagnosis and treatment of Hansen's disease, and demonstrated the different classifications of the disease as manifested among the patients at the Lubondai camp. The government subsidized the leprosy camps and every year provided a blanket, some cloth, and a small stipend to each of the patients. Not long after the Lubondai conference, the policy of the government changed. The noninfectious tuberculoid type of leprosy was to be treated in the villages on an ambulatory basis. The only patients the government would subsidize were the infectious lepromatous type and those that were too badly crippled to live in the village. As a result of this policy, the camp at Bulapé closed. The one at Lubondai was also closed and combined with a nearby camp that was run by the Catholics. I was able to cut the number of patients in the camp at Luebo to one hundred and seventy-four.

The leprosy conference was such an excellent opportunity for exchange among the missionary physicians that we started to have similar annual meetings to which we invited specialists from the States to give the main lectures. The first year, a surgeon from the University of Ohio led a conference at Lake Munkamba, going to Mutoto, the hospital closest to the lake, for one day in the operating theater. One year we held the conference at Luebo, at which our visiting speaker was an American pediatrician, a friend of Dr. Gladys Smithwick. She came from Ogbomosho, Nigeria, where she had visited a Baptist mission hospital. Subsequent meetings at Lake Munkamba featured a urologist and an orthopedist.

Toward the end of our second year at Luebo, I went to Lubondai for an IMCK board meeting. On my return trip, I was asked to take Winnited, Lach and Winnie Vass's youngest child, along with her nurse, Baba Kankolongo. We came through Luluabourg, where I placed in the trunk of the car a basket of money from Jim Halverstadt, the mission treasurer, to take to the Luebo station treasurer. Everything went well until we neared Luebo. About five kilometers from town, we rounded a curve and saw a truck coming down a hill toward us. The road was very narrow and sand had been piled on the banks on both sides. I tried to pull over to the right as far as possible. The truck apparently did not have good brakes. It was loaded with barrels of palm oil and had about a dozen or so riders perched on top of the barrels. The front part of the truck and cab scraped by my car but the back wheel rolled up over my front fender. Just before the wheel reached the windshield the truck turned over on its side, dumping its cargo and passengers on to the sandbank. My chin hit the steering wheel, bending the wheel and cutting the point of my chin. Winnited was beside me. She had fallen asleep and had slipped halfway behind Baba Kankolongo who was sitting by the window. Baba Kankolongo was thrown against the dash, but Winnited was cushioned and unhurt. Baba Kankolongo was bruised but had no serious injury. Fortunately no one on the truck was injured either. A car came along that offered to transport us to the District Hospital. I was covered with blood from the cut on my chin. We gathered up our baggage, including the basketful of money, and went on to the hospital. While the Belgian doctor was sewing my cut, we sent word to the station about the accident and asked that someone come to get us. The car was totaled. We towed it back to Luebo, where it sat in a garage for the rest of our term, while we tried to get an insurance settlement. We eventually got a small sum, though it dragged on for months.

Normally we would have been due a furlough the summer of 1955. Since we had spent a year in Belgium and our children were all still young, we decided to extend for an additional year. This made a total of five years overseas, four of them in the Congo, before returning to the States. We started planning with the Lach Vasses for a long trip home. They dropped out, and we pursued the plan to leave by rail via Victoria Falls, Rhodesia; Beira, Mozambique; up the east coast of Africa to Egypt; the Holy Land; then on to

England and the States. We used three different ship lines which had an arrangement for a through rate as if the whole trip were on the same line. The trip was planned to take three months. My mother decided to come and accompany us on the trip.

In April 1956, I drove to Luluabourg to meet Mother in the station pickup. She arrived in the morning; we had lunch with the Halverstadts and set out for Luebo. Normally the trip took around four or five hours. It was about midafternoon when we left and we expected to get in for a late supper. At that time, one still had to cross at least one ferry in addition to the one at Luebo. About two-thirds of the way to Luebo, there was a virgin forest with huge trees and dense foliage. It being the dark of the moon, the night was really black by the time we arrived there. I saw a fire in the road ahead. A group of people by a parked truck were huddled around the fire in front of a huge tree, four or five feet in diameter, which lay across the road. Obviously it would take days to clear the road.

The tree stump was about thirty feet from the road. When the tree fell, it left a gap of about fifteen feet between the lower end of the trunk and the stump. It appeared possible to dig through the banks and cut the underbrush to clear a passage between the trunk and the stump so that vehicles could bypass the fallen tree.

Those present suggested that if I would go call the road crew, they might start work immediately instead of waiting until morning. We had just passed some huts where they said the chief of the road crew lived. I left Mother in the car and took the flashlight to find help. Remember that she spoke neither French nor, of course, any of the local languages. The night was pitch-black and this was her first visit to Africa. I knocked at the first hut and found the chief of the road crew. He said we would have to awaken the others. We started knocking at doors, continuing up the road for a quarter of a mile or so. It took a half-hour or more before we got back to the car. They dug away the wall of sand and, with jungle knives, hacked away at the underbrush. When they had cleared a short distance, I drove the pickup as far as I could go and then backed up and waited for them to chop some more. It took most of the night to get the detour cleared. We finally arrived at Luebo at about five in the morning. Mother was a great storyteller, and when she later recounted this experience, the night grew darker and longer with each repetition.

The Grand Tour

About ten days before our departure from Luebo, Lee fell and broke his elbow. I had to set it and put it in a cast. Before we left, I split the cast and taped it together so I would be able to remove it later during the trip. We left Mweka by train going south to what was then Élisabethville (now Lubumbashi). A day there allowed a visit to the museum. After spending the night, we boarded another train for the border. In Congo the railroad was narrow gauge, in the Rhodesias and South Africa, broad gauge. It was necessary to change trains at the border, walking from one station to the other. Here we discovered that one of our checked pieces, a trunk, had not made the transfer in Élisabethville. We sent word to have it follow us.

A layover at Livingstone let us enjoy the impressive sight of Victoria Falls. The river plunges down the side of a long narrow gorge and then zigzags back and forth through a series of narrow gorges, each of which had been a former site of the falls. Repeatedly the water has cut another channel behind the falls, thus moving the falls back through successive channels. We could see where it was beginning to cut another channel back behind the present falls. There were baboons everywhere. We took a boat trip a short distance up the Zambezi River above the falls to an island inhabited by monkeys. While we stood listening to our guide, one of the monkeys snatched some bubble gum out of Lee's hands, much to his chagrin.

We had another day's layover at Bulawayo between trains. Lee had a high fever and was taking antimalarial treatment, so Katie stayed with him in the hotel. Mother and I took a sightseeing tour to Cecil Rhodes' tomb. He is buried on top of a granite *kopje* (hill), similar to Stone Mountain, Georgia, though smaller. There were some prehistoric cave drawings on the stone wall of a nearby grotto. From Bulawayo we went to Beira, Mozambique to board the ship. We had a couple of nights there, but our trunk did not catch up with us before we sailed.

East Coast of Africa

Our ship was the *Uganda* of the British India Line. It was one of the vessels that circled Africa, mainly to serve the British colonies, taking both passengers and goods. The crew was mostly Indian. Most of the passengers were from South Africa, headed to Europe. The children's meals were served first, separately from the adults. After they had eaten, they had to stay in a nursery with a caged portion of the deck as a play area. The boys especially felt this was a bit insulting. The ship made a call at Dar es Salaam, Tanganyika. Instead of going ashore, we opted for a picnic excursion in the lifeboats to a so-called Honeymoon Island at the mouth of the harbor. It had nice sandy beaches and lots of choice seashells, so it was a great day for the children.

The next stop was Zanzibar. As we approached during the evening, we began to understand why the island is famous for its spices. The unmistakable aroma of cloves, then its chief export, was wafted across the water as we neared the seaport, which bears the same name as the island. In 1956, Zanzibar was still a sultanate and a British protectorate, and strongly reflected Arab influence. After gaining its independence in 1963, the island merged with Tanganyika to form Tanzania in 1964. A highlight of our visit was a tour of the coconut plantations where we sampled fresh coconut milk while learning how they dried the coconut meat to form copra.

In Mombasa, Kenya, the boat stayed in port for a couple of days. We were on a pretty tight budget, so Mother offered to pay for a safari in the Tsavo game reserve. This was our first visit to such a reserve. We stayed overnight in one of the camps and were treated to our first glimpse of the snow-clad summit of Kilimanjaro high above the clouds. That fleeting image enticed us to return later for a longer look. We saw elephant, giraffe, zebra, several different antelopes, and hippos. I think we missed seeing lion on this trip. Our children ranging in age from two to nine years, were the only youngsters on the safari. Charmed from start to finish, they greatly enhanced the experience for their parents and the other adults by their appropriate expressions of delight. Not once did they frighten game with squeals of excitement.

The ship called briefly at Aden before proceeding up the Red Sea. Some of the passengers got off the ship at Suez for an excursion in Egypt and were going to rejoin the ship in Port Said. We were going to have a layover in Egypt, so we stayed on board for the transit of the canal. This was an interesting day. It is a sea level canal, so there are no locks. It passes through stretches of desert with sand on both sides. At the time we went through, it was only wide enough to allow ships to pass one way at a time. There is a lake near the middle where the northbound and southbound streams of traffic cross. En route we passed the King David Hospital on the bank of the canal.

It was after supper when we left the ship in Port Said. We hired a taxi to take us to Cairo, where we had a reservation at the Victoria Hotel. The driver went first to the native city and left us, presumably to get something. We weren't sure what was going on and were a bit uneasy, sitting in the dark in the native city until he finally returned. Our time in Egypt was split. We spent a few days there, then flew to the Holy Land before returning again to Egypt. The first morning when we walked into the hotel dining room, we were astonished to see George and Katherine Hudson sitting across the room. They had been at Jiaxing with us when we first went to China. They were now on their way home from Taiwan where he had been holding evangelistic tent meetings.

The Holy Land

The trip to the Holy Land was the highlight of our tour. In order to avoid flying over Israel to get to Jerusalem, we had to fly over Sinai, then over the Dead Sea. We could see the entire sea at one time. Its shape was familiar from maps of the Holy Land, which was now divided between Jordan and Israel. We could only visit the portion that was occupied by Jordan, for if we crossed over into Israel, we could not return to an Arab country, and we had to go back to Egypt to continue our trip home. We stayed at the American Colony Hotel on the Damascus Road. It was near the Mandelbaum Gate checkpoint where one could cross over into Israel, but from which there was no return. From our rooms we looked over into the Israeli portion of Jerusalem. The old city was in the hands of Jordan, so we were able to visit many of the traditional holy sites. The "Garden Tomb" was not far from where we were staying. It is located by a cliff which has a skull-shaped rock formation, and corresponds very closely to the description of the tomb given in the Bible. The traditional site of the tomb was encrusted with marble and enclosed in a large basilica with Catholic, Orthodox, and Coptic priests occupying different areas and vying for control. It bore little resemblance to the tomb of the biblical Easter story. The Garden of Gethsemane, however, is a site that made us feel that we were following in the footsteps of Jesus. The olive trees were so ancient and gnarled that one could easily picture Jesus praying among them.

The Moravian Church has a leprosy mission in Jerusalem and we asked our guide, Moses, to take us there. We found it down in the Kidron valley southeast of the city. We talked to the patients and found that the Moravian sisters in charge lived in Bethany, so we went there to find them. Their apartment was close by the traditional tomb of Lazarus. We had a memorable visit with them and they served us tea. What could be more appropriate than to have tea with two sisters near the tomb of Lazarus!

From Jerusalem we traveled south to Bethlehem. Here again, the traditional site of the manger was now a crypt under a large basilica. It was hard to picture it as a lowly stable. On this trip we also passed the spring where Philip is said to have baptized the Ethiopian. The water is only about six inches deep! We made a notable excursion to the Jordan River, Jericho, and the Dead Sea. Our third excursion away from Jerusalem was north to Shechem, where we saw the well by which Jesus sat when he talked with the woman of Samaria.

Egypt

After a week in Jordan, we flew back to Cairo, from which we took a taxi to Giza to visit the Sphinx and the Great Pyramids. At that time, visitors were still permitted to climb the pyramid of Khufu, the largest of the three, but only with a guide to lead the way. Efnowi claimed to have the record time in climbing to the top and back, as well as having served once as Marshal Tito's guide. We arranged for him to take Katie and me to the top, while Mother and the children waited. The outer sheath of smooth stones had long since been removed, and the blocks that now form the surface are three to four feet high, crumbling in places. The guide must pick and choose the route across broken stones in order to have firm footing and steps that are not too high. Efnowi pulled Katie up a few steps, then returned to pull me. About two-thirds of the way to the top, there was a small platform where Napoleon had a few stones removed to make a resting place. We finally made it to the top with Efnowi's able help. From Giza, we went on to visit the ruins of Memphis and the step pyramid of Saqqara. We were impressed by the similarity of the latter to Mayan pyramids. Of special interest in Cairo was a visit to the Cairo museum in which the golden treasures from Tutankhamen's tomb were on display.

One highlight of our visit to Egypt was a train trip up the Nile to Thebes and Luxor. It being midsummer and off-season, the old Winter Palace Hotel was practically empty. The temple at Luxor was apparently the inspiration

184 DOCTOR WITH BIG SHOES—AFRICA

for the design of the old First Presbyterian Church in Nashville, where I grew up. Interestingly, the temple itself was used as a church during the early Christian era.

We crossed the river on a ferry and visited the Valley of the Tombs of Kings where we saw the tombs of Tutankhamen, Seti I, a chief priest, and others. It was terribly hot there at the edge of the desert. We feared we might die of thirst, when across the sand came an Arab carrying a bucket with bottles of Coca Cola packed in ice! I thought I was seeing a mirage. After a cold drink, we then proceeded to Queen Hatshepsut's impressive temple at Deir el Bahari in West Thebes, before returning to Cairo.

On our departure from Egypt, we left Cairo before daybreak to drive to Port Said. On the way, we were stopped several times at roadblocks by soldiers. Our taxi driver seemed to think this was not unusual. Part of the route passed along the Suez Canal. We had passage on the old *Strathaird*, of the Pacific and Orient Line, which was on its last trip before being scrapped. Dirty and in poor repair, it was homeward bound to England from Australia, carrying about a thousand passengers. We sailed from Port Said around noon. About two hours after we left the harbor, we heard the announcement that Nasser had seized the Suez Canal.

The voyage through the Mediterranean was smooth. We went through the Strait of Messina and passed Stromboli at night for a spectacular view of the volcano's bright glow against the night sky. The ship called at Marseille and at Gibraltar, where we had an interesting tour of "The Rock." The boys were fascinated by the Barbary apes which inhabit it, and by the mystery of how they crossed over from Africa. There are no springs on Gibraltar. Water has to be piped from Spain. There are, however, large cement catchment areas from which rainwater is led into huge cisterns in case the Spanish cut off the water supply.

England

On arrival in England, we landed at Southampton. I had arranged to rent a small station wagon for our three-week stay. We traveled through southern England following the trail of King Arthur. We didn't quite make it to Land's End, but got as far as Tintagel on the Cornish coast. This is purported to be the castle of Uthur Pendragon, King Arthur's father. We then drove through Wales and finally ended up at Liverpool. We crossed the North Atlantic on the *Nova Scotia* of the Furness Line. It was our most unpleasant sea voyage, as the weather was foul and accommodations on the small ship were crowded. Mercifully it was short. Dad met us at Boston and we all took the train to New York City. My parents flew home to Nashville, while we picked up the 1956 blue and white Chevrolet station wagon, which I had ordered through a missionary purchasing service.

Furlough 1956-57

We made our furlough headquarters at Mission Court in Richmond, Virginia, in an apartment maintained for missionaries on furlough. We were located near Union Seminary and adjacent to some of the seminary student apartments. We were only in the States nine months, since we had taken three months for the trip. During those months, I audited a Bible course at the seminary and we spent a great deal of the time speaking and making visits to our families in Bethania, North Carolina and in Nashville.

We returned to Congo aboard the *Del Aires*, a Delta Line ship out of New Orleans. We were taking a lot of freight as well as the station wagon. We stopped in Mobile to visit my relatives on our way to New Orleans. When we boarded the ship, we discovered that it was going to call in Mobile before heading toward Africa. We surprised our relatives by a second short visit during the day the ship was in port. The ship made calls at St. Thomas, Virgin Islands; Freetown, Sierra Leone; Monrovia, Liberia; Port Gentil, Gabon; and Luanda, Angola before arriving at Matadi, the Belgian Congo's only port for ocean-going vessels.

Matadi to Kasai by Road

On arrival, the immigration and customs formalities were finished by late afternoon. This time the whole family would make the trip by road. In addition to the four children, the station wagon was fully loaded, including a luggage rack that had been installed on top. We decided not to spend the night at Matadi, but filled our gas tanks and headed up country. We drove most of the night, stopping to snooze for a short time. We made a wrong turn at one point and got onto a side road, but soon discovered our mistake. We finally arrived at Popokabaka in late afternoon, in time to cross the last ferry, and sought accommodations at the only hotel. The proprietor and his wife were both drunk and were not inclined to prepare a meal for us. The rooms they offered us were in an outbuilding and were filthy. We decided to push on to the Baptist Mission at Boko. We arrived there about ten o'clock at night. In spite of the late hour, we were welcomed and fed, before collapsing with exhaustion.

The next day we traveled on to Kikwit. We planned to continue via Tshikapa, and headed that way until we met a car. The driver informed us that a ferry on the route to Tshikapa was out of service, so we had to turn around and head for Port Francqui. We stopped at the Mennonite Mission at Nyanga for the night. The engine had not been running smoothly. It was dry season and the roads were extremely dusty. Before starting out the next morning, I had to clean the carburetor. We made it to Port Francqui in time to cross on the ferry before it docked for the night. The hotel there served us a good supper. We continued to Luebo, arriving there around nine o'clock in the evening.

Second Term at Luebo 1957 - 60

While in port in Monrovia on the way to Zaïre, we had gone ashore and visited a Methodist mission hospital. The hospital had jalousie windows that I thought would be just the thing for the Congo. Drs. John Miller and Carleton White had started on plans for a hospital building at Luebo, hoping that funds could be obtained from the Women's Birthday Offering. I had been working on these plans, drawing and redrawing them. I wrote to my brother Charles, who is an architect, asking him to get information about jalousie windows for me. He sent me several brochures. When we finally succeeded in getting part of the Women's Birthday Offering for the Luebo Hospital, I discovered that the windows best suited for our situation were available in Luluabourg.

The final design of the building contained a large foyer with a classroom behind it, separated by a folding partition so that the two areas could be thrown into one large meeting room. On the right of the foyer was the medical director's office with an adjoining examining room. There was a large White Cross linen storeroom and a pharmacy where drugs could be dispensed through a window to the back porch. The pharmacy adjoined another large storeroom with access to an attic storage space that ran the length of the building. A trapdoor in the ceiling of this storeroom permitted large cases and drums to be hoisted to the attic by a pulley. The east end of the building had two more offices, the laboratory, and an X-ray room with a darkroom. Aleck Shive had bricks already made when the funds became available. We had $25,000 for the building. This was the last building that Aleck built before

Breaking ground for new building in front of old wards, Luebo 1958.

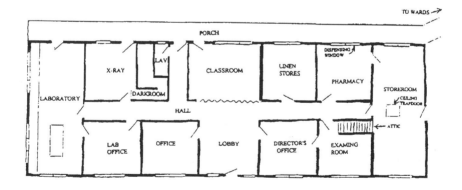

Luebo

McKowen Memorial Hospital
Administration Building 1959

Designer: H. S. Nelson
Builder: A. M Shive

retiring at the end of 1959. I had a great time watching the construction progress and often helped with such tasks as wiring and installation of the jalousie windows.

Not only did Aleck construct many buildings during his missionary career, he also added a word to the Tshiluba language. Bantu languages incorporate many terms from French, Portuguese, or English for items introduced from abroad, for which no name exists in the local language. In this case, Aleck was working and needed to use a crowbar. He pointed to it and when the worker finally picked up the correct tool, Aleck said, "Atta boy." Henceforth a crowbar has been known as an "attaboy" in that area.

In 1957, all the nurse aides on the mission were men, as were all the students at IMCK. The midwives were all older women who had received little formal training. We determined to seek young women for nursing service, and arranged to board our female students at the Girls' Home. We recruited a class of *aides-accoucheuses* (midwife aides). Each of the APCM stations was given an opportunity to send a student. At the same time, there was one female candidate who met the requirements for the nurse aide class, so we enrolled her in that program. Thus, we taught the first group of certified female medical workers on the mission.

Psychiatric cases presented a big problem, especially those of the manic-depressive type, because of our lack of appropriate hospital facilities. I have had a number of difficult experiences with these patients. The first was at Bulapé, where there was a woman who would usually enter the manic phase around peanut harvest time. She would be active all night, often waking everyone ringing the church bell in the middle of the night. She seemed to be harmless otherwise.

At Luebo we had mostly big open wards, but a part of the hospital porch had been enclosed to form a single room. A window between the ward and the room had been bricked up leaving an alcove in which shelves were installed. This was the only available room in which we could confine mental patients. The worst experience we had was with a man named Nkashama (leopard), who was especially violent and difficult to control. He tore off his clothes and climbed through the outside window of this room. We then covered the window with heavy wire mesh. Next he climbed up the shelves and got into the attic through a space between the top of the wall and the roof. The attic was not floored so he jumped around on the rafters. I put a ladder up and coaxed him down. We removed the shelves. He then climbed into the attic by pulling himself up on some electric wires. This time coaxing was to no avail. Finally I got into the attic with three assistants. Even then it was a struggle to bring him down safely. About this time, a new psychiatric hospital was completed outside of Luluabourg. It was only the second such institution in Congo, the other being far away in Lower Congo. With great relief, we turned him over to the care of state officials for transport to the psychiatric hospital.

One of our nurses also had a manic episode due to atabrine treatment that he was receiving for malaria. These and other cases finally led me to order a restraining sheet and a straight jacket. The latter was especially useful when a violent patient had to be transferred.

Later, after Independence, when we were at Lubondai, one of our older nurses had a son who was also manic-depressive. We had to deal with several of his manic episodes. He would be in constant motion, singing, and running from one end of the station to another. He would ask for food, but before it was set before him, would be off running again. He lost a tremendous amount of weight in a short time because of the expenditure of energy and lack of food. We persuaded the family to let me take him to the psychiatric hospital. They finally agreed and we arranged for the mission plane to come for him. When the plane arrived, I sedated him, put him in a straight jacket, and accompanied him to the hospital. He later escaped from the hospital. While he was running through a field, something jabbed him in one eye, causing blindness in that eye. The family always blamed me for that, even though they had agreed to his hospitalization.

On another occasion a man went berserk at Luebo. He killed one member of the family and attacked two of his brothers with a machete, before killing himself. I went out to the family's house in the city. The entire front and inside of the house were covered with blood. One of the brothers had a compound fracture of the arm, the other had been cut across the forehead, fracturing the skull. Amazingly both survived.

In all areas of medical service, we were often limited by the lack of updated equipment, adequate hospital facilities, and opportunities for referral of patients to medical specialists. These deficiencies seemed to be most keenly felt in relation to patients with mental problems.

The local people were also subject to hazards related to their particular lifestyle and technology. They were not allowed to have rifles. A few were allowed shotguns, but the great majority of the hunters used muzzleloading guns. Some of these were manufactured by the local blacksmiths. The barrel was made of a steel pipe. At the back end, the pipe was closed by a metal plug with a tail on it through which a screw was placed into the stock. The plug was made a little larger than the bore of the pipe. When the pipe was expanded by heating, the plug was inserted and the pipe allowed to cool, clamping down on the plug. Firing caps were often made from the heads of sulfur matches. The guns were loaded with black powder and all sorts of scrap metal. The missiles from these guns were low velocity, producing wounds that were jagged and irregular in shape, but with less widespread damage than missiles from high velocity rifles. On a couple of occasions, a barrel split and the plug was propelled back into the forehead of the hunter. In both instances the victims arrived with the end of the plug almost flush with the skin. On X-ray, the tail end with the screw was back in the frontal lobe of the brain. Amazingly enough following removal of these plugs, one of the patients survived; the other died of infection.

Another distressing neurological problem occurred in the case of an evangelist. He had been serving at Port Francqui where he was attacked and beaten unconscious, receiving a number of cuts on his arms and back. He had been treated at the hospital at Port Francqui. Later he came to Luebo, continuing to complain of back pain and a tingling sensation in the legs. I examined him several times and X-rayed his lumbar spine, but did not discover the cause of his complaints. Finally because of his incapacity, the presbytery was planning to discontinue his employment. The day before the final decision was to be made, word came to me that he was in the village unable to move his legs. We sent a stretcher for him. Another X-ray at a higher level revealed the broken fragment of a knife blade, just above the upper limit of the previous X-ray. It was about an inch and a half in length and was impinging on the spinal canal. It had gradually worked in by the action of the muscles. When attacked, he had so many little scars, no one was aware that he had been stabbed in the back. After removal of the knife blade, he was relieved of some of his symptoms and recovered most of the function of his legs, though he still had to walk with a cane.

Rainy season lasts for about nine months of the year in most of the area served by our mission. Especially at the beginning of the rainy season in September, the rains come in the form of tremendous thunderstorms which are accompanied by awe-inspiring displays of lightning and high winds. Since people are out in the elements a great deal, there are often deaths or injuries from the lightning. Some patients who thought they had been struck by lightning were just close enough to feel the discharge and were scared more than hurt.

When such a storm occurred at Luebo one night, we had already retired. There was a tremendous sound and Katie exclaimed, "That sounded as if the roof came off!" Since there were no leaks and no further sounds, we went back to sleep. Sure enough, in the morning we found that the roof had been ripped off over the storeroom across the back porch where we stored our grocery supplies. Most things were in cans so the losses were minimal. It must have been a tornado, as several of the other buildings on the station also suffered wind damage. Another storm occurred early one evening. When the lights died, I went out to determine the problem. Elder Mpoi David, our station electrician, was surveying the damage. The station generator was behind our house. A large tree had fallen across the main line. It was obvious that it could not be cleared until morning. About this time one of my nurses came saying, "You have to come and operate." I asked, "How do you know I will have to operate?" He replied, "Come and see." On arriving at the hospital, I found a couple of men sitting on the steps. I asked which one was the patient. One of them opened an apron that was soaked with the rain to show me his intestines. He had been walking in the path in the dark when a man on a bicycle, without a light, ran into him. He had a large hernia that was ripped open, spilling his intestines. We immediately started the standby generator, took him to the operating room, washed his intestines, replaced them, and repaired the hernia. He recovered without complications.

In February 1960, when Bill Rule became very ill with a gallbladder attack, it was decided to send him back to the States on a medical furlough. His absence would leave a tremendous hole to be plugged at the IMCK, as he carried a heavy teaching load. This was solved by asking me and Dr. Hugh Farrior, then at Bibanga, each to take a part of the teaching assignments. The schedule was rearranged so that Hugh would go one week, teaching the subjects for which he was responsible, then return to Bibanga. The next week I would go and teach. John Davis would fly to Luebo to get me on Monday and take me back after classes on Thursday. We continued that way for the remainder of the school year.

At that time, John Davis had taught John Miller to fly. During my weeks at Lubondai, he began flight lessons for me. John was an excellent instructor. He had helped to write the army manual on instrument flying. Emphasizing their importance, he had me flying on instruments early in my training. We used to get up early and go out to the airstrip at dawn. This was the best time to fly since the air was still. John was an avid cattle farmer. He had a personal project of raising cattle, teaching some of the locals to raise cattle and care for them properly. He would get them started and gradually build up their herds by breeding their cows with his bulls. Having one of his herds out on a plateau surrounded by streams, he built an airstrip there to make the cattle more accessible, and this provided another field for use in pilot training.

During our years at Luebo, the three river crossings between Luebo and Luluabourg had the ferries replaced by bridges. First the small stream about two-thirds of the way was bridged, and then a high arched bridge was placed across the Lulua River a short distance from Luluabourg. Finally work began on the bridge at Luebo in 1959. The new bridge crossed the rapids and was built on pylons of concrete with spans of prestressed concrete girders. The girders were made on the bank, then shifted into place. The concrete pylons had to be protected by coffer dams while they were poured and anchored in the river. Some of this work had to be done under water by French frogmen. Since there were crocodiles in the river, a man with a rifle stood guard on the bank. We once saw him standing guard while a big crocodile lay on a sandbank about fifty yards away from where the frogmen were diving. The bridge was finally finished in the fall of 1959.

It was during this second term at Luebo that Manford Saunders sold me an aluminum boat with a small outboard motor and a trailer for its transport. The motor was small and not adequate for the swift current of the Lulua. My mother sent us a more powerful motor which allowed us to ascend through the rapids and explore the river for several miles upstream. The boat furnished many hours of pleasure both on the river at Luebo and for family vacations at Lake Munkamba.

Onset of Tribal Conflict

In 1959, agitation for independence was becoming more and more persistent. As it became obvious that independence would soon be granted, the Bena Lulua awoke to the fact that they were less well prepared to take over positions of authority than were the Baluba. These two tribal groups came from common origins in southeast Zaïre, the region now called Shaba. One group came earlier to the western part of the Lulua River region and came to be known as the Bena Lulua (People of the Lulua). A related group of Baluba later migrated into what is now called East Kasai, and through time, in response to slave raids from the east, some moved westward into the region of the Lulua. In 1960, the Bena Lulua were still primarily a hunter-gatherer group and the Baluba were more agriculturally inclined. Many Baluba had settled in villages in the Lulua territory and taken advantage of the schools. Most of the clerks and assistants in the government offices were Baluba. Feeling threatened as time for independence approached, the Lulua chiefs held a meeting near Luluabourg and decided that the Baluba would have to leave their territory. They began attacking Luba villages, first in rural areas and gradually moving toward the urban centers.

In May 1960, there was a battle at Luebo, in the area surrounding the mission. I was operator for the radio schedule at noon every day. We had just finished when I heard the sound of gunfire. As I headed for the hospital, the first victims came staggering in that direction. The battle actually came onto the station, with some of the combatants being chased in front of the church. We only had one oper-

Lulua carving of mother and child.

ating room, with a small delivery room next to it. Dr. J.B. Jung, our dentist, was on the station at the time. J.B., Katie, and Mary Morrison helped with triage and took care of minor wounds in the delivery room. I placed a stretcher in the operating room. After caring for one major injury on the operating table, as soon as I could safely turn the patient over to one of the nurses to finish sewing up the skin, I would begin with another patient on the stretcher. I was kept busy until about nine that evening. Just when I thought I had finished, a colonial officer came with a pickup load of bodies, stacked like logs, with a request for examinations to determine the cause of death. The bodies had all suffered numerous machete wounds and then been partially burned. Many of the hands had been cut off. In fact, among the nine bodies, a total of nine hands were missing. One body was missing both hands, and one had not suffered this mutilation. I was proud of our nursing staff. I had not paid any attention to their tribal alignment. We had members of both tribes on the staff, but they all cared for the patients from both sides without discrimination.

The government decided to move all the Baluba to the mission side of the river and all the Bena Lulua to the government side. The government side was Bena Lulua territory and our side was actually Bakete territory. Most of the Bakete were aligning with the Bena Lulua, but Luebo city was considered a *centre extracoutumier* (non-tribal area). As a result of the government's decision, some patients were transferred to the government hospital, and we received some patients in return. We also lost several of our nursing staff, but were able to hire a couple of nurses who had been working across the river.

I had earlier taken charge of two rural dispensaries that had been provided by a special colonial fund for the well-being of the local people. One of these was near our leprosy camp on the Mweka road. The other was quite a distance by road, although not so far "as the crow flies." To visit the latter, I had to drive north to Mweka, then east on the Luluabourg road, and finally turn south off the main road, for a total of eighty kilometers (about forty-eight miles), making three sides of a rectangle. One of our nurses, Mushipula David, lived at the dispensary with his family. I usually made a trip once each month to take medicines and supplies and to see the patients for whom he needed my consultation. On June 10, 1960, I received an urgent letter from Mushipula requesting that I come to evacuate them. Not belonging to the tribe of that area, he felt threatened and feared for his family. It was not quite time for the usual clinic visit, but I went the next day to get them. When I turned off the Luluabourg road and started south, I came to a government rest house. A Belgian colonial officer was there with a group of soldiers. They were standing around looking as if they were not sure what to do. I stopped and spoke to them, but they gave me no advice or instructions. I drove on. A kilometer down the road, I met two men. One man was injured, stumbling, with one arm draped over the other man's shoulder. I stopped and asked what was going on. The injured man had a chest wound. I immediately put him in the car, turned around, and went back to the colonial officer, informing him that the wound required urgent attention in the hospital at Mweka. I started back down the road. For the next couple of miles, I passed through burned out villages. At several places there were human bodies as well as slaughtered goats and sheep lying by the side of the road. A little further down the road, I overtook the retiring raiders. They were all armed to the teeth with muzzleloading guns, spears, and machetes. They looked me over carefully, but let me pass without stopping the car. They recognized my car, as it was the only one in that area with a blue and white paint job, a rack on top, and red crosses displayed in the windows. The villages of the raiders, further on, were all empty, as the women and children were hiding in the forest in fear of reprisal. I collected the nurse and his family and returned to Luebo. On the way back, the villages were empty until I reached a small commercial establishment. The state officer was there interviewing the owner, whose wife and three children had just been murdered. His home and stores had been destroyed and he had barely escaped with his life.

Independence was scheduled for June 30, 1960. Our boys were both in Central School at Lubondai, Sperry in seventh grade and Lee in fifth. School was closed early so that the children would all be at home, or leave for furlough before Independence. We took the boys directly to Lake Munkamba for a short vacation and had a great time on the lake. Having the new motor Mother had sent added greatly to the pleasure of our family vacation. We returned to Luebo just in time for Independence.

Independence

Independence came so precipitously that no one was really ready for it. A few Congolese officials had been elected, but they had not been well oriented to their jobs. The Belgian colonial officers lacked sufficient instructions as to how they were to turn things over to the new officials. Mukeba Jean was to be the new *Commissaire de district*. He was a friend and a member of the church. The people in general had little idea of what independence entailed. I talked to some of the Belgian army officers. They were confident of the loyalty and competence of the soldiers. There was great rejoicing and celebration on Independence Day. Special services were held in the churches. We attended a gala event with speeches and refreshments at the state post. I had one medical emergency, a man who had made his own cannon, which exploded in his hand wounding a couple of fingers. All that was left of one finger was the skin which I used to cover the adjacent finger, which was salvageable.

The number of missionaries on Luebo station had been greatly reduced. The Hoyt Millers and Bill Reilys had left for furlough. The Shives and Kirk Morrisons had retired a few months earlier. The Rob Robertsons and their children were at Lake Munkamba for vacation, as was the Juengst family. Bill and Martha Worth were at the mission press. Dot Moore was also at Luebo. On July 8 we heard on the radio that the army had revolted in Léopoldville during the night. There were rumors that the revolt was spreading to other army units, elsewhere in the country. Sunday, July 10, we heard the army had revolted in Luluabourg. Since there was an army camp at Luebo, Mark Poole thought it best to evacuate the women and children to Bulapé, where he had his fuel supply. Mark made a couple of flights to take them all up there, leaving only Bill Worth and me at Luebo.

All the APCM stations were staying on the air almost constantly. Reports from Luluabourg confirmed that two or three expatriates had been killed, including one of the army officers. According to a contingency plan, all the remaining expatriates had taken refuge in a fairly new multistory apartment building. Arms and food had been stored there for just such an emergency. We could hear them calling to the air base at Kamina that they were under siege. They asked that the paratroopers be sent to protect them. The new governor came on the radio a little later and countermanded the request. After a short while, they began again frantically requesting the paratroopers. They said that the soldiers were setting up mortars and threatening to shell the building. Some thirty Belgian paratroopers arrived late Sunday afternoon. The planes circled the city and then the parachutes began blossoming to the north of the airport. As soon as the first chute appeared, the soldiers immediately returned to the army camp, which was also the military officers' training school for the Congo.

The paratroopers secured the airport, then organized convoys of cars to transport all the expatriates to the airport terminal. The next day, Mark Poole began evacuating the folks at Bulapé, including the Luebo women and children. John Davis started collecting the missionaries from the other stations, bringing them all to Luluabourg. Several of the stations had just completed airstrips in time for the emergency. Several of us were ham operators. Eric Bolton was able to contact a ham operator, Mollie Henderson, in Salisbury, Southern Rhodesia, and through her, Joseph Parker, the American Consul. We could not contact the consulate in Léopoldville. Mr. Parker was able to locate some planes. A Globemaster had just brought a satellite tracking station to Salisbury and was about to return to the States. He commandeered it, but the runway at Luluabourg was too short for it to land there. It could, however, land at the air base at Kamina. He was able to get a DC-3 that was assigned to the Ambassador of South Africa and also a Navy DC-3 that happened to be on the east coast of Africa. These were used to shuttle Americans from the interior to Kamina.

Evacuation

Mark evacuated some of those at Bulapé on Monday and the rest, including Katie and our children, on Tuesday morning. He then picked up Bill Worth and me at Luebo. We were limited on the amount of baggage we could carry, but I managed to take our wedding silver flatware, a treasured gift from my parents. Bill had the manuscript of the Bible commentary that had just been completed and was in the process of being type set. We went across the river in my station wagon. We did not have any Congolese chauffeurs, so I asked Jean Joseph, a Congolese business man and friend, to go with us. When we boarded the plane, I left the car in his care. The airport at Luluabourg was quite a scene. I rejoiced to be reunited with Katie and the children. Katie realized immediately, from the way I was carrying my bag, that I had brought the silver. The airport was packed with expatriates of several nationalities, and many were lying on the ground around it. The paratroopers had a machine gun nest on the roof and a number of foxholes at various points around the airstrip. In front of the airport, a large field had become a sea of cars, pickups, and trucks, of all sorts. A number of the pastors and Christians were there to see the missionaries, and to bring bananas and water. The missionaries stationed in Luluabourg were able to turn their cars over to these friends for safekeeping. The paratroopers took some of the businessmen into town to bring food out to be distributed, as some folks had spent the night at the airport. Belgium, Portugal, and Italy sent planes to evacuate their nationals. It was late in the day before the American planes arrived. We were ferried down to Kamina. There we were reunited with the Robertson family. They had tried to drive out in their car from Lake Munkamba, going south through Katanga Province. They had finally stopped at Kapanga, a Methodist mission station. From there they had been evacuated to Kamina.

We were only in Kamina overnight. On Wednesday, the first Globemaster flight took families with small children. There were about two hundred on our flight. There were no seats, just canvas benches along the sides. They had rigged up straps along the length of the floor. Those who were sitting on the floor had to hold onto the straps on takeoff and landing. In the front section of the cavernous interior, there was a double deck. We were seated on the upper deck. The plane was not soundproof. The roar of the engines was so loud one had to shout to be heard. The people in Salisbury had risen to the occasion and were well organized to care for us. On arrival, we were greeted and taken immediately to a canteen for hot soup and coffee. We were all dressed for the tropics. It was winter in Salisbury and the temperature chilly. We were next taken to a large warehouse where there were clothes for all ages. We found sweaters and warm clothing for the entire family. Many of the refugees were taken into private homes. We, along with the Robertsons, landed in the vacant house of the American agricultural attaché. It was a lovely home fully equipped with major appliances.

We had gone to Congo on one family passport. As independence approached we decided that we should have it split. We requested a passport for me, with a separate one for Katie and the children. Our passport had been sent to Léopoldville, but the new ones had not been received. We arrived in Rhodesia with no official papers. The next morning I went to the consulate to see about getting replacement passports. Katie stayed home and put all the children's dirty clothes into the washing machine. At the consulate I met Elizabeth (Liz) Shefelton, one of the Central School teachers, who had offered to take the children back to the States to our parents, so we could stay and further evaluate the situation. Places were available on a plane that was to leave in a few hours via South Africa, Europe, and New York. I called Katie and asked if she could get the children ready in time. She could, but most of their clothes were in the washing machine, soaking wet. There was not enough time to have passports issued for the children. The consul prepared a letter explaining that they were children of American parents who had been evacuated from the Congo, and requesting that they be assisted in their return to the States. I contacted my parents in Nashville and arranged for them to meet Liz and the children in New York. The girls were eventually to stay with Katie's parents in Bethania, North Carolina and the boys with mine in Nashville, Tennessee. At the time, we did not expect the separation to last ten months. In any case, the children were on the first plane to arrive in New York with Congo evacuees. Their photograph getting off the plane appeared in *Time* magazine.

The children have tall stories about arriving in New York City, not knowing how to operate a television set. They still delight to recall their grandmother's shock when she opened their small suitcase to look for their pajamas and found only the family silver.

After everyone had been evacuated, the two mission planes were flown to Salisbury. A number of the Presbyterian missionaries remained in Salisbury to await developments. After about a week, we held a meeting. It was decided that the two planes would go back with a team of men to visit all the stations and evaluate the situation. A proposed church-mission conference for turning over the affairs of the APCM to the Congo church was to be rescheduled. John Davis and John Miller piloted the planes; Dave Miller, Bill Washburn, Hugh Farrior, and I were the other missionaries on the team. One of my roles was that of radio operator. Mallory Davis, John and Emma's oldest son, also went with us to stay at Lubondai and take care of the Davis' cattle project.

Return from Rhodesia

We flew to Élisabethville and spent the night at the Methodist Mission. Small planes could land there, but the airstrip had some barrels placed on it to prevent large planes from landing. The next day we flew on to Luluabourg. It was weird flying over the city where not a single vehicle was moving, and very few pedestrians could be seen in the streets of the business area. The airfield was outside the city, on the opposite side from the big indigenous city. We landed and made contact with the pastors and elders of the church. We then visited all of the mission stations. In every case, the local church people had taken care to protect the houses and buildings of the mission. We were at Luebo just a couple of hours. I had to do an emergency Caesarean section while there. At all stations the missionaries were urged to return. A date was set for the conference, with Moma chosen as the site. One plane with John Davis, Bill Washburn, and Dave Miller returned to Salisbury. John Miller, Hugh Farrior, and Mallory Davis remained at Lubondai with the other plane. I caught a ride on a UN plane to Léopoldville where I joined Alex McCutchen, and crossed to Brazzaville for a flight to Salisbury. The missionaries met again. Mr. Parker would not give permission for the women to return. It was decided that those men who were willing, would go back. Nineteen men were prepared to go. In addition, Charline Halverstadt, Mary Crawford, and Katie were given permission to go to collect some needed documents and papers, on the condition that they return in the Rhodesian plane.

The DC-3 landed at Moma, which had a newly built red clay airstrip. It was the longest dirt strip on the mission; even so, it was barely long enough for such a large plane. Some of us got off there to prepare for the church-mission conference. The ladies and several of the men went on to Luluabourg to round up the pastors and elders who were to attend. At the Moma meeting, the process of dissolving the mission and turning over to the church was begun. The conference lasted several days. We ate a diet of *bidia* (manioc bread), greens, and beans, with meat furnished by slaughtering one of the cows of the Moma herd. Following the meeting, Charles Sthreshley, J.B. Jung, and I went to Luebo. Flo Sthreshley and Fran Jung had already returned to the States.

The situation at Luebo was extremely difficult. Ethnic tensions were increasing. The freight office on the river had closed, and the MAS truck transport service from Port Francqui had been discontinued. Mail and telegraph service had been suspended. Ham radio activity was forbidden, so we were effectively cut off from communication except through the mission radio net. It was difficult enough being there without our families, but Charles and J.B. were harassed constantly by the *jeunesse*, the Baluba youth vigilante group. At night they were often awakened by rocks being thrown on the metal roofs of their houses. After a couple of weeks, they decided to join their wives in the States. I decided to go to Rhodesia until I could return with Katie. The three of us traveled together to Bujumbura, now the capital of Burundi. We parted there; J.B. and Charlie went to Europe and on to the States, while I went to Nairobi. This was my first visit to Nairobi. The plane arrived after dark. As I rode into town, a herd of zebras crossed the road, clearly visible in the lights of the bus. I didn't take time for sightseeing, but caught the first plane to Salisbury.

Members of the translation committee, plus Katie and others, had been at work proofreading the new Tshiluba Bible translation. Mr. Parker, the consul in Salisbury, was reluctant to give us permission to return to Congo. We took the occasion to make a trip to the ruins at Zimbabwe, which gave the country its name after it became independent. Massive stone walls surrounded the prehistoric city. The houses and walls were built with stones dressed to fit together without mortar. One feature was a round tower that appeared to be solid. Its purpose remained a mystery.

Later, when Katie and Charline requested Mr. Parker's permission to return to Congo, he graciously responded with a smile, saying, "I cannot grant your request, but of course I cannot prevent you from going to Brazzaville." Brazzaville, the capital of the other new Republic of Congo, was just across the Congo River from Léopoldville. As they read his response, this amounted to his blessing. Jim Halverstadt was already back in Luluabourg, so the three of us flew to Brazzaville and crossed the Congo River by ferry. We were told we could go on at our own risk. United Nations (UN) troops were in the Congo to help maintain order and for relief purposes. Charline was able to obtain a ride for us in a UN cargo plane that was taking relief supplies to Luluabourg. We were offered the choice of taking a plane that was transporting two jeeps or one loaded with dried fish. Needless to say, the choice was easy! We actually flew to Luluabourg, sitting in a jeep.

8. The New Republic: 1960-71

Our Last Year at Luebo

When Belgium announced the date for independence, everyone was expecting the Belgian Congo to become the Republic of Congo. France, however, announced independence for French Equatorial Africa, a part of which, just northwest of the Belgian Congo, was also named Congo, with its capital at Brazzaville. This resulted in two Republics of Congo, leading to much confusion between Congo (Brazzaville) and Congo (Léopoldville) until the former Belgian Congo became the Democratic Republic of Congo.

We had just arrived back at Luebo and were being greeted by members of the staff at our home when Jean Joseph put the station wagon in the garage and brought me the keys. He had some repairs done on it at Port Francqui but would accept no repayment, since he had the use of the car while we were away. Bill Pruitt soon came to join us for the evangelistic work, including the school for evangelists. He was great support, though the Baluba *jeunesse* gave him just as hard a time as they had given J.B. and Charlie.

I not only had the work at McKowen Memorial Hospital, but was also called upon to help out at the District Hospital across the river. Dr. Grosjean, the Belgian doctor, had left. A couple of Belgian Catholic sisters were still there, working with a Congolese medical assistant. I went over several times to care for surgical patients. My insistence on serving patients of all tribes led to difficulty with the *jeunesse*, who objected to my going across the river to care for the Bena Lulua.

In the past, during Mark Poole's furlough, I had made regular trips to Bulapé for surgery. After spending the first night at Bulapé, seeing patients and arranging for those who needed operations, I then went to visit the dispensaries north of Bulapé. The second night was spent on a camp cot at Bambuyi. The next day I would go on across the Lubudi River to the Batua dispensary. After holding clinic, another night was spent at Bambuyi. Back at

Bulapé I would spend a couple of days in the operating room before return-ing to Luebo. After Independence, Gladys Smithwick was at Bulapé. I agreed to go there regularly to help out with surgery and the dispensaries. I always returned to Luebo via Mweka. One evening after one of my trips, there was an attack on some of the Luba villages north of Luebo on the Mweka road. The next morning it was reported to me that the *jeunesse* had taken the sta-tion truck. I went to search for it in the station wagon. I saw them driving down the road toward the front of the church. I drove up and blocked the road. There were twenty or thirty in the truck. They were armed with a mot-ley assortment of weapons including spears, machetes, clubs, and muzzle-loaders. One young man was standing with a shotgun pointed over the top of the cab. I got out and argued with them that the church's message was peace. I pleaded with them not to take the mission vehicle on an armed mis-sion. They should not involve the church in the conflict. They eventually relented and did not take the truck.

The family of the wife of one of our nurses lived in one of the villages that had been attacked. She had been visiting her father with her little baby. The nurse wanted to go out to see if she was all right. There was a UN contingent stationed at Luebo at the time. I arranged for us to go out with them to inves-tigate the situation. Our leprosy camp was on the section of the road that had been attacked. Several of our patients had been killed. The rest all scattered back to their own villages. This closed out our leprosy work permanently. We passed through a number of villages in which all the houses had been destroyed. Only mud walls remained after the thatch roofs had been burned. We found the house of the nurse's in-laws. The remains of the baby's crib were in the smoking ruins. At the next village, he finally located someone who told him that his family had all escaped and were hiding in the forest. I learned later that some claimed that I had been responsible for the raid, since it occurred immediately after I had returned down that road from Bulapé.

John Davis was soon to leave for furlough. Don Watt was the new pilot who came to fly the mission plane. The first time they flew into Luebo, both pilots were in the plane. John was orienting Don to the mission area and the various airfields. Charlie Ross was also in the plane. Dave McLean, who was visiting at Luebo, went with me across the river to the airstrip to meet them. We were standing by the plane talking when all of a sudden we realized that we were surrounded by soldiers pointing their guns at us. They threatened John when he tried to remove the keys from the ignition. They made us leave the plane and walk down to the district offices. The chief officer of the district had gone to Luluabourg leaving his deputy in charge. It was apparently on the deputy's orders that we had been apprehended. We were made to stand in the sun and take off our shoes and eyeglasses. He apparently wanted to harass the Protestants. Word was immediately taken across the river by passersby, so Katie soon learned that we had been arrested. A couple of the pastors and elders hurried over to give us support. The deputy still would not release us without first contacting the chief in Luluabourg. They tried for an hour or so before contact was made on the radio. He was instructed to let us go. All we suffered was several hours of uncertainty and discomfort.

Harlan McMurray, son of L.A. and Jean, came out to Congo to take charge of the J. Leighton Wilson Press at Luebo. He had been born in Congo and had been living in the States for several years. He lived at the press house next door and had his meals with us. Harlan was a big man, young, strong, good-natured, and spoke Tshiluba as naturally as English. His presence gave us a tremendous boost, especially at times. One day I saw a young woman in the clinic who had a tremendous enlargement of one breast, so large that it was an incapacitating burden for her. I talked to her about removing it. She left to discuss this with her family and to arrange for payment for the operation. As I returned to the house at noon, I noticed a gang of boys struggling with someone a short distance away. I went over to see what was going on. They were attacking the young woman. Four of them had hold of her four limbs, pulling in four different directions, while others were beating her. I stepped in and pushed them aside. As I was leading her to our yard, they grabbed her again. I argued with them that she was a patient at the hospital and that they should allow patients to come and go freely. Once more I was able to get her released. Just as we got to the gate of our yard, they grabbed her once more. Feeling responsible for my patient, I finally hit the leader on his jaw as hard as I could with my fist. They dropped her and turned their attention to me. At this moment, Harlan, who had been at our house, appeared by my side. Both of us were bigger than any of them, so they backed off. We were able to get the woman into the yard and up onto the porch. I credit Harlan with saving me. The woman stayed at our house for the rest of the day, until she felt it safe to return to her home. We learned later that the *jeunesse* had been hiding down at the bridge and taking note of all the women who were crossing the river. They suspected them of going over to be prostitutes at the army camp. That day they had caught and beaten all those that they suspected. The woman we had rescued claimed that she had just been going to the government hospital for treatment, which seemed plausible.

The last year at Luebo was a hectic time. The ethnic rivalry among the Baluba, Bakete, and Bena Lulua intensified. As station treasurer, I was often involved in mediating among the groups in the church and the mission school over division of funds. I was subjected to many false rumors and accusations by all sides, some of which were reported as fact over the government radio station in Luluabourg.

Anxious Last Days at Luebo

We continued to have daily radio contacts on the mission network. This was essential, since mail service was slow and not dependable. It was especially necessary to give weather reports to the pilot to arrange for flights of the mission plane. During my previous furlough I had taken a radio repair course, and had built my own ham radio transmitter, a Heathkit DX-100, which I enjoyed tremendously. Regular schedules kept us in contact with our families in the States. Hearing the children's voices occasionally gave us the courage to carry on during those ten months of separation. One day, just at time for the daily mission radio net, some officials came to confiscate the radios. I persuaded them to allow us to have one last contact to let the rest of the mission know we were going off the air. It was especially heart-rending to see the DX-100 go out the door.

Harlan McMurray had already left Luebo. We were due to go to Luluabourg in a few days for a meeting. The day before we were to leave, one of the elders came to inform me that the *jeunesse* were threatening to kill us. Katie had been told the same thing. We prepared to leave early the next morning before dawn. We went to bed very uneasy but praying, and trusting that the Lord would take care of us. Elder Mpoi, the station electrician, and Mukeba Jean, our good friend, who was the new district commissioner, were able to persuade them to leave us alone. This, in spite of the fact that they had badly beaten Mukeba a few days earlier. Apparently all my confrontations with the *jeunesse* had put me on their hit list. In Luluabourg, we were advised not to return to Luebo and were asked to go to Bulapé for the final few weeks of our term. Our passports and several other important papers had been left at Luebo. Dave Miller volunteered to go to Luebo and collect the things we needed. Bless the Lord for friends like Dave!

In planning for our furlough, I had explored opportunities for further surgical training. Knowing that Dr. Barney Brooks, Chief of Surgery at Vanderbilt, had died, I had written to Dr. William Meacham, Chief of Neurosurgery. He had been chief resident when I was a student and was an old friend. I wrote that I was due for a furlough and asked if there were any chance of an appointment to the surgical house staff. He turned the letter over to Dr. H. William Scott, Jr., then Chief of Surgery. I had kept a record of all the operations that I had performed in China and in Congo. On the basis of these, Dr. Scott placed me at the second year assistant resident level. We arranged with the Board of World Missions for a leave of absence and went on self-support, relying on the salary from my residency. I was able to sell the station wagon before leaving Luluabourg. We found a house for rent several blocks from the hospital, which was being vacated by our old friends, Lewis and Eliza Lancaster, retired China missionaries.

Nashville 1961-64

During my first year in the residency program, I finished a couple of months on the neurosurgical service and started on orthopedics. A new parking sticker was issued to be placed on the rear bumper of the car. In the parking lot at the rear of the hospital, I bent over to apply the sticker and couldn't straighten up without excruciating pain. I managed to hobble into the nearby house staff quarters and telephoned to arrange to be transported to the hospital for admission with a ruptured disc. Since I was on the orthopedic service, Dr. Eugene Regen, the chairman, took charge of my case. After a few days of conservative treatment, it became obvious that surgery was required. I was much relieved when Dr. Regen suggested that Dr. Meacham, the neurosurgeon, perform the surgery. I got immediate relief of the pain and was able to leave the hospital after one week. They gave me a couple weeks off for convalescence. I had begun taking flying lessons and used this opportunity to get in some more hours toward my private pilot's license.

During our first year back in the States, Katie was busy establishing a home, pulling the family together, and speaking on behalf of medical missions. Before the second year began, Katie was offered a fellowship for graduate study from the United States Public Health Service. She first earned her Master of Science in Nursing at Vanderbilt, and then continued work toward a Ph.D. at Peabody College (at that time not yet a part of Vanderbilt) majoring in comparative education, with social anthropology as a minor. Most of the anthropology was taken at Scarritt College with Dr. Ina Brown, who was a member of her doctoral committee. Dr. Brown and Dr. Stewart Fraser, her major professor, helped design a program which prepared her well for her role in transcultural nursing education.

The surgery program at Vanderbilt was usually a five-year program, preparing one for general surgery and thoracic surgery boards. As I was a special case, after two years as assistant resident, I was named a fourth year senior resident, working only toward the general surgery qualification. The last year was spent in the Vanderbilt program at Nashville General Hospital, with Dr. John Sawyers as Chief there, under Dr. Scott.

There was also a fifth year senior resident rotating through General Hospital. The fifth year resident did all the chest surgery; other assignments were shared between us. I was also involved in the Nashville Tumor Clinic for the entire year. Nashville General Hospital cared for most of the indigent patients in Nashville. It was an excellent experience, and Dr. Sawyers was a great teacher. A number of the staff physicians were old friends, many of them younger than I, having been in classes behind mine in medical school.

In July 1964, I had completed my program, but Katie still needed to take her preliminary examinations before she could return to Congo and collect data for her dissertation. Sperry was ready for his senior year in high school and Lee for his sophomore year. They were both to enter McCallie School in Chattanooga for the completion of their high school programs. Sperry had already been accepted for admission to Vanderbilt in 1965, under their early admission plan. I was to take the two girls with me, so they could enter Central School in August; Katrina was ready for seventh grade and Beth for fifth grade. As we left Nashville from Union Station by train, I spoke to Beth. She said, "My name is Elizabeth." Having always been known as Beth, from that moment on, she would only respond if addressed as "Elizabeth," that is, until baby sister Faye came along two years later and eventually changed her sister's name to "Bizza." We had a great trip, eating in the diner and traveling in the Pullman car.

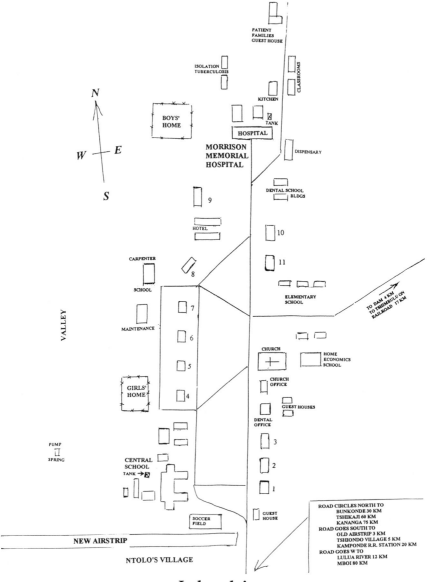

PATIENT
FAMILIES
GUEST HOUSE

ISOLATION
TUBERCULOSIS

CLASSROOMS

KITCHEN

BOYS'
HOME

TANK

HOSPITAL

MORRISON
MEMORIAL
HOSPITAL

DISPENSARY

N

W · E

S

DENTAL SCHOOL
BLDGS

9

HOTEL

10

11

CARPENTER

8

SCHOOL

7

ELEMENTARY
SCHOOL

TO DAM 4 KM
TO TSHIMBULU ON
RAILROAD 17 KM

VALLEY

MAINTENANCE

6

5

CHURCH

HOME
ECONOMICS
SCHOOL

GIRLS'
HOME

4

CHURCH
OFFICE

GUEST HOUSES

PUMP

SPRING

DENTAL
OFFICE

3

CENTRAL
SCHOOL

TANK →

2

1

GUEST
HOUSE

SOCCER
FIELD

ROAD CIRCLES NORTH TO
    BUNKONDE 30 KM
    TSHIKAJI 60 KM
    KANANGA 75 KM
ROAD GOES SOUTH TO
    OLD AIRSTRIP 3 KM
    TSHIONDO VILLAGE 5 KM
    KAMPONDE R.R. STATION 20 KM
ROAD GOES W TO
    LULUA RIVER 12 KM
    MBOI 80 KM

NEW AIRSTRIP

NTOLO'S VILLAGE

Lubondai

1965

Numbers 1 to 11 are missionary homes.

Our Return to Congo

In New York we stayed at the Prince George Hotel. A couple of days were spent at the World's Fair. We also went to the top of the Empire State Building. On the morning of our sailing date, we checked out of the hotel and arranged for our bags to be transported to the ship. We then took the ferry to the Statue of Liberty where we climbed up inside the Statue, going up into the head to look out of the crown. We were booked on the *Breughel*, a Belgian freighter on its maiden voyage. On boarding, we unpacked and settled in the lounge to watch television. Bill and Ruth Metzel and family, and Glenn and Betty Murray were also on the ship. We had just settled down when a man rushed in calling for Dr. Nelson. He said we were to get off the ship. It was already past time for the ship to sail, but loading was still in progress. The phone had already been disconnected. I rushed ashore to a pay phone and telephoned Katie in Nashville. She had been trying to reach us all day. The news had come that Burleigh Law, the Methodist pilot, had been killed at Wembo Nyama. The Simba rebels were advancing on Luluabourg. Katie wanted me to know before we sailed, but left to me the decision whether or not we should get off the ship. I went back with the news to consult with the others missionaries. The Murrays were alone, as their children were grown. They decided to go on to Africa. When they reached Matadi, they could either get off or come back on the ship, depending on the situation. I decided to take the girls back to Nashville to await developments. While the Metzels were discussing their plans, I sent the girls to pack our bags. I sat down with Glenn to give him all the papers relative to our baggage, so he could get it through customs for us. The captain held the ship long enough to let us get off. The Metzels and Murrays stayed on board.

The girls and I flew back to Nashville. In a couple of weeks, word came that the Simba rebels had been stopped short of Luluabourg. I flew out to Léopoldville, leaving the girls with Katie to attend the fall term of school in Nashville, while she completed her exams. I actually arrived in Léopoldville in time to greet the Murrays when they came up from Matadi.

We were assigned to Lubondai. The IMCK had been located there, but had just been granted a school concession at Tshikaji outside Luluabourg. The buildings had been constructed shortly before Independence, intended for a School of Administration to train the sons of tribal chiefs for roles of leadership. There were ten faculty homes, a couple of dormitories, a refectory, an administration building, and about twelve classrooms in two long buildings. These buildings were all badly damaged and occupied by squatters. Garland Goodrum had been repairing them and Drs. John Miller and Bill Rule were in the process of moving there. There was no hospital. The General Hospital in Luluabourg was in deplorable condition. During their last two years, the nursing students would spend half of each year at Lubondai for their practical experience. While they were at Lubondai, I was also to teach the obstetrics and pharmacology courses.

Lubondai 1964-67

Lubondai station was about a half-mile long. Morrison Memorial Hospital was located at the north end and Central School (CS) for missionary children was at the south end. The house we occupied was one of those nearer the hospital, numbered "8" on the map. The Lubondai Station Church, on the opposite side of the station, was about halfway between our house and Central School. There had been one or two dentists stationed at Lubondai, who had taught a dental section of the IMCK, training a couple of classes of dental assistants. This section of the IMCK was closed at Independence. The two dental school buildings were now being used by the hospital. About two miles from the station, a small stream had been dammed, forming a small lake. This lake furnished water for a small hydroelectric plant that produced power for the station. The current was not without interruptions, due to such things as snakes getting caught in the turbine. Also, in dry season the quantity of water was reduced, so the hydro had to be turned off during the day. The hospital and Central School both had standby generators. We frequently used the standby during surgery. One day the hospital generator quit while I was finishing my first operation. I had several more to do. I went out to the generator, still wearing my gown and gloves, to keep from getting too dirty. It so happened that a team of doctors who had come from the Presbyterian Board to survey the medical work flew in at just that moment. They were much amused by my "mechanic's garb."

Thanks to the missionary doctors who preceded me, the operating room arrangement at Lubondai was quite satisfactory. There were two operating rooms, a new room with terrazzo floor that had replaced a boiler room and the old operating room. I usually did major surgery in the new room. While the team was setting up for another operation, I would do a minor procedure in the old room. By shuttling back and forth between the rooms, I was able to reduce the amount of wasted time.

South of the station, were villages of the Bakua Tshipanga clan group. The chief of this group was Chief Ntolo Ngoy, who was paraplegic. Dr. John Miller had obtained a rickshaw which allowed him mobility. For old China hands, it was a shock to see a rickshaw in central Africa. The airstrip before Independence was located about three kilometers south of the station. After Independence, a new airstrip was constructed between Central School and the village of Chief Ntolo. The Lulua River was about fifteen kilometers west of the station. Tshimbulu, on the rail line, was about seventeen kilometers to the east.

In 1964, Lubondai was the only hospital in the area south of Luluabourg with a resident physician. Before Independence there had been physicians at several government and Catholic hospitals in the surrounding area, as well as at one company hospital. They had all left the country. The large Luluabourg General Hospital was staffed by some UN doctors on a rotating basis, so there was little continuity of care there. One hundred twenty kilometers to the east, the diamond mine hospital provided limited service to the general population. It was in Luba territory, so did not serve the needs of the

Bena Lulua. The nearest hospital to the south was the Methodist Hospital at Kapanga. As a result of the lack of other medical facilities nearby, we frequently received patients brought from all directions. This was especially true on weekends and holidays. The Catholic sisters often brought patients with obstetrical complications. John Miller and Bill Rule had heavy teaching schedules and could not get away during the week. They did some outpatient work, but had no hospital facilities. They would often fly down bringing patients needing hospitalization or surgery. There was an air charter service called *Air Brousse* that ran a weekly flight to Lubondai part of the time. It came down from Luluabourg, then went to Luiza before returning, transporting patients to and from Lubondai. We even had some patients come up from Léopoldville. There was a shed where patient families could stay and cook, but many of the patients who came by air wanted better accommodations. We turned some old dormitories into hotel rooms for these patients, charging them accordingly.

One day two Catholic priests came for a medical visit. The patient was Flemish and did not speak French. He brought the other priest along to translate for him. I discovered that the patient had been a missionary in China and, like us, was displaced to Congo. He spoke Mandarin, though from an area with an accent different from the variety I spoke. We managed to communicate with a combination of French and Chinese.

I was fortunate to have the assistance of a succession of three young doctors just out of internship. The first was Peter Gibbs of the Plymouth Brethren Mission, which was located north of the Sankuru River in an area where the Simba rebels were active. Since it was not safe for him to go there, he stayed and worked with us for about eight months. Peter was from Scotland. He had been an accountant working for a firm in Indonesia. Feeling called to be a medical missionary, he went back to medical school. Though he was just out of school, he was older than most beginning physicians. I tried to introduce him to surgery and prepare him for work in a bush hospital, though he really preferred other aspects of medicine.

The second doctor was Ralph Shannon. Ralph had been born in Congo at Shambungu in Bandundu Province. His parents were with the Unevangelized Tribes Mission. His father was American and his mother was Swiss. He arrived in August, then had to return to Léopoldville for his *stage*. This lasted about ten weeks. He was single when he arrived. While he was in Léopoldville, he met Elsbeth Scheidegger, who was working with Mennonite Travel Service. Like Ralph's mother, she was Swiss. Ralph came back to Lubondai in November and Elsbeth paid him a visit around Christmastime. Reassigned to Bibanga, Ralph left in the summer and they went to Switzerland, where they were married before going to their new post. Ralph had a good bit of experience in surgery at Lubondai, and I continued to go to Bibanga about once a month to work with him on his more difficult cases.

Soon after Ralph left, we received word that another young doctor was available. Neil Ratzlaf was a Mennonite conscientious objector, who was in Congo doing missionary service in lieu of military service. He, too, was just out of internship. He had been assigned to work alone in a bush hospital, but his mission wanted to place him at a hospital with an older, more experienced physician. We immediately jumped at the chance and requested him at Lubondai. He was a great help with the medical and pediatric patients. He was not surgically inclined, so when I went to Bibanga, we kept a radio contact in order that I could be called back early if necessary.

For the first year, in addition to Peter, there was a Plymouth Brethren nurse who worked with us, Eda Rogan from York, England. Nolie McDonald was our X-ray and laboratory technician. She was there for the first couple of years. She ran a boarding house for the single medical expatriates. I took my meals with her until Katie and the girls arrived in February 1965. After Nolie retired, I had to take my own X-rays. Ruth Worth came for brief visits to help supervise our laboratory technicians, and Elizabeth Templeton was there at Lubondai with us for a while.

One morning I went to Nolie's for breakfast. I was recounting a dream I had about snakes when Ilunga Paul who took care of the house came running over very excited. He said that there was a snake in my bed. We hurried over and sure enough, there was a snake about four feet long curled up inside the pillow slip beside the depression where my head had been. We took it out and needlessly killed it, as it was a nonpoisonous black snake. I took my bed apart to make sure that its mate was not there, and all I found was a missing grade book that had slipped under the box springs.

Mushrooms grew wild and were available early in the rainy season. One variety was a single large mushroom that sometimes grew to a foot or two in diameter. There were also some smaller varieties. We depended on the local people to know which were nonpoisonous and edible. One evening Nolie served us some mushrooms. Shortly thereafter I was called to the hospital to do a Caesarean section. Peter Gibbs was assisting me. I had just delivered the baby when I began to have waves of nausea. I managed to continue until I had closed the uterus and started the abdominal closure. I then had to turn it over to Peter to finish. I think it was the first case he had to sew up. I just made it to the X-ray room adjacent to the operating room before losing all that I had eaten. I can't remember ever feeling more deathly ill. I'm sure that I had gotten hold of the wrong kind of mushroom.

Patients sometimes showed amazing stamina in getting to the hospital. One man with a strangulated hernia had ridden the train for forty kilometers and then walked the seventeen kilometers from Tshimbulu to get there. Another man had been in a dugout canoe and was attacked by a hippopotamus. The hippo had been shot at several times, so was especially irritable. It turned the pirogue over, and almost amputated his leg at the hip joint. The deep wound exposed the joint. Somehow he managed to swim ashore. He was brought fifteen kilometers to the hospital on the back of a bicycle. We tried to clean the wound and close it, but he died the next day.

We always had a large prenatal clinic. It was much larger than our delivery service. About midway in their pregnancy, some women would ride the train to Tshimbulu from south or north, then walk seventeen kilometers to the hospital. They usually came for two or three monthly visits. If everything seemed to be normal, with no problem anticipated, they stayed in the village to deliver. When we anticipated some problem, they stayed close to the hospital for the last month, in order to deliver at Lubondai. Consequently we had a high rate of Caesarean sections.

Future Hospital for IMCK

When I returned in August 1964, the IMCK was in the process of moving to Tshikaji. The school buildings and residences were being renovated, but there was no hospital. I was named on a committee to search for a hospital site. We looked at a number of sites in and around Luluabourg. We had to consider such things as the availability of a good water supply and accessibility both for patients and for the students. When all was said and done, the best site seemed to be the plateau between the school and the main road at Tshikaji. It was occupied mainly with fields and just a few houses of native construction along the road, so the process of getting a concession for this was begun.

I was also asked to help work on preliminary plans for the hospital. To accomplish this, I tried to consult with all the doctors on the field at every opportunity. I obtained a book on hospital design from Duke that helped with a lot of the details such as room size, door size, hall dimensions, height and placement of sinks, etc. I also consulted on several occasions with Eric Bolton who had some architectural as well as engineering training. Bill Blake, an architect from Birmingham, was with our mission in Léopoldville building churches. I consulted with him and arranged for him to come up to Luluabourg to look at the site. The plans were drafted and redrafted several times. One of our goals was to have a hospital in which proper modern medical care could be practiced, yet one that was compatible with the type of institution in which our graduates would have to serve. In attempting to do this, many compromises had to be made.

After I left, the plans were reworked a couple of times by the architectural firm in Birmingham and I think by others as well. In any case, the eventual hospital followed pretty much the basic design. There were some glaring deviations which showed a lack of understanding of the environment and cultural habits of the population. For example, we had specified that the floor drains should be located adjacent to outside walls so that the drainpipes would be as short as possible. The prevalence of the fine sand made this imperative. Instead, they were placed in the middle of the halls, with the floors all sloping to the center. All of them promptly became clogged permanently. When the floors are washed, the water has to be raked out. The second major problem was placing the toilet facilities in the center of the ward buildings. We had placed them at the ends of the buildings, with the toilets on outside walls where the pipes were available for unclogging. This has been a major problem ever since.

Family Reunited

Katie and the girls arrived in February 1965. Both girls attended Central School (CS) that spring and the following year. In the fall of 1966, Katrina went to The American School of Kinshasa (TASOK) for ninth grade. The Methodist-Presbyterian Hostel (MPH) had not yet been built. The house that was serving temporarily was filled, so we arranged for Katrina to stay at the Disciples of Christ Congo Mission Hostel (DCCM).

While at Lubondai our girls lived and ate at home. Once a week CS served native food. Sometimes Elizabeth would swap with one of her class-mates. We would come home at noon to find a visitor for lunch. We became acquainted with some really neat kids that way! We enjoyed being there at Central School, and the association with the teachers. I also enjoyed seeing the children from all over the mission. Saturday evenings CS usually had some planned activity. Ballroom dancing was not allowed, because of the objection of some of the parents who had children at the school. Folk dancing was sanc-tioned, and one of the favorite activities was square dancing. We all partici-pated and enjoyed that very much.

Bill Worth did the maintenance at CS and Martha was in charge of house-keeping and the boarding department. Having great memories of our time together at Luebo as next-door neighbors, we enjoyed being on the station with them again. Bill was a great fisherman and often traveled the Lulua River. He had made the trip up the Lulua from the point nearest Lubondai to Moma. All of us were busy, but we finally managed to make the trip together, taking both our boats. Sid Langrall, the CS principal, accompanied Bill in his boat and Katie and I went in ours.

It was about sixty to seventy kilometers upstream, so we could make it in a day by starting early in the morning. There were practically no villages close to this section of the river, so it was a really peaceful voyage. We saw hippos in several places. About midway, there was an island where Bill had found crocodile eggs in the past. We stopped there to picnic, tying up to the bank, which rose sharply about five feet. We got out of the boat and started through the tall grass when there was a tremendous noise. A huge crocodile about ten feet long rushed by us and dived off the bank right beside our boats. Fortunately it missed the boats, as it could have damaged or overturned them. Bill collected a bunch of eggs from its nest and we continued up river.

Day and Blanche Carper were expecting us at Moma. When we reached the first road from Moma that came down to the river, our motor quit on us. We stayed there, while Bill went on to the ferry. He and Day brought the truck around to pick us up. Despite crocodiles and motor problems, after a pleasant visit with the Carpers, we made it back to Lubondai the following day.

Katie had plunged into the field study for her dissertation soon after arriving at Lubondai in 1965. She was undertaking an exploration of child rearing patterns and wanted to study one of the villages of the Bakua Tshipanga clan group, preferably one not too close, but easily accessible to

Lubondai. She consulted with Chief Ntolo. After a preliminary comparison of the villages in question, it was decided that Tshiondo village, two kilometers beyond the old Lubondai airstrip, was the best for her purpose. Chief Ntolo insisted that she should not stay all night in the village. She spent much of her time there and was out there at all hours, but never for a whole night at one time. In addition, she helped some at the hospital, especially when I needed a general anesthetic. Most of the time I could get by with either spinal, local, or nerve blocks.

Some of the crucial references that Katie needed were written in Flemish. There were a couple of Belgian Catholic sisters at Tshidimba who frequently brought patients to the hospital. Katie was talking to them about her study and Sister Stanislaus offered to translate the passages for her. Katie demurred, fearing that would take too much time. Sister Stanislaus replied that it was no trouble, she would just read it in Flemish and write it down in French, which she kindly did.

Radio communication both for the mission and for amateurs was permitted once more. After Independence, my call letters changed from OQ5FV to 9Q5FV. I had obtained another rig and did a lot of hamming in the evenings. I contacted over a hundred countries from Lubondai. I entered several contests and made the top score in Congo several times and the top in Africa on a couple of them.

Life at Lubondai took on a special glow when we learned that Katie was pregnant. She insists that the women in Tshiondo village knew it before she did. When Katie asked Katrina and Elizabeth if they would like to have a baby sister or brother for Christmas, Elizabeth said, "Where are you going to get it?" With a mother aged forty-one, not a stupid question! Since her prayers for a younger sibling had not been answered in all of twelve years, she thought we were planning for an adoption.

Katrina and Elizabeth became extremely solicitous of their mother's welfare. When Christmas passed and nothing happened, time began to drag for them. At lunch one day, Elizabeth said, "Gee, Mom, I'm glad you're not an elephant!" By that time Katie may have felt like one, but she unabashedly replied, "Well, so am I, but what do you mean?" to which Elizabeth answered, "It takes an elephant about two years!" From Christmas on, the girls regularly walked Katie all the way around Lubondai station every evening after supper.

Having opted for a home delivery, we found Elizabeth eager to assist, so I trained her to circulate for me. We stocked all supplies that we would need at the house. Katrina was not sure she wanted to attend, but when the time came, she couldn't resist, so all of us were present at the birth of Faye Wolff Nelson on January 4, 1966. She was born late in the afternoon; a couple hours later, atmospheric conditions permitted radio communication to the States. I was able to pass the word through a ham friend to our families. My mother called Sperry's dormitory at Vanderbilt with the news. She could hear the word echoing down the hall, "It's a girl; it's a girl!"

Visit to South Africa

In December 1966, we took our annual vacation in South Africa. Katie needed to do some research in the libraries there relative to her field study. We flew to Johannesburg, where she spent some time in the library, then rented a car and drove to Pretoria, for further library research, to procure copies of essential references. We then drove through Kruger National Park. Among the first animals we saw were three magnificent sable antelope. In fact, on our many subsequent visits to game parks elsewhere in Africa, we never again saw this beautiful creature at close range. We spent Christmas in a motel at Nelspruit southwest of the park. We then drove over and visited Sudwala Caves which had been used as a place of refuge by blacks trying to escape, at a time when they were being hunted. At the New Year we drove down to Parys in the Orange Free State. This is Boer country. We stayed in a motel and I visited a ham radio friend with whom I had frequently talked. There was a big celebration, held at the motel, similar to some Fourth of July picnics I have attended in the States. Boer farm families came from all over. There was an amateur contest in which the favorite vocal number "Edelweiss" was sung at least a dozen times with widely ranging degrees of perfection. Faye celebrated her first birthday, and started swimming in the pool with the aid of "water wings" (inflated cuffs) on her arms.

While in South Africa, I took the opportunity to purchase urgently needed drugs and medical supplies. At Luebo I had done refractions and kept a supply of frames and lenses of various diopter strengths. One purpose was to provide glasses for the elderly pastors and other church workers with presbyopia, so that they could continue to read the Bible. I continued this service at Lubondai. After Independence the mails became increasingly unreliable, especially for packages containing glasses, which were vulnerable to pilfering and so could no longer be ordered by mail. I found a supplier in Johannesburg and filled a suitcase with glasses and other supplies.

The months following our vacation in South Africa were busy, as we were to return to the States in the summer of 1967. The girls had to stay until their school term was completed. In order for at least one of us to get back to the U.S. for Lee's graduation from McCallie that spring, Katie had to leave early. She traveled by way of Brussels, as she needed a few days at Tervuren for a scheduled conference with Dr. Olga Boone at le Musée Royal de l'Afrique Centrale and to collect copies of references from the museum library. The three girls and I followed as soon as school was out. When Faye began to talk, she tried to say Elizabeth, but it came out "Bizza." The name still sticks.

Nashville 1967-68

Mother had located a house on Essex Place not too far from the university area. We settled there and the entire family went to school. I had arranged to take a year of pathology residency at Vanderbilt; Dr. Shapiro, the chairman of the department, was an old friend, having been a couple of classes ahead of me in medical school. Katie went to work writing her dissertation. Sperry was entering his senior year at Vanderbilt. He had been accepted at the University of Tennessee Medical School in Memphis and was to enter there following graduation. Lee was in his freshman year at Illinois Institute of Technology in Chicago on a U.S. Navy ROTC scholarship. Katrina was a sophomore in high school and Bizza in eighth grade. Faye was in day care. As the end of the school year approached, we recognized the girls' need to continue their education in the U.S. Through one of the pathology interns, Dr. Richard Callaway, from Maryville, I learned that his cousins Drs. Jim and Henry Callaway were temporarily in need of a third man in their surgical practice. Jim and I had been in surgical residency together at Vanderbilt. He and Henry invited us to visit Maryville and consider joining them for one year. Grateful for this opportunity and delighted with the location, we accepted. We located and bought a house that was nearing completion.

Maryville 1968-72

Sperry graduated at the beginning of the summer of 1968, but was enrolled at Vanderbilt for a summer course. Katrina was also in summer school. Katie was about to finish her doctorate and would graduate at the end of the summer. As soon as the girls were out of school, I moved to Maryville with Bizza and Faye. Katie, Katrina, and Sperry all continued in school in Nashville. Maryville, the home of Maryville College, is mainly a college and residential town and the Blount County seat. Alcoa, adjacent to Maryville, was originally a company town of the Aluminum Company of America, which has remained one of the largest employers, with three factories. Much of the business district is in Alcoa. We found a church home at New Providence Presbyterian Church.

I shifted into emergency medicine after one year, still hoping to return to Africa eventually. Emergency medicine was not yet a recognized specialty. St. Mary's Hospital in Knoxville was initiating a trial service. I joined Dr. Astor Jenkins and Dr. Thomas Ray in its organization. We incorporated as the Knoxville Emergency Physicians Group (KEPG). I was actively engaged in working out the contract with the hospital. In the beginning, we had to use residents for part of the coverage, but gradually replaced them with full-time physicians, as the emergency room had to have a physician on duty at all times. The American College of Emergency Physicians had just been organized and I joined it during its charter membership period. In 1970 we expanded to provide services at Fort Sanders Presbyterian Hospital. Again I was involved in contract negotiation. Bill Rule was retiring and coming home from Africa; he was among those we recruited to enlarge our team of emergency physicians.

Busman's Holiday in Congo 1971

Torn between family needs and the pull of needs on the mission field, we decided to take our month vacation by visiting Congo to see the situation for ourselves. We arranged with Medical Benevolence Foundation (MBF) to go under their auspices in May 1971 and took Faye with us. Our first week was spent at Bulapé. Dr. Birch Rambo was assigned there, but had to be away in Kinshasa (formerly Léopoldville). We filled in for him until his return. While there, we made the monthly air dispensary visits including the newer Shongamba dispensary. We next went to Bibanga where Dr. Walter Hull was medical director. He fell ill with malaria about the time I arrived, so I filled in for him for a week. I also made the Bibanga dispensary visits, which included a trip to Kasha. We then went to Kananga and to IMCK where they were still without a hospital. The land had been obtained and construction was to begin within a year. They had a clinic at a nearby government dispensary at Nkonku. I made visits to the places that IMCK was covering by air, which included Mboi, a couple of rural dispensaries, and the hospitals at Lubondai and Moma.

Several months after our return to Maryville in May 1971, I was contacted by an Arab student at the University of Tennessee. He was inquiring on behalf of Dr. David Dorr, a Baptist missionary in Yemen, about a temporary position in the emergency group. This gave me the opportunity to arrange with the mission board and with KEPG for us to return to Africa, and for David to take my place in the emergency group for one year. The Dorrs also rented our house for the year. By this time, returning to the country now called Zaïre no longer put the children's education in jeopardy. Sperry and Nancy Shelton had been married in Memphis on September 26, 1970. He had graduated from University of Tennessee College of Medicine, Memphis, was in a surgery residency at U.T. Medical Center in Knoxville, and was living nearby. Lee had graduated from Illinois Institute of Technology in 1971 and had married Roxanne Prince in Fort Worth, Texas on June 5, 1971. He was in the Navy, serving his required time in repayment for his scholarship. Katrina was at Peabody College (later to become part of Vanderbilt) in Nashville, pursuing a double major in elementary and special education. Bizza had just graduated from Maryville High School and was entering Southwestern at Memphis (now Rhodes College).

9. Zaïre: 1972-82

Zaïre

On returning to Africa in 1972, we found the Africanization of geographical terms had become more complete. Mobutu, army general who had taken over as president by a military coup, had instituted the change to the three Z's. The name of the country was now the Republic of Zaïre; the monetary unit was zaïre; and within Mobutu's realm, the mighty Congo River was now called the Zaïre. Many cities had resumed their African names. As to personal names, Western names were forbidden, so the Zaïrians were using only their traditional names. Coats and ties were outlawed; the men's garment was a suit with a special jacket style called the *abacost*, which had an open collar.

We arrived in Kinshasa to discover that we could not get a flight to Kananga (formerly Luluabourg) for two weeks. John and Jo Ann Ellington were working in Kinshasa, on loan to United Bible Societies. They had recently made a trip up river by boat and suggested that we investigate the possibility of going that way. A boat was leaving in a couple of days. We were able to get a first-class cabin. Jo Ann gave us tips on what we should take with us. This included insecticides, a padlock for the cabin, bottled water, and drinks for the five-day trip, as well as some food items to supplement the fare available on the boat.

Kinshasa-Kasai by Riverboat

The riverboat was fairly shallow draft and had two deck levels above the water. The bottom deck contained the engine room and crew quarters. Passengers occupied the upper deck. We had a private room at the rear of the ship for Katie, Faye, and me. Our meals were served in our cabin. On the same deck, there were second-class rooms with several bunks to a room, the

215

dining room, and the bar. The bridge was up front, one level higher. The double decked dormitory barge lashed to the right side of the boat had two more dormitory barges in front of it. The boat was pushing a flat barge on which a twenty-four hour market was in progress for the entire trip.

It was a fascinating trip. The boat maintained a steady speed against the current with only a few stops. Leaving the Zaïre River, the boat proceeded up the Kasai River to Bandundu where one of the passenger barges was dropped off. Another stop was at Leverville, the Lever Brothers palm oil plantation. We tied up to the bank the night before the end of the trip. Pirogues paddled out to meet the boat all along the way. A rope was thrown to them as the boat continued upstream, and they would tie up to the side for a short while to trade. All sorts of tropical fruits and other edibles, as well as goats, monkeys, ducks, chickens, green pigeons, gray parrots, and fish were offered for sale. On the barge in front, women cooked on *babula* (charcoal braziers) to feed those in the dormitories. Pirogues came bringing cases of empty beer bottles to exchange for a new supply of beer. Occasionally there would be a mishap, and one of the pirogues would capsize, spilling its contents and passengers into the river. The expanse of tropical vegetation along the riverbank was interrupted now and then by small villages, mostly of mud-walled huts with thatched roofs. Hippos and crocodiles were occasionally seen. On the Zaïre and lower reaches of the Kasai River, there were great masses of water hyacinths on which we saw jaçanas (lily trotters), long-toed wading birds that walk around with ease on the floating vegetation. The boat train was waiting at Ilebo, as Port Francqui is now called. Most of the passengers transferred immediately to the waiting train. It was an "express" stopping at only the most important stations.

Kananga 1972-73

At Kananga, Dr. John Miller and Aurie were waiting at the train station. There was no housing available out at Tshikaji, so we were to live in a house just obtained from Mr. Santos, a couple of blocks from Kananga station. It was located a block from the Centre Protestant, the old Hôtel Bon Auberge, which was bought by the mission shortly after Independence. The French-speaking congregation holds services in the Centre's auditorium. The house was only a few blocks from the building that the IMCK had rented for a clinic.

When we arrived, our new home was neat, clean, and empty of all furniture. Stacked in a corner were packages of Faye's first grade Calvert Course books that we had ordered. From a warehouse of furniture that had been brought to Kananga from other stations, mostly from Mutoto and Lubondai, Katie collected the furniture we needed. I had the house screened, including a back porch, which we used as a dining area. Since the city water was cut off intermittently, I eventually also installed a large cement water tank, arranging a float valve so that the tank filled whenever the city water came on.

We had just moved in and were getting settled when we had a visit from the daughter of Jean Joseph, our good friend at Luebo. Anne brought her daughter, Marie France, who was about Faye's age. The two girls were dashing around the house, when Faye ran into an open casement window, cutting her forehead, which bled profusely. I took her down to the clinic, but was totally unfamiliar with what was there, and it was after hours. I finally located enough instruments and supplies to suture the laceration.

Kananga seemed to be recovering from the turmoil following Independence. Several automobile agencies and repair shops including Ford, Chevrolet, Volkswagen, and Dodge were more or less in operation. There were several bakeries, a couple of butcher shops, four hardware stores, several grocery stores, and a number of general stores selling cloth and other items. In addition there were a large number of small African shops. Most of the larger stores were owned and directed by expatriates; many of the small shops were their subsidiaries. There were enough expatriates in town that the club named Le Cercle was functioning. It had a large swimming pool and restaurant, both of which we enjoyed occasionally that year. There was a pizza parlor next door to our house with a small ice cream store adjacent to it. On the other side of the house a small hotel often provided loud music. Two doors down the street, a discotheque blared music long into the early morning hours. The first couple of nights this disturbed our sleep, but we soon became accustomed to it. The missionaries no longer placed large food orders in the States as we did during the early years in Africa. Many things were available in the stores, and in addition Don Brew had organized a *procure* (commissary) for the missionaries. He placed orders in South Africa, so anything one wanted could be obtained, for a price.

Funds for the new hospital had been obtained from the PCUS Women's Birthday Offering, USAID, and from the American Leprosy Missions. Sam Ediger, a Mennonite builder, was living at Tshikaji, and the hospital construction was proceeding rapidly. I was disappointed to find that I was too late to correct the placement of the toilets and drains. A Mennonite cabinet maker, Olin Schmidt, was there, building cabinets for the nurses' stations, and other furniture. Medical consultations were being held in a rented house near the train station in Kananga. I went out to Tshikaji a couple times a week to teach classes in the nursing school and took occasion to follow the construction closely. Sam asked me to help design the scrub sinks for the surgical and the obstetrical suites. He built them in place, using terrazzo to match the floors.

Lake Munkamba

Lake Munkamba is situated about sixty kilometers (some thirty-seven miles) east of Kananga. It is the largest of a series of lakes, which are thought to have some underground connections. Surrounded by rolling grasslands which are practically treeless, there are no streams entering or leaving the lake. Parts of the lake are shallow, but the center of the lake is very deep. It is apparently fed from underwater springs. In any case, the water is clear and has a remarkable ability to cleanse itself. Munkamba is irregular in shape, with several bays. It is roughly two and a half miles long and has a large bay extending toward the east. (See map.) The church conference center was located on the western shore of the lake at the edge of Bakua Luntu territory. The southern and eastern shore was in Baluba country. Following Independence, the tribal conflict was intense around the lake.

Not long after we arrived back in Zaïre in 1972, we went to Lake Munkamba with John and Aurie Miller. All the buildings on the conference grounds had been almost completely destroyed after Independence. The roofs and all the wood had been removed. The buildings constructed of sun-dried brick had melted away in the rains. Houses made of cement block had only the walls standing. Before Independence, a number of missionaries and some of the mission stations had built vacation houses on the mission concession. The concession now belonged to the church. A new dormitory and a kitchen with dining hall had been built. A number of the houses had been reconstructed. John Miller had restored the house that he and his father, the Reverend Hoyt Miller, had once built.

Just south of the church concession were two private concessions. The one adjacent to the church property had belonged to a Belgian. The walls of the house were still standing. Ralph and Elsbeth Shannon arranged to get this concession and rebuild the house. Dr. Hugh Wilds had the next concession, which was five hectares (12.35 acres), extending from the lake back to the main road. He had built two houses on it. The first was built of stabilized brick, a mixture of cement and dirt dried in the sun, but not kiln fired. He lived in this while building a larger house in which they retired in 1958. He also had a small dental office and a house for a sentry. They had to evacuate when all the other expatriates left at Independence in 1960. The sentry house and dental office were completely gone. The walls of the front half of the first house were standing. Most of the walls of the second house, which was built of cement block, were also standing, but the cement floor was cracked. A large tree, reaching above the height of the walls, was growing in the living room area. John Miller inspired us to contact Dr. Wilds, take over the concession, and rebuild the house. He had the Wilds' power of attorney and helped us to arrange for the purchase and transfer. We received a new twenty-five year concession from the government.

Rebuilding the house was quite a project. We changed the floor plan somewhat by eliminating some of the interior walls, enclosing a back porch for a kitchen, and making the old kitchen into a storeroom. The original store-room was made into a third bedroom. Partitions were removed, throwing the old living room, dining room, and hall into a large living-dining area. Instead of a small front stoop, we built a long porch across the entire front of the house. I found a local contractor to hire workmen and oversee the day to day construction, and I bought the necessary hardware and materials in Kananga. There was a sawmill between Kananga and Tshikaji which cut the lumber to

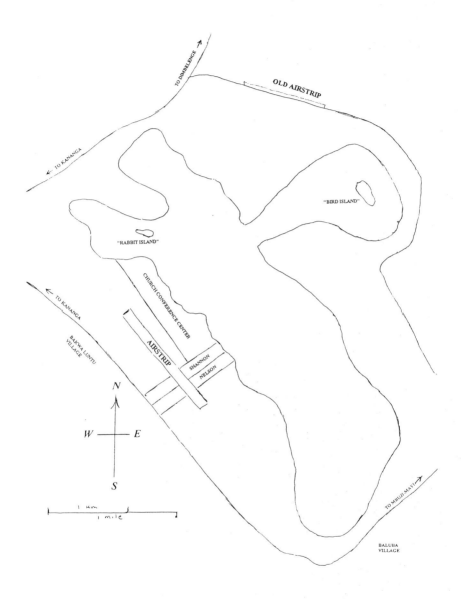

TO DIMBELENGE

OLD AIRSTRIP

TO KANANGA

"BIRD ISLAND"

"RABBIT ISLAND"

CHURCH CONFERENCE CENTER

TO KANANGA

BAKWA LUNTU VILLAGE

AIRSTRIP

SHANNON

NELSON

N

W — E

S

1 km
1 mile

TO MBUJI-MAYI

BALUBA VILLAGE

Lake Munkamba

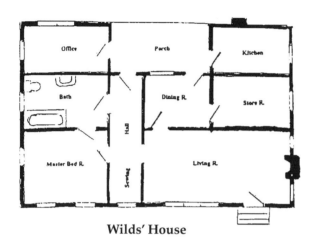

Wilds' House

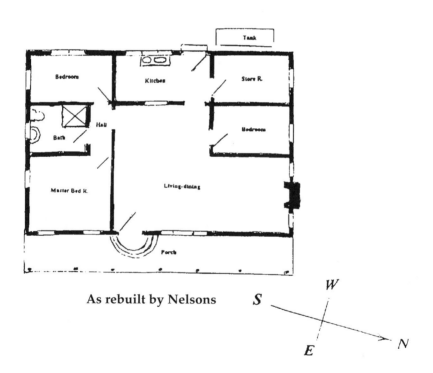

As rebuilt by Nelsons

Lake Munkamba House

specifications. Sam Ediger helped me design and lay out the roof trusses at Tshikaji. The various pieces were cut to size. I then rented the Tshikaji truck to transport them to the lake for assembly. The window frames were made at Tshikaji, where they had jigs to drill the holes for reinforcing rods used as security bars. Jalousie window frames were available in Kananga. The Catholic carpenter shop made the door frames with doors attached. I bought a pickup from the Reverend Levi Keidel, a Mennonite missionary, one which he had used as a bookmobile. It had a large cover over the bed, with built-in cupboards. The road to Munkamba was in fair condition, so frequent week-end trips allowed the transport of supplies and supervision and direction of the contractor. Some of the work I did myself, such as installing the jalousies, cutting the glass panes to fit, installing wiring for lights and plumbing for toilet and sinks. The Reverend Archie Graber, a senior Mennonite missionary, happened to be out at the lake on vacation. The Mennonites had rebuilt one of the houses on the church concession. Archie had a long standing reputation as an expert builder. After the roof was framed, he helped put the galvanized roofing on the house. John Miller had a rectangular galvanized water tank which he was replacing with a larger one in order to supply water to two adjacent houses. I bought the tank from him so I could install it under the eaves of the house to collect water from the roof in rainy season. As you can see, I used help from many sources. All our friends, Zaïrians and missionaries, were interested in the project.

During this era, we had an opportunity to buy a canoe from Mark Grings to replace our old aluminum boat which had been sold to Bill Pruitt. Mark was from a family of independent missionaries that had a couple of stations on the Sankuru River. The canoe was equipped with a water jet driven by a small gasoline motor, which was not powerful enough to be used against the current on the Sankuru. I never used the jet; instead I made a sail conversion by rigging a short mast and a lateen sail. I made dagger boards which attached to the sides of the canoe. Munkamba rarely has a day without wind. There is usually at least a gentle breeze during some part of the day. One day Katie, Faye, and I went sailing. One of the violent storms so typical of Munkamba suddenly arose. Trying to make it to shore, we were caught in deep water. When the canoe capsized, high wind and waves defeated our efforts to right it. Fortunately, Dr. Zook had a motorboat which his sentry's son operated with skill. Ruth Worth saw our difficulty and sent the sentry's sons to our rescue. They took Katie and Faye into the motorboat, swam for things floating in the water, and towed me in close enough to shore so that I could right the canoe. Fortunately we did not lose anything. I had a pair of binoculars which were tied to the boat. They were thoroughly soaked, but I was able to dry them out in a desiccator at the hospital laboratory.

To prevent a recurrence, I redesigned the conversion of the canoe, by fashioning a frame for outriggers which could be attached to it. A balsam log was split in two and shaped for a float on each side, with a dagger board attached to each float. In use, the float and dagger board on the lee side would tip into the water and the one on the windward side would rise out of the water. With increased stability, a larger sail could be employed. This was a big improvement and afforded us much pleasure during our subsequent times at Munkamba.

Lake Fua

Lake Fua is located about twenty kilometers (twelve miles) east of Munkamba and a few miles north of the main road to Mbuji-Mayi. The lake is a collection of crystal clear springs which reminds one of Silver Springs, Florida. One of the springs has an opening about ten to fifteen feet across, into which one can see down thirty feet or more. The clear water boils up out of it constantly. In parts of the lake that are fifteen to twenty feet deep, the water is so clear one can see pebbles on the bottom. The banks are lined with trees. It is truly an idyllic spot. Many years ago the Belgians built a hotel there, planning to turn it into a major tourist attraction. It was soon discovered that the water, which looked so clear and pure, was infested with schistosomes (liver flukes), parasites that are transmitted through an intermediate host, a small aquatic snail. The parasite causes a disease called schistosomiasis, related to the disease I had seen in China, but caused by a different species of the parasites. This is a very debilitating disease which eventually can lead to liver failure and death. Plans for the tourist site had to be dropped, and the old hotel stands abandoned. Dr. John Miller planned a public health survey to determine the incidence of the disease there. Ruth Worth was at IMCK at the time and we took a group of students to help carry out the study. In addition to searching for the eggs of the parasite in the stool specimens, we also gave immunizations and held abbreviated clinics. We found that villagers living on the bank of Lake Fua had an infestation rate of about 70 percent and those living in a village a few kilometers from the lake were about 33 percent infested. The same disease is also found in some of the rivers in the Mbuji-Mayi and Bibanga areas of East Kasai. Most of our work has been done in West Kasai, where the lakes and rivers are free of the snails that are essential to complete the life cycle of the parasite.

Road Hazards

In 1960, the only paved roads in the Kasai were in the two major cities, Luluabourg (Kananga) and Bakwanga (Mbuji-Mayi), and a couple of the larger towns. Roads for the most part were sandy, though in the Moma area there was a lot of red clay, and in the eastern Kasai, there were rocky areas. During the rainy season the roads washed badly and there were often large pools of water in the low places. In dry season one had to contend with fine dust, grit, and deep sand pits. Prior to Independence, roads were kept passable only by the constant efforts of local road crews, as required by the colonial authorities.

Following Independence, there was virtually no maintenance, and travel became increasingly difficult. The roads were narrow and visibility on curves was often obscured by tall grasses. In addition to oncoming traffic, one had to watch for women with loads on their heads, hunters with their dogs, children in the villages, and bicycles with enormous loads tied to them. Sheep, goats, and occasional pigs were hazards to be avoided. I never tried to avoid chickens, as the sandy surface was too treacherous, so they frequently became casualties when they tried to dash across the road. Because of all these hazards, I preferred to travel at night whenever possible.

Tire treads lasted longer than when driving on paved roads. Tire failure was more often the result of climate and rough roads, which were particularly hard on the sidewalls. Shock absorbers also succumbed frequently to the constant pounding. The climate took its toll on batteries; one had to be careful to keep the fluid levels up. Fortunately, the hospital had a still for distilling water. Batteries required frequent filling, but did not last as long as in a more moderate climate.

A number of times I was forced to make major repairs on the road. Cleaning the carburetor and complete carburetor overhaul under the dusty conditions was a challenge. Filling stations were available only in the larger cities, so most refueling was done from fifty-gallon drums with small hand pumps. I filtered all my gas through chamois skin, but even then it was not possible to keep the tank from becoming contaminated with sediment. Gas lines became clogged, requiring them to be blown out. In spite of greasing, universal joints were vulnerable to the grit, often requiring replacement.

Returning from Lubondai during our second term at Luebo, with a load of children from Central School, a rear mainspring broke. We were about halfway between Luluabourg and Luebo. Fortunately we stopped in a village beside the home of an evangelist. We sent word to Luebo for someone to come and get us. The car was left there in the care of the evangelist until I could obtain a replacement spring leaf. I returned later to rebuild and install the spring.

On another occasion, I was in the Luebo pickup. The road was badly rutted, and a front wheel fell into a deep rut. The tie rod between the front wheels bent, and the front wheels were turned outward so that they were at right angles to one another. After removing the rod, I was able to straighten it using a fork in a nearby tree.

Conditions on the road to Lake Munkamba tended to vary widely. At times four-wheel drive was essential, and the forty-mile trip usually took anywhere from one and a half to four hours. We learned that it could take much longer! We were once returning to Tshikaji from Munkamba on a Sunday evening in our pickup, with Anita Janzen, then director of the laboratory school at IMCK. Just before leaving the lake, an elderly woman had come to me, severely ill with congestive heart failure. I agreed to take her to the hospital. We had gone a short distance when we had a flat. I changed to the spare, only to have it go flat, too. We were about halfway to Tshikaji. A big MAS truck, of the local freight and mail service, came by. Katie and Anita were able to get a ride and took the two wheels into Kananga, leaving me in the pickup with the sick patient. It was already nearing nightfall. Katie arrived in Kananga while the missionaries were at English services. Jim Branch, the mission pilot, recognized the seriousness of the situation and took Katie and the wheels to the hangar at the airport where the tires could be repaired. They then brought them out to me about midnight. The night was chilly and dark, and the old lady's labored respiration had given me concern as to whether she would last the night. She made it to the hospital and recovered. I was later able to give her a ride back to the lake. Never had a pilot more graciously rendered overtime service for us on the road. We have always been grateful to Jim.

Katrina's Visit

In December 1972, Katrina came out to visit us during her winter break from Peabody College. At that time, the mission board financed one round trip for each child during the college years. The house at Lake Munkamba was almost completed at that time. The roof had just been finished, but we were having some leaks. Christmas found Katie and Katrina on the roof, caulking some of the leaks with roofing cement. When it was time for Katrina to leave, she developed a severe case of malaria. We had a rough time with her, as she could not keep anything down. I had to resort to intravenous medications and fluids to gain control of the disease. The malarial attack delayed her return to class. We were just thankful that she had developed it before she left, as so few doctors in the States were experienced in treating malaria.

Before the year was over, it became apparent that there was a need for us to stay a second year. Dr. John Zook, the Mennonite surgeon, and his wife Jean, who was directing the nursing school, were due for furlough. I was needed to take over John's classes and surgical responsibilities, and Katie was asked to be director of the nursing school. When we contacted Dr. David Dorr, we discovered that they too needed to extend a year. Thus it was advantageous for both families to continue our arrangement for another year.

IMCK Tshikaji 1973-74

When the Zooks left, we moved to Tshikaji. The General Hospital in Kananga had two sections. One was the large hospital built for the population at large. A smaller and newer section was called La Clinique. It was completed shortly before Independence as a hospital for expatriates. This was now being used for private patients. John had worked out an arrangement to do his operations at La Clinique. He had been assigned an office and examining room in the building. A Catholic sister was in charge of the surgical suite and kept the sterile techniques up to standard. John had a Zaïrian nurse assigned to him who assisted him at his consultations at La Clinique and at

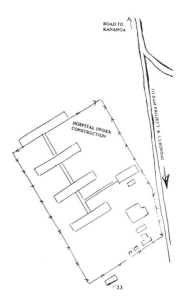

Original Buildings:
School
Dining room and chapel
Administration
Boys' dorm complex
Faculty houses 1-10

Additions by I.M.C.K.:
Duplex
Girls' dormitory
Houses 11-13
Hangar
Chicken project

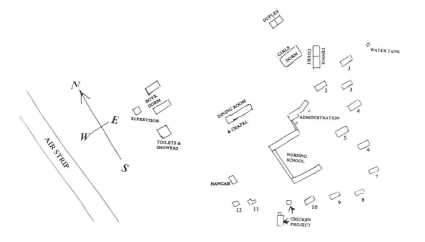

I.M.C.K. Tshikaji
1972-1973

the IMCK clinic. She also followed his postoperative patients. He had to supply his own gloves, instruments, sutures, and gauze. He also had to supply the medications for his patients. The nurse was responsible for seeing that the patients received them. Otherwise, one could never count on patients in the general wards receiving drugs that had been ordered. He turned this all over to me. I continued the practice, operating as well as delivering several expatriates at La Clinique during that year while we lived at Tshikaji.

Katie replaced Jean Zook as director of the nursing school. At this time, the upper classes were spending part of the time at Bulapé Hospital for their clinical work. When the students began their clinical nursing, Katie and the other instructors took them to the General Hospital in Kananga for experience. This was quite an ordeal. They had to be transported into the city by truck, taking with them everything they needed—linens, basins, soap, etc.— as nothing was available at the hospital for nursing care.

Another job that John turned over to me was a chicken project. He had built a large chicken barn near his house. It had four large cages, each of which held about fifty chickens. It also had a large storeroom for feed. Another small house was used for raising chicks. He had a worker that did the daily chores of putting out the feed and collecting the eggs. There was an agricultural school near the airport. John had arranged to place a couple of large incubators there. The school was allowed to use them in payment for their supervision of the incubators. Sixty eggs were started every week. Some of the settings of day-old chicks were sold to Zaïrians to get them started raising better stock. About every four weeks, a setting would be kept for the project. The old hens were also sold, as new hens came along. The excess eggs were sold to missionaries and some of the expatriates in town. Feed had to be bought from a company in Katanga (now Shaba), a carload at a time, both growing mash and laying mash. Some we used for our own flocks and some we sold to Zaïrians who had bought chicks. It was quite an operation. I took eggs into town every time I went in for clinic. From the profits, I bought a deep freezer in which we stored the hens as we killed them, since we often killed more than we could immediately sell. It later became increasingly difficult to get feed and the incubators became more of a problem, so John Zook had to abandon this project eventually.

For a while, it seemed that Zaïre might be on the way toward economic recovery following the setback at Independence. Abruptly this changed when Mobutu confiscated all expatriate businesses. Some of the expatriates also had their personal furniture and belongings taken. The business establishments were turned over to Zaïrians who were supporters of Mobutu. A few of them tried to operate the businesses. Many just sold off inventories without any effort to maintain capital to order new stock. When they tried to place orders, they found that the suppliers demanded payment before shipping orders. Most of the expatriates fled the country. Some businesses depended upon the skill or training of the owners. For instance, there was a German cabinetmaker in Kananga who made beautiful furniture. When the new owners sold what he had made, there was no one to replace him. The same was true of the machine shop. The workers could do some of the welding and other tasks, but without the direction of the engineer and machine operator, the business ground to a halt. An Italian who ran an ice cream shop, with several employees selling ice cream from carts in the city, left with practically nothing. The new owners could not keep the business going. Many other examples could be given.

Several other events of note took place during this two-year term. The elected governors from all the provinces were called to Kinshasa. On arrival they were told that there was to be a general fruit basket turnover. They were all assigned to different provinces. This was an effort to cut down on nepotism. The theory was to get them away from areas where they were under constant pressure from relatives. Higher education was reorganized. The universities were combined and different sections located in several of the larger cities. There were three medical schools —the Catholic school, Louvainium, in Kinshasa; a small government school in Lubumbashi; and a recently organized Protestant school in Kisangani. These were all combined into one school, located at Kinshasa.

The owner of the IMCK clinic building in Kananga decided to terminate the lease, as he needed it for other purposes. A nearby lot became available and was purchased. It contained a house, a large garage, storerooms, and an old store. The church dental office already occupied half of the store building. Mr. Kabamba Sekomba, a dental assistant trained at IMCK Lubondai before Independence, was in charge with an active practice. I was assigned the task of converting the house and garage for use as a clinic.

In 1974, we decided to return to the States by way of the Far East. We were eager to visit the Presbyterian missions in Taiwan, Korea, and Japan, and took the occasion for visits in Kenya and India on the way. Bizza came out in the spring of 1974 on the trip allowed college students, and arranged to do an independent study during the time, for credit toward her anthropology major at Southwestern. Before leaving the States, she also worked with a travel agent to arrange our itinerary. We wrote ahead to friends on each of the missions. They graciously helped to plan our program in the respective countries.

Trip Home 1974

The first part of the trip home was arranged by a local travel agency, AMIZA. We wanted to leave via the Kivu and visit the game park and also go see the mountain gorillas. We left Kananga on an Air Zaïre plane, which sat on the apron for over an hour after we boarded. It was terribly hot and the air conditioning was not working, because there was no ground power supply. We found out later that in order to restart the engines, they needed a Phillips head screwdriver to open a cover. Finally they borrowed one from the mission hangar, and we were able to depart. The delay made it too late to get to Goma before sundown, but the pilots did not want to spend the night in Kananga. The flight was diverted to Kisangani for the night. The only hotel in town did not have enough accommodations for all the passengers. We were fortunate that the AMIZA agent for the office in Goma was on the plane. He had priority for a room at the hotel which he turned over to us, and he spent the night in a chair in the lobby. We have been recommending AMIZA ever since! The next morning the plane continued to Goma.

Kivu

Goma is at the northern end of Lake Kivu at the foot of a volcano which is active from time to time. The most recent lava flow was very close to the hotel where we stayed. AMIZA arranged for a car to take us north to Rwindi in the game park. On the way, we crossed the continental divide between the Zaïre and Nile watersheds. There we stopped at some hot springs. The hotel in the game park at Rwindi overlooks Lake Idi Amin (formerly Lake Edward). Below the hotel, a river enters the lake, in which there were a large number of hippopotamuses. Our rooms in the hotel were in round cabins called *rondavels*. These had conical thatch roofs and contained two rooms with two cots in each room. Katie and I were in one room and Faye and Bizza were in the other. There was no adjoining door. Hippos stay in the water during the day to keep cool, coming out during the night to browse on the grass. After we had gone to bed, we could hear them snorting and moving around outside the *rondavel*. Bizza knocked on the wall, waking us to say that Faye was sick. Katie went out the door and around to the other side of the *rondavel* to enter their room. Bizza had failed to unlock the door, so Katie had to bang on the door to get in and escape from the hippos. Happily, Faye recovered from her stomach upset the next day. A guide took us for a drive in the park, though the wildlife was not as plentiful and varied as in some of the east African parks. From Rwindi, we went back south.

To reach the gorilla preserve from Goma, we crossed Lake Kivu to Bukavu. The gorillas inhabit the mountains above the city. When we arrived, we learned that Faye would not be able to go because she was under the age limit. In the morning, we were taken to a tea plantation on the mountain, where a missionary pilot, Jack Spurlock, and his family were living. I had met Jack, but he was away. His wife very graciously offered to keep Faye while Katie, Bizza, and I went in search of the gorillas. We hiked out through the plantation with the park guide to the area where the gorillas were last seen. The guide tracked them to where they were having their midmorning siesta in a clump of bushes. We could hear them shifting about and grunting from time to time. We were warned to sit still and if the gorillas came our way, to pick some leaves and nibble on them. They say the gorillas understand that if you are eating, you are no threat, and they will not bother you. We waited patiently, picking out some choice leaves to munch on. When the gorillas had finished their naps, they left the bushes on the far side and went up a hill. We saw their backs at a distance, but were disappointed not to get a closer look.

The guide gave us a rain check and offered to take us out again the next day, but our schedule did not permit us to stay longer. A few years later, we were distressed to learn that Jack Spurlock had died in a plane crash near Bukavu.

Kenya

We returned to Goma and left Zaïre for Nairobi. We hoped to arrange a night at "Treetops" but it, too, had an age limit which excluded Faye. Instead we went to the "Ark," a similar situation, where you spend the night in a lodge located by a salt lick that is floodlighted at night so you can observe the animals. The Ark is located in a forest. We arrived by tour bus. We were welcomed and given a brief introduction by a man in a safari suit with a huge elephant gun, which he propped muzzle down on the toe of his boot while he gave his talk! The path led only a couple hundred feet to the Ark, which was built high off the ground and took roughly the shape of a boat. From inside, one could also go underground to a pillbox on the edge of the salt lick. Before dark there were plenty of buffalo at the lick, and while I was in the pillbox, some came within a few feet. We had small rooms and bunks, but we didn't sleep much. Every time there were some interesting animals in view, they rang a buzzer to alert us. One of the animals often seen there was a rare forest antelope, the bongo. A number of other animals came that night, but we had to wait to see a bongo later at the Tokyo zoo.

From Nairobi we continued on around the world, spending a week each in India, Taiwan, Korea, and Japan. We enjoyed seeing not only the Presbyterian mission work in those lands, but also friends and some of our former missionary colleagues who were working there.

Maryville 1974 -78

On returning to the States in 1974, we remained for another extended period. I resumed work with the Knoxville Emergency Physicians Group (KEPG). It soon became apparent that Blount Memorial Hospital in Maryville was ready to try having a full-time emergency service. At the hospital's request, I organized Blount Emergency Physicians (BEP), so during most of this time, I worked near home in Maryville, while maintaining my ties to the KEPG. Katie returned to Maryville College to teach anthropology and sociology.

In 1976, when Bizza graduated from Southwestern at Memphis, she volunteered for two years of service with the Peace Corps. She expressed a preference for Zaïre, but was assigned to Benin. At the end of her first year, conditions in Benin were so bad that the Peace Corps gave volunteers the opportunity to return to the States or transfer to another country. She chose the latter, was transferred to Zaïre, extended for a third year, and was assigned to IMCK, arriving there in the fall of 1977.

The Good Shepherd Hospital at Tshikaji had been completed and dedicated on January 20, 1975. Bill Rule went for the dedication. I could not get away for that, but kept hoping for a chance to see it in operation. The call to missionary service was becoming too strong to resist. The Zooks were to leave definitively in the summer of 1978; Katie and I became increasingly eager to go back to Zaïre for another term.

In preparation for Zaïre, I purchased a four-wheel drive Ford pickup with a crew cab, and, hence, a very long wheel base. Over the rough Zaïrian roads, this proved to be the most comfortable riding four-wheel vehicle on the mission. Before shipping it, I had a cover made for the bed and an extra gas tank installed. I gave it to Medical Benevolence Foundation (MBF) for the IMCK. This made it possible to ship it through Church World Service and have it cleared through customs by the church in Zaïre. It was assigned for our use during our term in Zaïre, but remained the property of the IMCK. We shipped the truck far enough in advance for it to reach Zaïre about the same time that we arrived in May 1978.

Back to Zaïre

On arrival in Kinshasa, we found that fighting had broken out once again in the southeastern province of Shaba (formerly Katanga). This was primarily a resurgence of long-standing ethnic animosity. It was feared that the fighting might spread. Understandably, the central government was gravely concerned, so army roadblocks were reportedly set up all over the country. The pickup had arrived at Matadi, so we waited until it had been cleared through customs and we were able to claim it. Rob and Loobie Robertson, former missionary colleagues in the Kasai Region, were now living in Kinshasa, working with USAID and the American Embassy. They graciously hosted our family, making the forced wait thoroughly enjoyable. It seemed best to delay driving upcountry until the situation settled down, so I stored the pickup at Methodist-Presbyterian Hostel (MPH) for children attending The American School of Kinshasa (TASOK). We finally flew on to Kananga.

IMCK 1978

The Good Shepherd Hospital was in operation at Tshikaji. Dr. John Miller was in charge of the pediatric service and community health. Bizza was working with him and the health teams. Dr. Walter Hull was the obstetrician and gynecologist; Dr. Birch Rambo was in charge of the surgical service. Dr. Ralph Shannon lived in Kananga and limited his work to ophthalmology. He came to Tshikaji for surgery and consultations, but most of his work was in the city.

The arrival of Dr. Ed Williams and his wife Kathie was anticipated. Until he came, I was asked to cover the internal medicine service, in addition to my surgery responsibilities. We each had consultation schedules, some days in

Kananga and some days at the Good Shepherd Hospital. Most of us also had teaching responsibilities at the school.

Dr. Nzengu Benoit was a graduate of the IMCK. Following his education as a nurse, he had received his premedical education at Davidson College, then went to Belgium for his medical program. After his residency in Canada, he returned to IMCK, where he became the first Zaïrian doctor to serve in our hospitals. He and his wife Michelle left Tshikaji to return to Belgium in 1978 right after we arrived. We regretted missing the opportunity of working with them.

Katie was asked to replace Jean Zook as director of the nursing school. She agreed to do this if she had a Zaïrian associate who would then replace her. For the first year she directed, working with Associate Director Musumadi. For the next three years their roles were reversed.

Origins of the Central Pharmacy

The government's system for procurement of drugs and medical supplies had become a shambles. This meant that not only were the hospitals poorly stocked, but there was a total breakdown of the system of rural dispensaries. In order to address this need, the Communauté Presbytérienne au Zaïre (CPZ) began to establish church-sponsored rural dispensaries. A few of these had already been opened. Dr. Nzengu had begun a service of procuring drugs for them. A few shelves in the drug storeroom at Tshikaji had been allotted to him for this purpose. I was asked to take over this responsibility. World Health Organization (WHO) had developed a basic list of drugs for developing countries. I used this and modified it to fit our situation. I limited our list to those drugs which I felt could be utilized by nurses working in a more or less unsupervised situation in the rural dispensaries. I had to stretch the criteria a little, so that they could treat some of the tropical diseases that were endemic to our area. The dispensaries were set up with local committees in charge. They were self-supporting and relied on fees to provide for the salary of the nurse and the purchase of their medicines and supplies. The Central Pharmacy was run on a strictly cash basis. The nurse would deposit his funds with the church treasurer. He would then come to the pharmacy with an authorization to purchase a certain amount of drugs. Their drug requests were often unrealistic, both as to the amounts of certain drugs that they could reasonably use, and also the amount that their funds could afford. I tried to fill their requests as reasonably as possible. It soon became obvious that the nurses needed more direction in their use of the drugs available to them. Consequently I did two things. First, I compiled a list of the drugs that we stocked with indications, instructions, and recommended dosage for each. This filled a couple of mimeographed pages which were furnished to each nurse and dispensary. Secondly, about every month or so I would write a one-page discussion of some condition or medication. Subjects were chosen which seemed to be causing difficulty or were not being handled properly. These were available to the nurses when they came to pick up new supplies.

Third Road Trip to Kasai 1978

The situation in Shaba improved and the threat to the Kasai was averted. It became safe again to make the trip from Kinshasa. IMCK had purchased a truck in Kinshasa, so we decided to drive our pickup to Tshikaji at the same time. Lushimba Pierre, the IMCK head mechanic, and another worker went down to drive the truck. Katie, Bizza, Faye and I went to bring our pickup. The new IMCK truck had a bare chassis, as they planned to build a bed on it to carry personnel after getting it to the Kasai. We lashed some boxes on the chassis and put an extra fifty-gallon drum of gasoline in our pickup to refuel both vehicles. In addition to the gasoline, we had a full load of supplies that we purchased in Kinshasa. Lushimba got a head start on us, leaving in the wee hours of the morning. We left after daybreak in the pickup. Since my last trip, a paved road had been built directly from Kinshasa to Kikwit. This avoided the long swing down south near the Angola border, eliminated many ferry crossings, and shortened the route over a hundred miles. The road was several years old. With all the heavy traffic, torrential rains, and little maintenance, it was already developing large potholes in many places. We caught up with Lushimba at Idiofa in the evening. Here we refueled the truck and added to our pickup tanks. In the early hours of the morning, shortly before arriving at the first ferry crossing, we stopped by the side of the road and napped until just before sunrise. We then went to the ferry just before dawn to be among the first to cross. It was dry season, so the rivers were low and ferry crossings slow. There were now only three ferries on the entire route. We reached the last one, a large motor ferry that crossed the Kasai River at Ilebo, late on the second afternoon of our trip. Both vehicles were able to get on the same ferry. Leaving Ilebo in the pickup ahead of the truck, all was well until about halfway to Mweka, where we became stuck in a long deep sand pit. Even with four-wheel drive, we couldn't get out. In a short while Lushimba came along and helped dig us out. We had to back out and detour around the sand pit through a small village that paralleled the road. Even at best, the road was extremely dry and sandy. In the past, the villagers were required to repair the ravages of the rainy season during the following dry season. Since Independence, this was being done less and less, so the roads were becoming worse with each passing season. We finally pulled into Tshikaji around daybreak. We had made the trip in a record breaking forty-eight hours. Lushimba arrived in the big truck a couple hours later. We hate to think how long it might have taken us without his help!

Kananga

Economic conditions in Kananga seemed to be recovering somewhat. A number of the expatriates had returned. They were operating their businesses and stores, usually with Zaïrian partners. The generators for the city were in poor condition, so there were frequent power outages which were often rotated from one section of the city to another. The water system was also in poor condition, and during this period, was completely overhauled, with new water mains and treatment plant installed by an Italian firm of engineers. The roads in the city often developed potholes, which were patched haphazardly from time to time. All the paved streets were in need of resurfacing, but this never happened. It had been increasingly difficult to get feed for the chicken project, and Dr. Zook had discontinued this before our return. The buildings of the chicken project at Tshikaji had been turned over to the Zaïrian staff for conversion to a primary school for their children.

Dam Project

Tshikaji was too far from Kananga to get power from the city. IMCK depended upon a pair of large diesel generators. These were operated alternately, running one while the other was shut down for maintenance. Current was on most of the time, but was sometimes shut off during part of the afternoon. The water supply came from a spring in the valley near the station. The lift was about one hundred feet, and the spring was about a kilometer from the water tower. Since fuel was so expensive and supplies were sometimes limited, ways were sought to develop hydroelectric power. The Lubi lua Mpata, a stream located about two miles from the station, seemed to have an adequate flow of water, even in dry season. There were rapids at a bend in the stream. It was hoped that by placing a dam at the head of the rapids and diverting a portion of the stream through a canal around the bend, enough drop could be obtained to power turbines. Funds were obtained through Medical Benevolence Foundation (MBF), USAID, and the German Protestant Church. The latter agreed to provide the turbines. The Reverend Gene Sharp, a builder who had gone into the ministry, came out to begin the project. He was hampered by a limited work force, working with hand tools only. Most of the dam was earthen, but the center portion with spillways was constructed of concrete. The stream had to be diverted, while this portion was being built.

Occasionally on Saturday afternoons, we enjoyed hiking down to the dam site to see the progress and to bathe in the Lubi. One of the concerns was how far the water would be backed up by the dam. There was no good topographic map or survey available which could tell us. A road and railroad crossed the stream some distance above the dam site. No one knew if the lake would reach that far. Katie and I brought our canoe to Tshikaji to explore upstream. A short way above the dam site, the stream was choked with *tshikakakaka*, which has spikes similar to the leaves of a pineapple plant. It has long woody underwater trunks covered with large thorns. The back of each spike also has a triple row of thorns. One row of thorns points in one direction and the other two point in the opposite direction. In order to go upstream, we had to hack and saw our way through these plants. We used a machete (jungle knife), hedge clippers, and a saw, clearing a few hundred feet farther upstream each trip. We eventually made our way up a couple of kilometers, still far from the road. We did get up beyond small rapids and concluded that there would be no danger to the road from rising water.

The dam soon proved to be a much bigger project than had been anticipated initially. Gene made a good start on the dam, but the project took a lot more funds, time, and the efforts of a number of others to complete. In fact, it was more than ten years before it was finished.

INGASHABA, Air Traffic, and Guests

During the late seventies, an American engineering firm, INGASHABA, was building a power line from Inga Dam on the Zaïre River below Kinshasa to Shaba Province in the southeast, to provide power for the copper mines. Because of the long distance, high voltage direct current was to be used. This required a large inverter to change the direct current to alternating current before it could be reduced to usable voltages by transformers. Since an inverter station for high voltage is extremely costly, the power line passed by Kananga, one of the larger cities in Zaïre, with no provision to furnish it power. In fact, the power line could be seen from Tshikaji and it passed within a hundred yards of our dam site. The INGASHABA engineers were very cordial to the missionaries. They often had movies on Saturday night to which we were invited. They also helped Gene Sharp on a couple occasions with their earthmoving equipment, and used their road scrapers on the Tshikaji airstrip when needed. INGASHABA also had a helicopter which would occasionally land between the hospital buildings bringing injured workers.

The Tshikaji dirt airstrip was in constant use. Several of the missions had small Cessna planes. Almost daily one or another of the planes would fly in, bringing patients to the hospital. One patient I remember vividly was a priest who was at one of the Catholic outposts when he developed appendicitis. The pilot of the plane that picked him up was new to the area. He lost his way and was getting low on fuel, when he landed at Bulungu, a Seventh Day Adventist station, halfway between Luebo and Kananga. They were able to give him a little fuel. He asked about landmarks as he was flying by visual flight rules (VFR). He was told to fly south until he saw the INGASHABA power line and then follow it to Tshikaji. He found the power line, but turned right instead of left, 180 degrees from the correct heading. He eventually ran out of gas and crashed in the forest. The priest had to be carried in a hammock about five kilometers to a road and brought by jeep over terribly rough roads. He had a ruptured appendix with peritonitis, but responded to treatment and eventually recovered. He gave me a beautiful Zaïrian carving of a Madonna and Child in appreciation.

Mission stations were located where there were no hotels, and Tshikaji was no exception. Guests and patients from afar had to be housed and fed. The families on a station usually took turns providing meals on a rotating basis. At Tshikaji there were enough families that each household had a day of the week on which they were responsible for guests. This made it easier to plan ahead in relation to other scheduled duties. We had guests every Wednesday, but never knew in advance how many might be there. In 1980, we understand that there was at least one guest rotating on the station, every day of the year. We never had guests at our table without remembering with gratitude the many times our family had been graciously received and entertained by perfect strangers, African, American, or otherwise. The friends and strangers who came and went at Tshikaji added greatly to the joy of living there.

South Africa

We planned to visit South Africa with Bizza and Faye in the summer of 1979 when Bizza terminated her Peace Corps assignment. Our visas did not arrive in time, so we had to wait until December to go with Faye during her winter break at TASOK.

One purpose of our trip was to obtain some much needed supplies, drugs, and eyeglasses for the hospital. I contacted our supplier in Johannesburg and placed enough orders to fill a large suitcase. Since our first visit to South Africa, there were a few evidences of weakening of segregation. The major hotels admitted blacks, most of whom were from abroad. Elevators in the buildings were no longer segregated and the streets and stores were teeming with blacks. Many store and product names were familiar. Supermarkets, malls, roads, and bustling traffic all reminded us of home.

While in Johannesburg we visited our friend Lee Standish-White. We had first met her when we were evacuated to Salisbury, Rhodesia at the time of Independence. Her husband Dennis was a mining engineer and had since died. Lee taught political science at Witwatersrand University and her son was following his father's footsteps as a mining engineer. They gave us some insight into the political situation of the time.

Lesotho

We rented a car and drove to Lesotho to visit the Dave Millers, then assigned there. As we crossed the border near Maseru, the capital, the border control station was crowded with men. A large number of Lesotho men work in the mines and factories of South Africa. They live in large dormitories and only return home once a year at Christmas vacation time. When we visited the Millers' mission station, one of the highlights for us was attending the church service during which the babies born during the year were baptized. The front and sides of the sanctuary were lined with nearly fifty couples, all with babies about three months old. September must be a busy time for the midwives!

Lesotho is a mountainous country and for a time was under British protection, although never a part of South Africa. Completely encircled and with so much if its work force employed in South Africa, it is economically dependent on that country. We enjoyed very much our visit with the Millers. As we left, Dave took us to see some recently discovered dinosaur footprint fossils.

Road Trip to Cape Town

Leaving Lesotho we followed the road to and along the southern coast. Since it was summer, the coastal villages were crowded with vacationers. We visited the small Bontebok National Park, named for the rare antelope, only found there in its natural state. While there, I heard a birdcall that I recognized as the sound that identifies Radio South Africa. It is unique and sounds something like a squeaking barn door. I followed the sound and discovered that it was a sugarbird, the only bird species peculiar to South Africa.

There were a number of other birds that sparked our interest. Long-tailed widow birds were often seen sitting on fences, resembling our redwing blackbirds, except for those long flowing tails. Many fields were filled with several varieties of migrant storks. We were especially interested in the black-bellied storks which we saw in great numbers. They were familiar to us, as they pass through Zaïre on their migration from northwest Africa. This occurs at the beginning of the rainy season when there is a great deal of lightning. They are often seen circling in large flocks high in the sky. They are called *midinga* and are said to be lightning men (witches) looking for their victims, since this is the time of year when many of the lightning deaths occur.

We drove down to Cape Agulhas, the southernmost tip of Africa. Since we had sailed past the western, eastern, and northern extremes of the continent, we wished to visit the southern extremity. Huge rocks lined the coast. A side road led to a small Moravian community of Cape Coloured. Much of the architecture reminded us of Zeist, Netherlands and Old Salem in North Carolina. We met the pastor and his wife and they showed us the church which was still decorated for Christmas.

The wine country around Paarl was the next stop. Paarl sits at the foot of a rounded granite mountain, resembling a pearl, hence its name. We were there on a Sunday, so the wineries were not open. We lodged at a rural hotel surrounded by lush gardens. It also had a bowling green. A group of vacationers in crisp all-white clothes contrasted with the brilliant green of the grass. They explained the game to us. A small white ball was first rolled onto the green. Then the players bowled black balls, attempting to roll closest to the white ball.

Cape Town

Pretoria and Cape Town share the functions of government, Pretoria being the administrative capital, and Cape Town, the legislative. We visited the old government buildings in this southern capital. We went to the top of

Table Mountain, which dominates the city and overlooks the harbor. A drive down the peninsula and along the coast of False Bay took us by some of the black townships. Parades and dancing were part of the New Year festivities and we attended a contest in which many of the groups competed.

There were two famous luxury trains. The blue train traveled the Cape Town-Johannesburg route, the green train the Johannesburg-Durban route. The blue train was booked a year in advance for the holiday season. Fortunately for us, the green train had been added to the Cape Town-Johannesburg route for one trip that coincided with the time we needed to return to Johannesburg. We enjoyed the overnight sleeping car and meals in the diner.

Departure from Johannesburg

The supplies I had ordered were collected and we prepared to return to Zaïre. The flight was delayed. We learned later that Mobutu had commandeered the plane, to return his mother's body to Zaïre, following her death in Europe. It was Sunday morning. The hotel was in the center of town. Katie attended a church close by while Faye and I went to a park. We sat for a short while to read the morning paper. As we got up to leave, we were suddenly surrounded by three young blacks with knives drawn. While two stood in front of me, the third tried to grab my billfold out of my hip pocket. It was a pickpocket-proof billfold made of suede, so it did not readily slip out. He yanked on the billfold and pocket, ripping my trousers down to the ankle. Immediately the three scattered in three directions. I chased the one who had the billfold. He jumped over the fence and disappeared in a crowd. Faye and I returned to the hotel, meeting Katie on the way. The experience was really traumatic. I called my friend in the medical supply business. He came to the hotel to be with me when the police came to interview me. Luckily, the billfold contained just enough money left to pay our taxi fare. The main loss was my credit card. The police assured me that the blacks would have no way of using the cards and had probably disposed of the billfold in the trash as soon as they had removed the cash. They said there was little that they could do and commented that I should have known better than to go to the park. In any case, my friend agreed to contact American Express on Monday morning to cancel the card. I was very grateful to him, as he helped calm me down and transported us to the airport.

Sky Watch

In Zaïre one becomes keenly aware of the heavens. On the mission stations, there are no street lights and the generators usually shut off by 10 P.M., "Zaïre midnight." In the villages, the only light is from fires and kerosene lamps. The phases of the moon vitally affect the nighttime rhythm of activity. Moonlit nights at full moon are filled with the throbbing sounds of drums, singing, and dancing. In 1957, when Russia launched the first satellite, we saw Sputnik the first night it passed over. The villagers were much concerned and frightened by the unusual sight of a star that traversed the sky, unlike a meteor which flares and is quickly extinguished.

We learned the next day on the Voice of America that it was a satellite. Our location near the equator proved to be ideal for viewing satellites. The best time to see them was in the first hour or two after sunset. As the years went by and the number of satellites increased, it was not unusual to see several pass overhead in a single evening.

Total Eclipse

On February 16, 1980, a total eclipse was visible across central Africa. Many people went to Nairobi to view it. We were fortunate that the path of the eclipse passed directly across Tshikaji. This was a phenomenon that we had always wanted to observe.

We prepared for the eclipse by instructing the students in the proper way to watch the eclipse indirectly, using a pinhole to project the image on a white sheet of paper. The foundation of a house under construction, for which the cement floor had already been poured, made a perfect platform for setting up my camera on a tripod. We had an ideal day for it. When the eclipse neared totality, it seemed as though waves of darkness were approaching us. When totality came, we heard a cry go up from all over the village as darkness fell. I took some pictures and, in doing so, burned out the light meter in my camera. It was an exciting event, one we shall never forget.

In Kananga, Jim Branch, the mission pilot, had been called to go to Mbuji-Mayi to get Marcia Murray, who had broken her arm. He was on his way to the airport on his motorbike when the eclipse became total. An old lady got so frightened and confused that she ran out across the road in front of him. He could not avoid her. Fortunately, she was not killed, but did require hospitalization for several days. Jim was thrown from the bike, knocked out, and fractured his ankle, which required a cast. After applying the cast, I flew with him over to Mbuji-Mayi to get Marcia.

Jim had suffered a tragedy early in 1979. He had been on a flight and was returning home. It was customary to have someone follow the mission planes by radio at all times when they were in the air. Jennie, his wife, performed this function for Jim. She had just signed off with him after he had arrived at Kananga airport. She went out in her yard to talk with Ralph Shannon, when she suddenly had a cardiac arrest. Ralph attempted to revive her with CPR, but to no avail. Jim arrived only a short while later. Her death was a great shock to Jim, the missionary community, and her many Zaïrian friends. Their daughter Jennie, who was at TASOK in Kinshasa, was flown back to Kananga for the funeral. All of us were deeply touched by the evidence of love and the sense of loss that was shared by our Zaïrian colleagues.

Kenya

Before returning to Zaïre in 1978, I had planned to attend a continuing medical education (CME) seminar on primary health care that was scheduled for March 1979 in Nairobi. It coincided with a TASOK school break. The mission plane needed a major overhaul, which was to be done in Nairobi. Jim Branch took Katie, Bizza, Faye, his daughter Jennie, and me with him to Nairobi. I planned to attend the seminar while the plane was being over-hauled. When we arrived in Nairobi, I discovered that the seminar dates had been changed. We could not return until the overhaul was completed. Jim suggested that we go deep-sea fishing, so we took the train to Mombasa. Bizza decided not to go fishing, but to spend a day sightseeing while Katie, Faye, and I went with Jim and Jennie. We didn't have much luck with the fishing, but did enjoy our day in the boat.

On returning to Nairobi, Katie, Bizza, Faye, and I decided to climb Mt. Kenya. Jim and Jennie had other plans. We took a bus to a lodge at the foot of the mountain, where we were able to rent boots, sleeping bags, and arrange for porters and provisions. The next morning, a jeep took us up to the ten thousand foot level to begin the hike. As we entered Mt. Kenya National Park, a young man who had stayed at the lodge and was in the jeep with us learned at the gate that he would not be allowed to go up alone. An Egyptian hiker was waiting at the gate, so the two of them teamed up. The Egyptian was wearing open sandals with socks. The ranger asked him if he had some more shoes, and he said that he did. The trail was rather steep and part of the trail passed through an area described as a vertical bog. It was covered with a thick carpet of moss, full of moisture like a sponge. One had to climb up stepping from clump to clump. As we went up, a rescue squad came running down bearing a stretcher with hooks on each end that fitted over the shoulders of the two men carrying it. A young woman on the stretcher was suffering from altitude sickness. I was amazed at how sure-footed the men were as they bounded down the mountain. It was reassuring to know that such a rescue squad was stationed up there!

At 13,500 feet, we arrived at the shelter in Teleki Valley where we were to spend the night. This fairly level valley looks up toward the peaks of the mountain. The highest peaks are accessible only by Alpine mountain climbing techniques. We were striving toward Point Lenana. The shelter was built of boards, but was quite open. There were bunks at one end for the hikers, and at the other end for the porters, with a fireplace in the center. It was cold at night and in the morning there was ice on a little brook that ran nearby. Our Egyptian friend and his partner stayed in the shelter, too. The Egyptian had only a prayer blanket for cover, so someone lent him another blanket. It turned out that his spare shoes were another pair of sandals! I don't know how he tolerated the cold. We were short on time, but planned to go as far up as we could the next morning, then return to the base. After crossing the valley, the trail went up very steeply across a bank of scree, formed by a landside of loose gravel. It was difficult going, as with every two feet up, we slid down a foot. Faye and I turned back, as the altitude was beginning to make her feel ill. Katie and Bizza continued on for a short way before returning.

Katie and I went back to Kenya at a later date to attend the delayed seminar, which I found very interesting. Following the seminar, we joined the group of physicians from the U.S. on a three-day tour. We visited Taita Hills and Salt Lick Lodges in southeast Kenya. The latter were built on pilings in a semicircle around the floodlit salt lick. We also visited Mt. Kenya Safari Club at the foot of Mt. Kenya, a fabulous hotel with beautifully manicured lawns, occupied by an amazing collection of birds, the most spectacular being the crested cranes. They also had a number of peacocks. These were not native to Africa, but had been imported from India. There is an African peacock, but it is very rare and is limited to the deep forest of Zaïre.

Our appointment was for a three-year term. Katie's mother was in failing health, so we requested permission to return to the States for a month in December 1980 at our own expense. This was granted on condition that we extend for a fourth year. Our house was rented, so Dr. Jim Proffitt graciously invited us to use his house in Millers Cove out in the foothills. We visited all the children, as well as Katie's family in Bethania, North Carolina. We collected supplies for a planned expedition to the Ruwenzori Mountains. These included sleeping bags, dehydrated foods, and camping equipment.

The Ruwenzori Range

We had often wished for an opportunity to hike the Ruwenzori, purportedly the famed "Mountains of the Moon." These mountains lie on the border between Zaïre and Uganda. The highest peak, Mt. Margherita, at 16,798 feet is the third highest mountain in Africa, after Mt. Kenya and Kilimanjaro, but it is not accessible from the Zaïre side. The Reverend Fay Smith, Methodist mission pilot in Kananga, and his wife Sally were also interested in such a venture. We planned to do this during the spring break in 1981, so that our daughter Faye and their son Steve could join us. The approach to the mountains from the Zaïre side is rather remote, though there is a dirt airstrip about three or four kilometers from park headquarters. We had to take all needed equipment and supplies, as nothing was available there for rent.

We flew from Kananga north to Wembo Nyama, a Methodist station in the Otetela tribal region, where we spent the night. The flight from Wembo Nyama to Goma passed over some sparsely inhabited plains where we saw a small herd of elephant and some African buffalo. After refueling we went on to the hotel at Rwindi in the game park. The next day, after a flight across Lake Idi Amin, formerly Lake Edward, we landed at a little village near the base of the mountain. Fay tied the plane down and arranged for a man from the village to guard it. There were plenty of volunteers to help us carry our equipment as we hiked to park headquarters. A park ranger guide was

Katie, Faye, and porter beginning descent in snow, Ruwenzori, Zaïre 1981.

required and porters were available for hire. Their pay included enough for them to supply their own food. They cooked their food, but we were responsible for our own food and its preparation. Because of weight limitations in the plane, Katie had planned our menus with as little cooking as possible. We used a small portable Sterno stove for boiling water and doing the necessary cooking. This was not entirely satisfactory at the higher altitudes, as it does not produce a very hot flame.

The park headquarters were at an altitude of about five thousand feet. Each day's hike ascended three thousand feet or more. We passed first through a village, then by rural huts in lush tropical gardens with banana and plantain groves, pineapple, citrus trees, corn, and manioc. Soon the trail plunged into dense rain forest. Since it had been about three months since the last hikers had used the trail, it was grown up with brush and dense canelike grass. Steve and the porters took turns chopping a path with jungle knives. At one point the trail passed by the body of a dead chimpanzee. I couldn't tell whether or not it had died a natural death. We kept hoping to see some live ones, but were denied the opportunity. Our porters had a young member of their family accompany us for the first day leading a young pig. The first night, they slaughtered the pig and had a feast. There were separate shelters for the hikers and porters. For each of the three nights on the mountain, our shelters had cots though no mattresses or bedding. We had to patch together the springs of several of the cots. Fortunately we had good sleeping bags.

Sally and Fay Smith decided to stay at the first shelter and wait for the rest of us to do the remainder of the climb. About a half-mile above that shelter we came to a rushing stream some twenty feet wide. We had waded one stream the previous day. Faye and I were together. We took off our boots and socks and tossed them across the stream. One of Faye's boots hit a limb and was flipped back into the stream. It was immediately carried swiftly over a cataract and out of sight. This was a disaster, as there were four more days of hiking ahead of us. The porters came along and made a search, but couldn't find the boot. Finally one of them went back to borrow Sally's boots. By the time he returned, another of the porters had gone farther down the stream and finally located the boot floating in circles in a whirlpool. The sock that had been in it was gone, but Faye had a spare pair, so the day was saved.

The path continued along the side of a cliff that dropped off to a stream at its base, and narrowed, until it was only six or eight inches wide with a fifty foot drop to the stream below. At this place on the bank above the path, there was a strong root that we could grasp to help get by the narrow spot. The path was slippery. As I negotiated the passage, my feet slipped out from under me and, only by hanging on for dear life to the root, was I saved from a fall. The path on the cliff ended at a crevice in the rock, where there was a chain attached to help us climb up to the top of the cliff.

The vegetation began to change as we reached higher altitudes. The trees were small evergreens similar to our cedar. The path had washed out into a deep narrow gully that was crisscrossed by the roots of the evergreen trees. Everything was damp and the roots were slick. Climbing over all these roots made this section the most difficult part of the hike. The second shelter was just above the tree line. It was surrounded by thick moss, similar to the moss we had encountered on Mt. Kenya. There was water available at a shallow surface well, which did not look very clean, so we used only water we had brought with us.

The vegetation on the third day's climb took on yet a different character. The most prominent plants were strange looking Alpine types with long thick leaves growing off of thick stalks. The third shelter was at an elevation of almost fifteen thousand feet, on an exposed shoulder about two hundred feet below the highest peak to which one could hike from the Zaïre side. The altitude was beginning to affect Faye, so she stopped there. We had arrived in the late afternoon, but enough time remained for Katie, Steve, and me to climb to the top and return before nightfall. We could look across a narrow valley to the tallest peak, which could only be scaled by Alpine methods. Down in the valley, a glacier fed a small lake

Diamox, a diuretic, had been reported to be useful in the prevention of altitude sickness. Katie, Faye, and I took this before starting the climb. In spite of this, Faye suffered some altitude sickness, but less severe than on Mt. Kenya. Steve also became sick in the evening with what appeared to be a combination of altitude sickness and malaria. We gave him an antimalarial, but there was not much to be done for the altitude sickness until we could go down the mountain in the morning. We awoke to discover that there had been a two-inch snowfall during the night. It was an awesome sight to see the weird Alpine plants all covered with snow there less than one degree from the equator. This was our only experience of snow in Zaïre.

We called the porters, whose camp was located on a knob a couple hundred yards from our shelter, and started down. The goal on the fourth day's hike was to descend from the topmost shelter to the first shelter where the Smiths were waiting for us. The first hour we were trudging through snow. I fell twice, twisting my knee. This slowed me down considerably. The others pushed on ahead, while the park ranger stayed with me, as I hobbled along. It was getting close to sundown and we still had about a mile to go before we reached the cliff. The guide kept urging me on, threatening that if we did not reach the cliff before nightfall, we would have to camp out in the open and wait for daylight. It was getting dark when we reached the cliff. Katie had reached the shelter and sent one of the porters back with a flashlight, but it was almost burned out. This time I managed to negotiate the narrow path without mishap. Everyone collapsed into exhausted sleep that night.

The last day we hoped to get down to the airstrip in time to fly back to Rwindi before sundown. We were all footsore, and I was hampered by my knee. We made it back to the small village, but too late to make it by foot to the airstrip. I inquired about the possibility of hitching a ride to the airstrip, and found a storekeeper who had a truck. As providence would have it, he had trained as a nurse with Dr. Helen Roseveare at Nyankunde. When he learned that I was her friend, he was delighted to furnish us transportation and would accept no payment. The airplane had been well cared for. We quickly loaded it and flew back to Rwindi before nightfall. The real beds and meals at the hotel were never more welcome. We stayed there an additional day, soaking in the swimming pool and recovering from the hike. An elephant that commonly visited the hotel came to drink from the pool. He was quite accustomed to people; in fact, too well accustomed, as he fell prey to poachers about six months later.

Hôtel Pax - Polyclinique

The IMCK's need for expanded clinical facilities was fulfilled when the Hôtel Pax (Peace Hotel) in the center of Kananga became available. It was ideally located for a clinic, in the heart of the commercial district, a two-story structure with plenty of rooms to be converted to consultation space, laboratory, X-ray, pharmacy, and chart room. On the second floor, there was sufficient space to make two small apartments. It also had a restaurant, which was later converted to the dental department. The floor above the restaurant became Ralph Shannon's ophthalmology department. There was also a movie theater which was useful for meetings. The facility was named the Polyclinique, but often continued to be referred to as the Pax. This was a

DOCTOR WITH BIG SHOES—AFRICA

tremendous improvement over the crowded clinic space we had been using in the old residence, which could now be used by IMCK as a residence for Administrator Shamba Manenga. The store nearby was turned into an apartment for Dr. Mulaja Mukendi, one of the Zaïrian physicians. The old garage was turned over to the Central Pharmacy, which had outgrown the shelves assigned to it at Tshikaji. This made the pharmacy much more accessible to the nurses, when they came in from rural areas to purchase drugs. Although retired, Nurse Wenu Isaac, who had worked at Mutoto and later at Tshikaji, agreed to help me on a part-time basis. The church kept adding to the number of rural dispensaries and the pharmacy kept growing. Shortly before we completed our term in 1982, Bill and Sarah Altland arrived. I was then able to turn the pharmacy over to them, both of whom were pharmacists.

Kenya CME Conferences

Beginning in 1978, the Christian Medical Society in cooperation with Louisville Medical School organized continuing medical education (CME) conferences in Africa. These were primarily for the purpose of aiding American missionary physicians working overseas to fulfill their continuing education requirements. These were held in Africa in the even numbered years; in odd years they have had similar conferences in southeast Asia. The first of the African conferences, which none of us attended, was held on the west coast. Starting in 1980, they were at Brackenhurst, a large church conference center not far from Nairobi, Kenya. In order for our physicians to attend, Medical Benevolence Foundation recruited physicians to come to Zaïre as locum tenentes for our hospitals. As we began to get a few Zaïrian physicians, permission was obtained to take some of them to the conference as well. I was privileged to attend the conferences in 1980 and 1982. When I left Zaïre later in 1982, I promised to be available to cover for the next conference in 1984.

Return to the States 1982

After returning to the States in 1979, Bizza entered a nursing program at the University of Tennessee, Knoxville, designed for students who had a B.S., other than in nursing. It led to a Master of Science in Nursing in about three years, depending on the content of the student's earlier studies. In the spring of 1982, Bizza's faculty advisor encouraged her to take a break, so she decided to come back to Tshikaji to visit and accompany us home. We had decided to return to the States by circling the globe once again. This time, we wanted to visit the south Pacific area. Bizza worked out the itinerary and obtained air tickets and reservations. The trip took us to Burundi, Tanzania, Madagascar, Réunion, Mauritius, Australia including Tasmania, Papua New

Guinea, Trobriand Islands, Fiji, New Zealand, Tahiti, Mooréa, Los Angeles, Fort Worth, and home to Maryville, Tennessee. The first three places visited are the only ones that qualify as part of our African experience.

Burundi

One of our IMCK graduates, after working at Tshikaji for a short while, left to visit her sister in Burundi. There she met and married an agricultural agent. When we found that we would have nearly a day in Bujumbura between planes, we wrote to her and gave her our schedule. She met us at the airport and efficiently got us through customs. She and her husband had driven forty miles to come and see us and to show us a little of their country, a small mountainous country off the northeast shore of Lake Tanganyika. They had a coffee plantation and she was working as a nurse. It is always gratifying to find former students functioning successfully in the real world.

Kilimanjaro, Tanzania

Our plane called at Moshi at the base of Kilimanjaro, but we had to go first to Dar es Salaam in order to request a visa for Madagascar, since there was no Madagascar consulate in Kinshasa. After making our requests, we returned to Moshi. Kibo Hotel is on the lower slopes of Mount Kilimanjaro, near park headquarters and the foot of the hikers' trail. Equipment for the trek is available for rent, though we had our boots and sleeping bags. We arranged at the hotel for porters and for food. The porters prepared hot meals at each of the three camps. The climb took three days up and two days down. Each stage going up was easily done in a day, but it was necessary to take this much time in order to become acclimated to the altitude. On the hikers' route, most of the trail was not too steep, but was an unrelenting steady uphill grade. Other more difficult routes could only be attempted by serious mountain climbers. We met a group of primary school children who were hiking up to the first camp. They were not allowed to go higher because of the altitude. The camp sites for the first and second nights had wooden A-frame lodges with bunk beds. The second camp was on the upper edge of the tree line, at the top of a short steep section of the trail.

As we left the second camp, we got a magnificent simultaneous view of both peaks for the first time. The trail skirted Mt. Mawenzi, the lower peak of the mountain, and then crossed a broad saddle to the third lodge, Kibo Hut, on the slope of Mt. Kibo, the highest peak in Africa at 19,340 feet. The saddle was almost devoid of vegetation. The ground was dusty, with a few scattered volcanic rocks. This third camp, at over 15,000 feet, had a stone building which contained several large dormitory rooms, each with multiple beds. We arrived late in the afternoon. After claiming our bed space, Katie and I walked a short distance up the trail toward the peak. It rose at a very steep angle over loose scree. I found that I could not take more than ten steps before stopping to catch my breath, because of the thin air at that altitude. Faye began to feel ill at 15,000 feet. There were rescue squads at each of the camps, and at the highest camp, oxygen was available. We let her breathe some oxygen, which helped a little. Katie decided to go back down with her as soon it was daylight.

It was necessary to begin the climb to the peak in the middle of the night while the scree was frozen, in order to arrive at the top before the ground thawed on the slopes. There was another group going up at the same time. Shortly after midnight, Bizza, our guide, and I joined the other group and their guide, making a party of about twenty. Bizza did not feel well after we had gone a short distance, and returned to the camp. The trail zigzagged back and forth across the frozen gravel. I was much slower than the younger folks in the other group, so our guide stayed with me and the others went on ahead. The last short section was covered by snow. I reached Gilman's Point just as the sun was coming over Mawenzi, the peak to the east. I could look down on the glacier in the crater. Gilman's Point is at 18,651 feet. The other group had gone around the rim of the crater to a higher point and returned to Gilman's just as I arrived. I had to settle for Gilman's, as I not only had to go back to the third camp, but also had to hike down to camp number one that same day. The guide locked arms with me to descend the scree in a straight line taking giant steps. With each step we slid six or eight feet in the loose gravel. It was like coming down in an elevator. Bizza had recovered after resting a bit and came part of the way up to meet us.

A couple from Netherlands had climbed to the third camp along with us. They had been traveling in east Africa for a couple of weeks, but had not been taking antimalarials. The man became very ill with a combination of malaria and altitude sickness. The rescue squad had to evacuate him on a stretcher. On Kilimanjaro, the rescue stretchers had two large wheels, like bicycle wheels, mounted on an axle in the center of the stretcher. A rescuer held each end of the stretcher. The trail was smooth enough that wheeled stretchers were practical.

Katie and Faye met two exhausted hikers when we arrived at the first camp. Hikers arriving back at park headquarters that have made it as far as Gilman's Point were given certificates. At age fifty-nine, I was one of the oldest to have made it that year.

Before going back to Dar es Salaam, we went to Moshi to visit the mission hospital there. I had met some of the doctors at the CME conferences in Kenya. The hospital was well-known for its excellent orthopedic service. It was older than Tshikaji, but the facilities were comparable.

Madagascar

From Dar es Salaam we flew to Antananarivo, capital of Madagascar. This large island lies east of Africa and is separated from it by the

Mozambique Channel. It was formerly quite wooded. At one time buildings, by law, had to be constructed of wood. As a result, much of the island was deforested. As we flew in, we saw bare, orange clay hills. The law was changed to make it illegal to build with wood, and all the newer buildings we saw were built of stone. At one time it was under French control, so French was widely spoken. We understand that the native language, Malagasy, is unrelated to most African languages. Animals on the island are quite different from those on the continent of Africa.

When we visited, Madagascar (Malagasy Republic) was a Communist state. We were given quite a hassle on entry. Our passports and yellow books (immunization records) were taken up, in spite of the fact that they were in order. I had to spend a large part of the next day getting them back. We stayed at the Lutheran Hotel which was in the center of town. Having arrived the weekend of the lantern festival, we found the streets filled with booths selling brightly colored paper lanterns, as well as all sorts of other goods. I'm afraid the unpleasant entry had taken the edge off our visit, so we were happy to continue our trip home via the Pacific.

Bizza returned to University of Tennessee, Knoxville, to continue work toward her M.S. in Nursing, which she completed in December 1983. She and Edward Cameron Britton (Ed) were married at New Providence Presbyterian Church in Maryville on December 28, 1982. Faye entered Maryville High School for her junior and senior years, graduating in 1984.

10. Short African Assignments: 1983-93

On our return to Maryville in 1982, I went back to work in emergency departments at Blount Memorial Hospital and at Knoxville hospitals, but kept in mind my promise to return to Zaïre in 1984 to cover for the CME conference in Kenya. Dr. Kenneth and Nancy McGill were stationed at Bulapé and due for furlough in the summer of 1983. Arrangements were made to cover his furlough by getting several physicians who had previously worked at Bulapé to go for several months in turn. We agreed to go to Bulapé for two months, then move to Tshikaji to cover for the doctors there during the Kenya conference.

Bulapé 1983

By this time, Bulapé hospital had begun using solar power. John Gutzke, an engineer and a solar expert, had made several trips to our mission hospitals in Zaïre, Malawi, and Haiti as a specialist in mission, to install solar systems. He had done the solar installations and was at Bulapé most of the time we were there, then constructing one of the buildings for the nursing school that was being started. Solar panels charged batteries that furnished a couple of lights in each ward. The delivery room and operating room had solar lights. The operating room also had an inverter that provided 110 volt current for suction and cautery machines. The old X-ray unit had worn out. A new U.S. Army portable unit had just been sent to Bulapé, but was not yet installed. It was similar to the unit that I had used in China, so John and I had no difficulty assembling it and putting it into operation, using the inverter power.

We shared the McGills' house with John, Dr. Muambi Kabongo, and visiting doctors. The house was also wired for solar power. It had an inverter that powered a small microwave oven, the use of which was a new

248

Group of Bakete, Bulapé 1984.

experience for us in Zaïre. There was also a TV with a VHF player, although there were no TV stations close enough to tune in. We used a wood stove in the kitchen to cook breakfast and the main meal at noon. A small butane hot plate or the microwave oven served for heating the evening meal. The refrigerator operated on kerosene, like the ones we had used for years. We had never before "had it so good" in the bush!

There were several Peace Corps volunteers in the Bulapé area, whom we saw from time to time. A couple of them once took us to a restaurant on the Mweka road, which was housed in a semipermanent building owned and operated by a Zaïrian who specialized in dishes prepared from game. He served us python, antelope, and bustard, a large turkey-sized bird. A truly novel meal, and also tasty!

Tshikaji 1984

On our return to Zaïre we found that conditions had remained fairly stable. A television tower had been built within sight of Tshikaji and there were a few hours of programming each evening. The hospital even had a TV set up so that the ambulatory patients could watch. INGASHABA had completed the power line and their camp was closed down, except for a few maintenance people. Bill Swanson, an engineer, was at IMCK, continuing construction of the dam. He had enlarged the work crew, revised the canal, and gotten some equipment from INGASHABA which speeded up work on the project. Even then, it would be a couple more years before the project was completed.

Several other doctors also came to cover for the CME conference. One of them was a thoracic and vascular surgeon whom I assisted with a couple chest cases. He also came prepared to perform an operation for a large abdominal aneurysm on a gentleman from Mbuji-Mayi, with which I was privileged to assist. If not a first for Zaïre, it was certainly a rarity .

Malawi 1989-90

On returning to the States in 1984, we received an invitation to go back to China. We finally arrived there, as teachers with Amity Foundation under the auspices of the Presbyterian Church (U.S.A.), in 1986. Three years later we returned to the States from Beijing following the Tiananmen demonstrations and massacre. Soon thereafter, the Global Mission Unit asked us to go to Malawi to work with Dr. Kenneth McGill at Embangweni. We gladly agreed to go for five months until the spring of 1990, when Katie was committed to return to China as a nursing consultant for Project HOPE.

Malawi, formerly Nyasaland, is a narrow country along the west bank of Lake Malawi, which lies in the Great Rift Valley of Africa. Most of the country, except for the extreme southern portion along the Zambezi River, lies at a fairly high altitude. It is divided into three regions, northern, central, and southern. Embangweni is located near the southern border of the northern region and is close to the border of Zambia. The mission was established by the Church of Scotland and continues to have fraternal workers from Scotland, as well as a few from the Presbyterian Church (U.S.A.).

Dress in Malawi tended to be more formal than in Zaïre. The men wore coats and ties, which often seemed inappropriate for the climate. Women were forbidden by law to wear pants. We had not been informed of this, and Katie traveled on the plane in a pantsuit. On arrival at the airport in Lilongwe, one of the officials politely informed her that women were not permitted to wear pants. He directed her to the women's room where she could change to a skirt.

Like many countries in Africa, Malawi was rife with ethnic tensions. The party in power was primarily from the Chewa tribe. This was the tribe of Dr. Hastings Banda, the first and, until then, the only President of Malawi. He had graduated from Meharry Medical College in Nashville, Tennessee and was a somewhat benevolent dictator, then in his eighties. He had systematically suppressed anyone who showed promise of replacing him, setting the stage for an eventual power struggle.

Over centuries, peoples had migrated into the area from north, east, and south, providing the basis for ethnic rivalries and tension. Around Embangweni, the Tumbuka predominated. They had originally migrated into the area several centuries earlier, from the same region of Shaba that had given rise to the Luba groups with whom we had worked in Zaïre. Since Malawi had been an English colony, educated people all spoke English. At Embangweni, however, Chitumbuka, the language of the Tumbuka, was also in general use. We could get along in the medical work with English, but felt

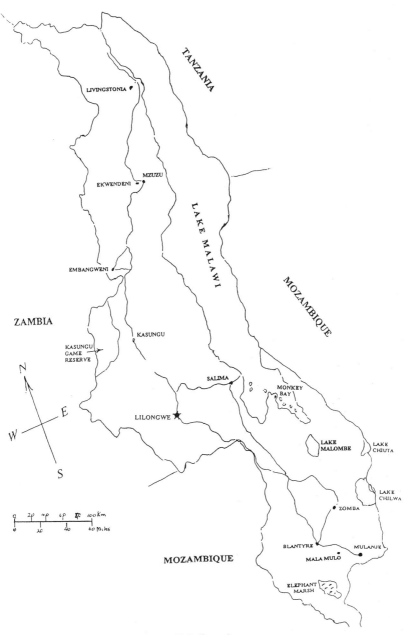

TANZANIA

LIVINGSTONIA

MZUZU
EKWENDENI

LAKE MALAWI

MOZAMBIQUE

EMBANGWENI

ZAMBIA

KASUNGU

KASUNGU
GAME
RESERVE

N

W E

S

SALIMA

MONKEY
BAY

LILONGWE

LAKE
MALOMBE

LAKE
CHIUTA

LAKE
CHILWA

0 20 40 60 80 100 Km
0   20   40   60 Miles

ZOMBA

MOZAMBIQUE

BLANTYRE
MALA MULO

MULANJE

ELEPHANT
MARSH

Malawi

Author studying language with Mr. Jere, Embangweni, Malawi 1989.

the need for some knowledge of the local language. We studied Chitumbuka with Mr. Francis Jere, one of the primary school teachers, and found many similarities to Tshiluba. One main difference was that Chitumbuka had lost the tonal characteristic which is still very important in Tshiluba.

Whereas the Tumbuka tribe was predominant in the area, the chiefs were Ngoni, a branch of the Zulu tribe, who had migrated up from South Africa and conquered the Tumbuka many years earlier. Through time, there had been considerable admixture of the tribes through intermarriage. The Ngoni demonstrated active leadership not only as chiefs, but also as teachers, and in agricultural development. The local culture was being vitally affected, as chiefs and others visited abroad and imported new knowledge and "new ways," mainly from England and the United States.

While at Embangweni we lived with Ken and Nancy McGill. John Gutzke was also there with us for a couple of months. Power lines had not yet reached Embangweni, so John had installed solar power at the hospital. Batteries furnished lights to the delivery and operating rooms and to the wards at night, but the X-ray was powered by a standby gasoline generator. John was also installing solar power in the McGills' house. During our stay, an engineer from the Netherlands came to install an oxygen concentrator in the operating room. He had developed the machines and was installing them in a number of hospitals in Malawi. This was the first one to be operated on solar power by means of a battery and an inverter.

Embangweni is located about fifteen degrees south of the equator. The dry season lasts about seven months, with most of the rain falling between November and March. The dry season here is at least twice as long as in south central Zaïre, which is nearer the equator; consequently, the shortage of water is a serious problem. A small creek in the valley below the station had been dammed and was the source of water, which was pumped up with power from the station diesel generator. The demands of school, hospital, and staff houses exceeded the system's capacity, however, so there was a constant hassle about the water.

*Author with Dr. Ken McGill,
Embangweni, Malawi 1989.*

Embangweni Hospital consisted of several buildings, including a dispensary, maternity, men's ward, women's ward, pediatrics, and separate buildings for the surgical suite and for X-ray. All the wards were constantly filled. Pediatrics was especially crowded and has been expanded since we were there. The Malawian staff consisted of three or four medical assistants (men), a number of nurses (women), several midwives (women), and a number of orderlies (men). Since nurses were in short supply, the wards were manned by the orderlies at night. They also gave a lot of the injections. We were concerned about the possible transmission of AIDS, since needles and syringes were reused, so Katie and the other nurses spent a lot of time working with the staff, especially the orderlies, trying to improve the sterilization routines.

AIDS was an enormous problem, as in all of east Africa. We did not test all patients, only those who were suspected of having AIDS. Potential blood donors were always tested. About 20 percent of those tested were HIV positive. In some areas of the country, the rate was reputed to be 50 percent positive. About 20 percent of our inpatients were suffering from AIDS, or AIDS related illnesses. Most of the deaths that occurred in the hospital during our stay were AIDS related. In the pediatric wards, malnutrition was our biggest problem, and many of those who failed to thrive and to respond to treatment proved to have AIDS. Tuberculosis was also quite prevalent and was frequently associated with AIDS, as was shingles (herpes zoster). One of the medical assistants was assigned full time to education for AIDS prevention. He gave talks at schools and counseled with patients and their families. Government policy forbade informing a patient's family he was HIV positive without his consent. At Embangweni Hospital the laboratory used a code to indicate positive tests. Polygamy was prevalent among the more affluent and contributed greatly to the spread of AIDS. Cases came to our attention in which a man had transmitted the disease to several spouses and subsequently to their children.

In Malawi, one main highway, most of which was paved, ran north and south, the length of the country. The section between Embangweni and Mzuzu was under construction when we arrived and was completed before we left. Mzuzu, north of Embangweni, is the site of government offices and the

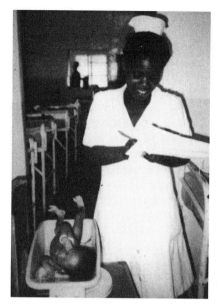

Embangweni Hospital chaplain with patient, 1989.

Embangweni Hospital nurse weighing newborn, 1989.

headquarters of the Presbyterian Church; the Presbyterian Hospital at Ekwendeni is nearby. Since the soil was thick red clay for the most part, our first few trips to Mzuzu required about three hours with four-wheel drive. After the road was completed, it only took about an hour and a half to make the trip.

While in Malawi, we happened upon the memoirs of Sir Martin Roseveare, the father of Dr. Helen Roseveare, mentioned heretofore. Nancy McGill told us that his widow, Lady Margaret, was living near Mzuzu. We contacted her and she invited us to visit. Sir Martin had come to Nyasaland in 1957, before it became Malawi. He had been named principal of the newly built teachers' college at Soche Hill, which eventually became part of the University of Malawi. He contributed greatly to the development of the education system and was held in high esteem by the Malawians. He died a few years before our visit. Lady Margaret lived in the home he had built just east of Mzuzu, situated on the edge of the plateau, overlooking Lake Malawi. We were interested to find that the climate varied within just a few kilometers. On the east side of Mzuzu, where the land descends steeply to the lake, there was much rain and the vegetation was lush. On the west side around Ekwendeni, it was very dry with little rain and a long dry season. Lady Margaret, a delightful hostess, found pleasure in sharing pictures and items of interest with us. Her electricity was supplied by a small private hydroelectric plant installed on a small stream that rushes down to the lake. Dr. Helen Roseveare, now retired, had visited her recently, before returning to visit Zaïre.

John and Ishbel Dorward, doctors from Scotland, worked at Ekwendeni. They kindly invited us to go with them on one of their regular dispensary visits. We drove north in their four-wheel drive Land Rover to Livingstonia. When the first missionaries came from Scotland, they established a mission station at

Monkey Bay on the southern end of Lake Malawi, then called Lake Nyasa. To get away from European influence, they later moved to the north. Livingstonia was established on a high plateau overlooking the lake, placed at a high elevation to avoid the mosquito-infested lowlands. They were told it was impossible to build a road up the steep escarpment. The missionaries accomplished it anyway, by means of eleven sharp switchbacks. Going up, we took a back road which was somewhat less steep, but we did drive down it on leaving.

The population around Livingstonia has declined, as the people have followed a widespread trend of moving into urban centers and out of rural areas. The church offices, formerly located there, have been moved to the more central location of Mzuzu. There is a rather large hospital, with more adequate buildings than at Embangweni. Due to the relative inaccessibility of Livingstonia and the lack of a resident doctor, however, there were very few patients. The medical work was being carried on by two medical assistants with direction and periodic visits from the Ekwendeni doctors. The old doctor's residence stood empty, but was being restored. The local personnel were pleading for a resident physician. There were very few Malawian physicians practicing in the country; nearly all the hospitals were staffed with expatriate doctors. Since there was no medical school in Malawi, the few Malawian physicians had attended medical schools in Zimbabwe, South Africa, or elsewhere. Nearly all were practicing in other countries. One Malawian physician from Livingstonia, who owned a house within sight of the hospital, was practicing in Lesotho.

At Livingstonia, we saw a number of buildings of historical interest. The stately church has a beautiful stained glass window. The post office in the center of the station is an interesting structure with a clock tower, the circle in front of which contains a tablet to commemorate the founding of the mission. Practically all the buildings in Malawi were built of brick or concrete. One of the early missionaries imported masons who quarried and built a house of stone. It was said to be the only stone house in the country at that time. The "stone house" at Livingstonia had been declared a National Treasure. Part of it is now a museum and part is used as a guest house, in which we stayed. On the return trip, we descended the winding road to the lake and stopped at two rural dispensaries, both on the shore of Lake Malawi. Each of these consisted of a maternity and dispensary with a nurse and a midwife in residence. We picnicked on the beach at one of them.

At Embangweni, the laboratory technicians had limited preparation, but there was a man in training in the school for technicians at the Seventh Day Adventist Hospital at Mala Mulo. The director of the school, who was from eastern Europe, had some reconditioned laboratory equipment which he made available at very reasonable cost to hospitals where his graduates were assigned. During our stay, Ken McGill asked us to go there and get the equipment that was available for Embangweni.

We drove south and spent a night near Salima on the shore of Lake Malawi, at Livingstone Motel. Our cabin was a *rondavel* on the beach, from which we looked across an arm of the lake to a peninsula where the first mission station had been located on the shore of Monkey Bay. As we headed south, we drove through the old capital at Zomba and then on to Blantyre, where Otis and Wilma Rowe were headquartered. Otis, a Presbyterian missionary, is a hospital maintenance engineer. He helped to install and repair equipment for all the mission hospitals and dispensaries in Malawi, not just the Presbyterian hospitals. He had in hand equipment that he had repaired for the Mala Mulo Hospital and for the Mulanje Presbyterian Hospital located on the eastern border of the country, at the base of the Mulanje Massif. He invited us to join him for these hospital visits.

The Seventh Day Adventist Hospital was quite large, with a large nursing school in addition to the laboratory school. They had a fairly new school building that was built with USAID funds, and a large, well-designed premature nursery, with several oxygen concentrators. They also had several of these units in the operating room and intensive care. This was one of the areas of the country with a high incidence of positive HIV blood tests. We met the young man who was soon to complete his training and obtained the equipment for Embangweni.

The drive to Mulanje was through rolling country, with rich farmlands. The mountain presents an impressive wall rising with almost vertical cliffs for a thousand feet. A couple of months after our visit, there was a terrible landslide from these cliffs that resulted in a number of dead and wounded. The southern part of the southern region gets a lot more rain than much of the north, and is much lower in elevation, as it is part of the Zambezi valley. The lush tropical vegetation was much the same as that we were accustomed to seeing in Zaïre. Rice is the principal crop and a major staple of the diet in Malawi.

The southern region of Malawi is surrounded by Mozambique on three sides. Returning to Embangweni, the highway ran along the western border, and in some places, the road was right on the border. On the right side of the road was Malawi, and on the left was Mozambique. All the buildings on the left had been destroyed, as far as the eye could see. We were told that many of the refugees living in the camps would slip back across the border during the day to tend their fields, returning at night to Malawi. We saw the result of the ethnic fighting in Mozambique, as Malawi was swamped with refugees. We passed a number of large refugee camps and saw long lines receiving relief supplies.

There were three other missionaries at Embangweni, teaching in the high school. Ann Dawson, the school director, was from Scotland; Mark Gray was from Belfast, Ireland; and Betsy Cameron was a Volunteer in Mission with the Presbyterian Church (U.S.A.). On one occasion, the school had a soccer game with a Catholic school at Kasungu about sixty miles away. They sent a truck loaded with the team and a number of the students. Betsy went with them, riding in the cab. As they passed through a village north of Kasungu, a little boy darted across the road in front of the truck. The driver tried unsuccessfully to avoid the child. The boy was killed and the truck turned over across a ditch. The students were dumped out, but the front and back ends of the truck were held by the sides of the ditch so that no one was crushed. Betsy had hot crankcase oil poured all over her, suffered some second degree burns, and was as black as any of her students. Several of the students suffered broken bones. Three of them had to be hospitalized for a couple of weeks at the Catholic Hospital before they could return to Embangweni. It was a tragedy that the child died, but a miracle that no one else was killed.

There is no longer a mission organization in Malawi. As is the case in most countries, all the expatriate missionaries are there as fraternal workers at the invitation of and under the direction of the church. As far as the hospital was concerned, this made for a somewhat cumbersome organization. The hiring and firing of hospital personnel and other decisions all had to be approved by the station church committee, requiring frequent lengthy meetings.

The church at Embangweni was a huge brick cathedral-like building. There were only a few benches with backs, occupied mostly by elders and women leaders. Most of the congregation sat on backless benches or on the floor. Services were two to three hours long. We especially enjoyed the music. One of the early missionaries had encouraged the writing of hymns by sponsoring an annual hymn writing contest. Most of the hymns in use were written by Malawian Christians and were sung to local tunes.

Much attention was given to carrying on traditions that had been established by the early missionaries. The Communion service was preceded by a session meeting, which admitted new members, but also carried on routine business. The meeting was held in the church, so the congregation had to wait outside for the meeting to be completed. The church was usually packed for the Communion service. The Communion elements were brought in on the heads of women all dressed in white. The last women had large buckets containing the wine. They used common cups which were replenished as needed from the buckets. At the conclusion of the Communion service, the elements were again carried out of the sanctuary.

After one of the long services, I was walking back to our house which was a half-mile from the church. About halfway, I suddenly had an episode of weakness and numbness of my legs and had to sit down until they recovered. This happened again on a couple of occasions.

Ken and Nancy McGill both developed severe upper respiratory infections in November 1989. Ken could not seem to overcome it. Finally in January, they returned to the States to try to get the problem diagnosed and cured. I was left in charge of the hospital. Dr. Stanley N. Jones arrived from Alaska in February to give some relief for a month. We were scheduled to return to China the first of March for Katie to participate in nursing seminars sponsored by Project HOPE and China Nurses' Association. The McGills returned just a week after we left.

1990 in the States

After two months in China, we returned to the States in May. On arrival there, we became occupied with plans for Faye's wedding, which was set for

June 23. She was to marry William Henry Maynard III (Bill), who was then attending University of Tennessee College of Medicine, Memphis. The wedding was to be in Nashville at Second Presbyterian Church, where Katie and I, as well as our older daughter Katrina and William Rucker Manier IV (Bill) had been married. Faye was to wear the same wedding dress that Katie and her two older sisters had worn.

Despite limited mobility relative to spinal stenosis, the result of arthritis and scarring from my previous laminectomy, I managed to stay on my feet through the ceremony and reception. As mentioned earlier, a second laminectomy the following September gave me miraculous relief.

APCM - CPZ Centennial
1891-1991

On April 18, 1891, the pioneer Presbyterian missionaries, William Sheppard and Samuel Lapsley arrived at Luebo and founded the American Presbyterian Congo Mission (APCM). The successor to the mission was the Communauté Presbytérienne au Zaïre (CPZ). When we learned that a group trip was being organized to attend the Centennial ceremonies, we decided to join them. The tour was to last two weeks, spending a day in Brussels, a couple of days in Kinshasa, and about a week in the Kasai. We felt that this was all too short a time, so arranged to travel with the group to Zaïre, then to stay on for several weeks after the ceremonies to work at Bulapé.

Virginia Pruitt was the tour leader. There were several members of the missionary family in the group, including retired missionaries, Mary Crawford and Anne B. Cleveland Crane, and children of missionaries, Anne Louise Crane, daughter of Hank and Anne Crane; Edna Vass Stucky, daughter of Lach and Winnie Vass; Russell Smith and Ruth Smith Gilmer, children of Plumer and Katie Smith. In Brussels we were met by the Reverend Alastair Scougal, formerly a missionary to Zaïre and for many years minister to the international students in Belgium. His office was at the Royal Protestant Chapel. He had arranged a supper for us there with some of the African students. We were pleased to see Professor Mubedi Ilunga, a former science teacher at the IMCK, who had earned his Ph.D. and was teaching in Belgium. He was planning to return to Zaïre to teach at the University in Kinshasa. Mr. Mukuakua Bertin, one of our former nursing students, studying community health at Liège, also greeted us enthusiastically. We had not been in the Royal Protestant Chapel before. Belgium is predominantly a Catholic country, but Leopold I was a Protestant. When he accepted the crown, a former Catholic chapel, built by the Duke of Lorraine, was converted to a Protestant chapel. Leopold I remained a Protestant, but his children and the kings who followed him on the throne were brought up Catholic. The chapel is located near the palace and is quite beautiful, with a balcony that circles it. Columns still have the Duke's symbols on the capitals. There is an impressive lovely fresco behind the pulpit.

The group stayed at a Catholic hostel in the Uccle section of Brussels. We had a few hours free in the afternoon and went for a walk. A furniture refinishing shop now occupied Mme. DeGueldre's once beautiful home where we lived in 1952. The school next door, which the boys had attended, was unchanged. Hospital Edith Cavell, where Katrina was born, had burned and been rebuilt. The surrounding streets were familiar and brought back fond memories.

In Kinshasa most of the group were housed at the Methodist-Presbyterian Hostel. Mr. Kalonji Isaac, son of Pastor Kabongo of the Luebo area, had several members staying with him. Mr. Kalonji had served in the parliament for many years. He arranged for us to stay with his good friend, the retired Ambassador Tshimbalanga, who had been ambassador to Canada, Switzerland, Burundi, and then for ten years to the Vatican. The Ambassador's wife, now deceased, was originally from Luebo. Two of his grown daughters lived with him in their home not far from the university. The Ambassador graciously gave a dinner for our entire group during our stay in Kinshasa, as did Mr. Kalonji.

We met a number of church leaders of the Communauté Presbytérienne de Kinshasa (CPK). The CPK was established as an offshoot of the CPZ. The American Baptist Foreign Mission Society (ABFMS) had been responsible for Kinshasa, but the city had grown so large that they requested the Presbyterians to share in the ministry. Many of the pastors and members of the CPK are from the Kasai, so they, too, were celebrating the Centennial. We attended a banquet for over four hundred persons in a huge warehouse converted to a restaurant. We saw a number of old friends from the Kasai Region.

One interesting occasion was a meeting with the alumni of Katubue, our first high school in the Kasai. We were greatly impressed when each one introduced himself and told what he was doing. They were all in positions of leadership and responsibility in business or government. With such potential for leadership, we felt hope for the future, if the country rids itself of the oppressive yoke of dictatorship.

On our first Sunday in Zaïre, our group was divided among the different churches in Kinshasa. We attended the Limbe Church which had two services. The first was in French, followed by one in Lingala. We ate dinner with the church leaders after the service, during which time the conversation was mostly in Tshiluba. Sunday afternoon, there was a concert in the Théatre du Zoo at which several of the church choirs each sang two numbers.

An opportunity was also given to see some of the activities of the CPK. We visited a church that had been built with the aid of the Project for Evangelism and Church Growth in Africa (PECGA). The tour included one of the CPK dispensaries, a community center, and a community development cooperative. One of the major functions of the latter was to help in the construction of housing, with equipment for building available on loan. Cement blocks were being produced and there was a carpentry shop where furniture was being built. Kinshasa was tremendously overcrowded, with about a fourth of the population of Zaïre concentrated there. Large areas of the city appeared to be glorified slums, so the need for housing was acute as more people continued to pour into the city.

Charles and Florence Sthreshley were in Kinshasa. Flo had been in our appointees class in 1946, expecting to go to Brazil. Her assignment was later changed to Africa. They were retired, but had returned for a short assignment to build one of the dispensaries in a newly developed residential area out beyond the airport. We went there for the dedication of the dispensary. Their son, Larry, was then working with the CPK in the public health project.

On May 7, we flew from Kinshasa to Kananga, where we were greeted by Dr. Tshihamba Remy and other church officials. The following day, Virginia Thornton, Katie, and I flew to Bulapé and Luebo in the church Cessna with Pilot Pierre Mukengeshai. We wanted to make arrangements to work for a short while following the celebration and also to have an opportunity to visit Luebo. Virginia, a church leader from Texas, was especially interested in Bulapé and wanted to see the equatorial forest. During the few hours at Bulapé, Katie and I spent most of our time with Dr. Tshibangu Mangala.

We arrived at Luebo just before a rainstorm. A celebration had been held at Luebo on April 18, the anniversary of the arrival of Lapsley and Sheppard. The station had been cleaned up for this and was still in good order. The clock in the church tower was running and on time; the cemetery was nicely groomed; and the grass was cut. We met with church leaders in the house that had been occupied by the Robertsons (Number 7 on the map), where Dr. Kasonga Mbuyi was now living. They sent word to our old friend Jean Joseph and he came to visit. He was quite thin but in good spirits. This was to be our last visit with him, as he died in 1993. His grandson attended Maryville College for a couple of years, so we had news of him up until his death.

At Luebo we visited the hospital, where most of the staff members were former colleagues. The old section of the hospital building was in poor repair, which is not surprising, when one remembers that it had been condemned when we were there thirty-five years earlier. I was pleased to see that the building I had designed was being adapted to changed conditions. It was now being used as the outpatient clinic. The folding partition was kept open and the large lobby and classroom served as the waiting room. The laboratory and pharmacy were both convenient to the outpatients. The former dispensary had been converted to a maternity. The rooms in the old maternity wing were being used for medical and surgical cases. The roof of much of the older section leaked so badly that they were unable to use a couple of the wards. The outpatient and maternity services seemed to be the most active, as there were few other inpatients. Dr. Kasonga was also doing some work across the river at the government hospital.

From Luebo we flew back to Kananga. Before leaving there the group visited the Faculté de Théologie Réformée au Kasai (FTRK) at Ndesha, on the western edge of the city. The Rev. Dr. Wakuteka Hanyi-Muanza was Rector, and the Rev. Dr. Mulumba Musumbu-Mukundi, General Secretary of the CPZ, was among the professors. This school prepares ministers at the university level, and students come from all over Zaïre, not just the Kasai.

A tour of the IMCK revealed a number of changes. The dam had been completed. Two large turbines were in place and much of the electrical system had been renovated, so there was twenty-four hour current, supplied by the hydroelectric installation. Drs. Dick and Judith Brown were at Tshikaji and had developed a continuing education program. A center for this had been built and dormitories for those attending the conferences were under construction. The number of girls in the nursing program had increased, making it necessary to build a second girls' dormitory. Both nursing school and laboratory school were under the direction of Zaïrians, Professors Mpoi Lumpungu and Lufu Luabo. The director of nursing at Good Shepherd Hospital was Mputu Tshiondo. All are friends and former students.

The main Centennial celebration was scheduled for May 14 at Lake Munkamba. At first glance, it might seem strange to place it in a rural location, especially with transportation such a problem and the cost of fuel very high. The lake, however, is on the main road between Kananga and Mbuji-Mayi, the largest centers of West Kasai and East Kasai. It is about halfway between the two cities and on the border between the two regions. We went out to Munkamba a couple of days early to get our lake house cleaned up so we could accommodate some guests. The house had not been used for several months, so it required the usual raking out of a few termite hills, sweeping up of thousands of termite wings, and the removal of some dead bats. Other than that, it was in good shape. The celebration was a huge success. The weather was beautiful, and the ceremonies took place on the lawn at the edge of the lake. As director of the Global Mission Unit (GMU), the Rev. Dr. Clifton Kirkpatrick represented the Presbyterian Church (U.S.A.). The church leaders of East and West Kasai, the Governor of West Kasai, and many of the missionaries were there in addition to a crowd of over four hundred. A number of choirs from both Kasais, and even one from Kinshasa, sang. It was a joyous occasion, and much appreciation was expressed for the work of Presbyterian missionaries in Zaïre.

At the close of the celebration, priority for transportation was given to the foreign participants and to the church leaders who needed to return to their work. Consequently we had a couple of days to enjoy the lake. Pierre came to get us in the plane on Friday. The church Cessna had conventional landing gear; that is, it was a tail dragger with no nose wheel. As he was landing, some goats dashed across the runway in front of the plane. Pierre was alone in the plane with no weight in the rear seats or baggage compartment. He applied the brakes to avoid hitting the goats, and the plane nosed over. Fortunately this occurred after the plane had partially slowed in the landing roll. The propeller was bent as it struck the dirt strip but there seemed to be no other damage. Pierre was able to contact a newly arrived Catholic pilot in Kananga, who brought out a spare propeller. Within five hours the two of them installed the new prop and flew a couple of test flights. Pierre then flew us back to Tshikaji.

We had hoped to make a visit to Lubondai before going to Bulapé. The Lubondai Land Rover was in the church maintenance garage. It was found that it could not be repaired in time, so the trip was canceled. Word was then received from Mbuji-Mayi that Angie Anderson was seriously ill there. Angie had been a missionary in Zaïre, serving at Mbuji-Mayi and teaching at the theological school at Ndesha. More recently she had been assigned to Yaoundé, Cameroon. She came back to Zaïre for a visit and had gone to Mbuji-Mayi after visiting in Kinshasa. She was staying with the Metzels, who found her unconscious when they returned from a meeting.

Dr. Barbara Nagy and I flew over with David Law, whose plane could accommodate a stretcher. Angie was hospitalized at the MIBA (diamond mine) Hospital where Dr. Ngoyi Kadima, who had formerly been on the IMCK staff, was medical director.

Angie was in a deep coma, apparently from some intracranial lesion. We decided to transport her to Tshikaji. It soon became apparent that there was no reason to try to evacuate her to the States. Her condition deteriorated rapidly. Katie, Jeanne Steele, and Patricia Marshall, a nurse of the Plymouth Brethren Mission, who was then at Tshikaji, took turns caring for her around the clock until her death on June 1, 1991. The funeral service was held on Sunday, June 2, at Ndesha. The church was packed and there were many eulogies and individual witnesses to Angie's influence on their lives. She was buried at Ndesha, and the primary school there was renamed the Angie Anderson Primary School in her memory. It serves the children of students at the theological school and also the nearby village.

We finally flew back to Bulapé to spend a couple of weeks. Since our last stay at Bulapé in 1984, a new operating suite building had been constructed beside the administration building. It was dedicated to the memory of Dr. McGill, and contained two operating rooms. The larger one accommodated two operating tables, a situation not too uncommon in hospitals in developing countries. The second operating room was used mainly for orthopedic and minor surgery. There was also an X-ray room and dark room, with a small room for the batteries and inverter that supplied both DC and AC current to the operating rooms, X-ray, and administration building. There were several solar panels on the roof. I was kept busy during most of my stay with surgical cases.

A new pediatric building was filled with patients. It contained two large twenty-bed wards and several small isolation rooms. The nursing school was in operation and students stood oral examinations while we were there. The solar lighting system for the wards was performing well. We stayed in the house where the McGills had lived. It was serving as a guest house, beautifully maintained by Dr. Tshibangu's wife, Thérèse.

We spent a few days with Marge Hoffeld in Kinshasa on the way home. We had an opportunity to attend the International Church on Sunday and saw a number of friends, both missionary and Zaïrian. We arrived back in the States in late June, in good time for a reunion of our family at Seagrove Beach, Florida. By then, we had already accepted an invitation to go to Cameroon in August, to relieve Dr. Daniel Etya'alé.

Cameroon

To get to Cameroon, we first flew Lufthansa to Frankfurt, Germany. There was a lot of construction going on at the airport. To board the flight to Douala, Cameroon, we took a bus from the terminal to the plane, which was parked on an apron. All the seats were taken, so we walked to the rear of the bus. An African gentleman rose to offer Katie his seat. She was astonished to recognize him as Manenga André, an old friend from Bulapé, who had since become second vice-president of the parliament of Zaïre. He did not recognize her until she spoke and he saw me coming down the aisle. When we were in Zaïre for the Centennial, he had been out of the country on a diplomatic mission to Japan. He was now on the way back to Kinshasa. We had an animated conversation with him, passing news of mutual missionary friends.

International flights were not yet landing at Yaoundé, the capital, as the airport there was being enlarged. We had to transfer to Air Cameroon in Douala. Mr. Elogo Metomo, the Director of Medical Services for the Presbyterian Church in Cameroon, and Mr. Ela Aboo, the head nurse of Enongal Hospital, met us. They put us in a hotel for the night and Mr. Ela drove us south to Ebolowa the next morning.

Cameroon was a German colony which was split up after World War I under League of Nations mandates. It was larger under the Germans, as portions remain in Equatorial Guinea, Congo, Central African Republic, and Nigeria. The northern portion of what is now Cameroon was part of the English mandate that was administered as part of Nigeria. The central and southern portions were administered by the French. Since Cameroon was partly under the English and partly under the French, both languages are official. We were asked to go to Cameroon as they needed a French-speaking surgeon to relieve Dr. Etya'alé, so that he could take a much needed vacation with his family. Enongal Hospital was located just outside the town of Ebolowa, about three degrees north of the equator, on the edge of the equatorial forest which reaches across the Congo basin to Bulapé, about three degrees south of the equator. The climate was very similar, though the seasons were reversed.

The mission station was located on a beautiful knoll. We lived in a guest house next door to Dr. Etya'alé's home. Both yards were filled with flowering plants and trees. There were a number of rose bushes in front of our house, which allowed us to keep a rose on the table during most of our stay. There was almost a three hundred sixty degree view of the surrounding countryside, with hills in the distance. Birds were abundant and most were species present in the Kasai, so were familiar to us. The hospital was about three hundred yards down the hill, in front of the house.

The hospital was old, but had a number of features which I wish we had incorporated into the buildings at Tshikaji. The administration building also housed the outpatient clinic, laboratory, and X-ray department. The roof had been blown off in a storm not long before we arrived and had been replaced. There was a large central court, or atrium, which was open to the sky. In the

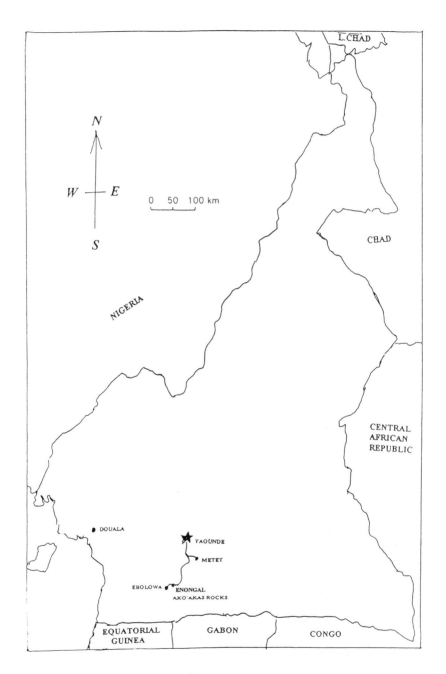

Cameroon

center of this was a small garden with a tree, providing a very attractive setting and allowing light into the center of the building. The maternity building and the surgical buildings both had halls down the center. These were filled with light, as the roofs had been designed with clerestories. This would have been a great feature at Tshikaji, as it would have made it unnecessary to have artificial light in the nurses' stations during the day.

Dr. Etya'alé spent a few days finishing up some of his administrative duties before he left with his family. They returned just before we left, so we were not privileged to work with him very long. There were two other expatriate doctors present, both young graduates from the Netherlands. Dr. Froika Hingtsman was in charge of obstetrics. Dr. Girard Haggart was covering pediatrics and internal medicine. His wife Esther Caes was a pharmacist. Mr. Ela and some other medical assistants and nurses performed hernia operations and some other surgery. Dr. Etya'alé is an ophthalmologist, but when present did other surgery as well.

Ebolowa was not far from the southern border, and patients frequently came across from Gabon and Equatorial Guinea seeking medical care. We were told that the medical services in those countries were inadequate. Our maternity service had a high incidence of premature infants, infected abortions, and contracted pelvises requiring C-sections. A number of these came from south of the border. Froika took care of most of them, though I was called upon to do a couple C-sections. Tubal ligations were done routinely after the sixth or seventh pregnancy. Otherwise, family planning was geared toward child spacing. Most of my routine surgery was thyroidectomies and hernia repairs.

While we were there, President Paul Biya paid an official visit to Ebolowa, his first visit as President, to the southern region. There was a lot of ethnic tension, especially between the English-speaking northern peoples and those in the French-speaking areas. Biya was from the central region, but the people of the south were politically ambivalent. His visit was intended to try to gain more support among them. Bus loads of people from all over the south were brought in until the population of the city was multiplied several fold. One of the trucks overturned, injuring a number of the passengers. For us it was a disaster situation, with a number of injured, including several with open fractures. The operating room was a long room with three operating tables. Again, a design that does not conform to the best surgical standards, but which is fairly common in developing countries. We kept all three tables occupied. I took care of the worst cases. Froika and Girard took care of some at my direction, and Ela and other nurses sutured some of the minor wounds. When the President heard of the accident, he sent one of his ministers the next day to see the wounded, and promised to pay all the hospital bills.

There had formerly been a dental school at Enongal for training dental technicians. The building was there, and one of the graduates was carrying on a dental practice. The facility reminded me of Lubondai. Much of the laboratory equipment was still there, gathering dust. Since Dr. Etya'alé was an ophthalmologist, he had trained an optical technician to do refractions, grind lenses, and fit glasses. One advantage that the hospital had over the hospitals in Zaïre was the availability of electrical power.

While there, we enjoyed a number of walks observing the birds and the nearby countryside. The cacao plant, source of cocoa and chocolate, was new to us. The pods grow on the trunks and branches of the plant. We saw two varieties, one had red pods and the other yellow when ripe. Cacao was long one of the main cash crops of the country, with cacao beans a principal export. We enjoyed their locally made chocolate bars. The world market was declining, however, as South America had become a major competitor, so the economy of the country was vitally affected.

We were given the opportunity to take an excursion to the country south of Ebolowa, to visit an interesting formation called Ako'akas Rocks, a tall granite column, that jutted up out of the forest for several hundred feet, with nearly vertical cliffs. One of the nurses came from a village nearby and we stopped to meet his family and to see their church. We also had an opportunity to observe their method of drying the cacao beans. These were spread on racks, with thatched roofs on rails that could be pushed over the racks in case of rain, and pulled back when there was sun, to dry the beans.

There was a large school at Enongal where Angie Anderson had once taught. Near the school was the large mission church. We worshiped there once, but usually attended a small chapel near the hospital. The services were somewhat more formal than those in Zaïre. The choir processional was beautifully rhythmic. As always, the Africans excelled in singing, and hymns had the distinctive character of local melodies.

When we left Enongal we stopped to visit the Presbyterian Hospital at Metet, about halfway between Ebolowa and Yaoundé. Built on a hillside, with a number of one-story buildings and pavilions, it did not seem to be as conveniently arranged as the hospital at Enongal, but it had a good many more patients. Before leaving Yaoundé, we passed by Djoungolo Hospital, but did not have the time and opportunity to visit it.

Illness Strikes Home

As we were preparing to leave for Zaïre in April 1991, Katrina's husband, Bill Manier, asked me to look at a lump in his neck which he had just noticed. It appeared to be an enlarged lymph node beneath his left jaw. He had no evidence of an infection, so I advised him to consult his physician right away. After unsuccessful trials on antibiotics, the node was removed for biopsy and proved to be metastatic squamous cell carcinoma. The primary site was not initially evident, but was eventually found to be the left tonsil. For the next two years he fought a losing battle with the cancer, undergoing removal of nodes in the neck, radiotherapy, and eventually a radical removal of the tonsil with portions of the palate and tongue. Katie and I were thankful to be present to lend support to Katrina and the girls, especially during the last few months. We had never experienced a greater outpouring of love on the part of family, neighbors, Bill's lifetime friends, and acquaintances from far and near. Bill and Katrina were courageous throughout the struggle. He died on their seventeenth wedding anniversary, July 17, 1993, at age forty-five. We were all grateful for the active assistance and support of Alive Hospice in Nashville, Tennessee during the final months of their ordeal. Having struggled against illness wherever we find it, throughout our lives, this was our first experience with untimely, fatal illness within our own family. It deepened our appreciation of the ties that bind and our gratitude for sustaining love.

Arthritis had bothered me for a number of years and during this period, my right knee gave me increasing difficulty. Finally in May 1992, Dr. William Youmans performed a total knee replacement on the right. He had been an intern at Vanderbilt during my last year of surgical residency and had then become an orthopedist specializing in sports medicine. The first couple of months following surgery required intensive rehabilitation, and improvement continued for more than a year.

Zaïre 1993

In 1993, we were invited to return to Zaïre to lend assistance at Bulapé and Tshikaji. We responded by returning for three months, September through November. The political situation in Zaïre had long been in turmoil and the economic situation continued to plunge. Efforts to oust Mobutu from power had resulted in a stalemate between rival factions. Some months after the Centennial celebration in 1991, the soldiers became so discontent from lack of pay that they ran amok, pillaging and looting the stores and warehouses in Kinshasa. Most of the stores in the business area were not only sacked, but had the windows and doors destroyed as well. Similar pillaging occurred in the major cities, including Kananga. A second pillaging occurred later, this time targeting the native stores and homes, since nothing was left to target in the business district. Torture and murder of members of the opposition to Mobutu had been documented by Amnesty International.

Kinshasa

Arrival at Kinshasa's Njili Airport in the past had often been an unpleasant ordeal. This time, in September 1993, thanks to Bill Simmons and his well-organized assistants, everything went smoothly. Kinshasa was calm and a few of the major stores were back in operation. The store windows had been replaced by solid walls of cement block, and guards armed with automatic weapons were posted day and night. The economy was in shambles, with inflation out of control. We became instant billionaires when Marge Hoffeld gave us two billion zaïres, slightly more than three hundred U.S. dollars, since the exchange rate was 6.35 million zaïres to a dollar. The largest bill in circulation was a note of one million zaïres, worth about sixteen cents, so billfolds were useless. To go shopping, we had to carry around sacks of bills.

Willie Simmons was then teaching at TASOK. We spent an interesting evening at their home. Larry Sthreshley was in the Kasai doing a survey of the medical work, but his wife Inge, a former schoolmate of our daughter Faye, was there. The other guests were TASOK teachers and a doctor who worked at the Baptist clinic. I spent a good bit of the evening talking with the doctor. She told me that 25 percent of the patient and donor population at the clinic were HIV positive. The rate for the entire country was reported to be about 10 percent, the last survey at Tshikaji, about 8 percent. More recent reports, in March 1994, stated that the epidemic is accelerating at a startling rate and may exceed the infection rate of the east African countries before long.

Tshikaji

At Tshikaji we were welcomed by many old friends, among whom were Dr. Walt and Nancy Hull, and Dr. Sue Makin. Dr. Ralph and Elsbeth Shannon and Dr. Bob and Sharon Gardner were all living in Kananga. Bob, a dentist, was working in the dental training program at the IMCK Polyclinic. Tshikaji had recently gained two Zaïrian physicians. Dr. Mubikayi Léon, a gynecologist, was working with Walt Hull. Dr. Mvita Pierre was formerly professor of pediatrics at Lubumbashi. Our old friend Dr. Mulaja Mukendi was then in South Africa for additional study. During his absence, Dr. Sue Makin was in charge of the internal medicine service. Dr. Nzengu Benoit was covering surgery, having returned to Zaïre for several months. Since he was to be at Tshikaji until the middle of October, it was decided that we should spend the first six weeks at Bulapé and return to Tshikaji when he departed.

There had been some additions to the buildings at Tshikaji since our last visit. The dormitories for the continuing education program had been completed. An extended care facility had been built in front of the hospital. This was used for patients receiving tuberculosis treatment on an ambulatory basis, as well as for others who came from a distance and were being treated on an outpatient basis. An additional faculty residence had been completed, and construction had begun on housing for residents. A guest facility had been built, where we were housed. This consisted of an enclosed courtyard with four rooms on each side. Each pair of rooms shared a bath. Across the end of the courtyard were the kitchen and dining room. The showers were equipped with solar water heaters, so that warm showers were a novel luxury. We had brought a footlocker of foodstuffs with us from the States. Before going to Bulapé we supplemented this with some items from the Catholic Procure in Kananga. We spent half a billion zaïres, roughly eighty dollars, and our purchases just filled a cardboard carton.

Bulapé

On returning to Bulapé, our first African post, we had gone full circle. It was the beginning of rainy season, but the grass on the station was already quite high. Cutting such a large area was an expense the church could ill afford. A number of hogs ran uncontrolled on the station and kept a lot of the ground plowed up with their rooting. We stayed in the house that the McGills had last occupied, which had been prepared for us. The woodwork had been recently painted, and all the furniture was intact. The solar panels were in place and a battery had been brought in, so that we had lights at night. The regulator burned out one day and we were without lights for one night only, as it was replaced the next day. What a contrast to life at Bulapé forty years earlier! To think that unharnessed solar power had been there all the while! There was wood for the old stove, but refrigeration was out of the question. We managed well, as rice and beans were plentiful. The abundance of bananas, pineapples, and papaya made a feast of every meal, and friends were all too generous with their chickens.

We were enthusiastically welcomed and royally entertained. The *bashashenge* (village elders) came bringing a chicken and some eggs; the Presbytery gave a dinner for us in the refectory of the nursing school; several members of the hospital staff and the pastor all invited us to dinner during our stay.

Several buildings had been added for the nursing school, including classrooms, two dormitories, and a refectory. One evening there was a terrific storm which blew the roof off one of the classrooms. Fortunately, no students were in it at the time, and no one was hurt. They were able to salvage the roofing and repair the building. The solar system at the hospital was operating, though they have just about exhausted their spare parts. I had brought my notebook computer and took it to the hospital in the morning to recharge the batteries on the inverter, so that I could use it to write in the evenings.

With the encouragement of Mobutu, the Baluba of Shaba had embarked on a program of ethnic cleansing. Reportedly, they had driven out more than three hundred thousand people who were originally from the Kasai. The trains were running very irregularly so that there was not enough transportation for all the refugees. Stations in Shaba were swamped with crowds trying to get places on the train. Many died en route, especially the children. Families were torn apart, as men who had married women from the Kasai were forced to reject them and send them away. The rail centers in the Kasai were all swamped with refugees. Oxfam was helping to coordinate relief work through church organizations.

About a fourth of the patients at Bulapé were refugees. The relief committee was paying for their medical care, so it was not too great a financial burden for the hospital. Several medical problems were direct results of the refugee influx. AIDS had not been as prevalent at Bulapé as in some other areas of Zaïre, such as Shaba, where the rate is much higher. Among the refugees, AIDS and AIDS associated tuberculosis were common. Sleeping

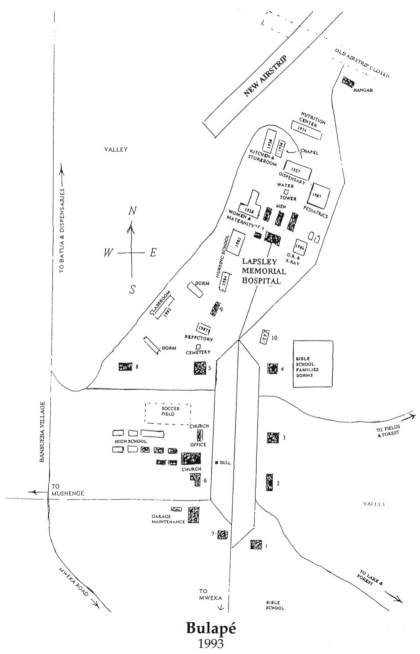

Bulapé
1953

Buildings existing in 1953 are shown in black.
Dates of construction are shown on newer buildings.

sickness had been largely eradicated in the Bulapé area; I saw a dozen patients who had contracted the disease in Shaba. Since the tsetse fly which transmits sleeping sickness is prevalent in the Bulapé area, we fear that it will again become endemic. Sanitation in the refugee crowds was a problem; dysentery, typhoid, and other enteric diseases were rife.

Prior to this time, my "new right knee," dating from a total knee replacement in May 1992, had not been thoroughly tested. When we decided to return to Zaïre, this had been one of our concerns. Gratefully, I had no difficulty standing in the operating room for several hours nearly every day. In fact, I performed over fifty major operations and a number of minor ones during the six-week stay. We dealt with an interesting mix of surgical problems, a number of them in children: pyloric stenosis, harelips, and hernia operations. Among adults, hernia repairs and thyroidectomies were the most common, but the list also included gynecological procedures, plastic repair of a lower lip, amputations, and three splenectomies.

A number of the Bulapé hospital staff had been educated at Tshikaji, and some of the older staff members were still active, so we knew most of them. At the time of our visit, Dr. Tshibangu was studying in South Africa, and Dr. Beya was medical director. Bulapé hospital was serving the needs of a large area stretching north into the equatorial forest. Lack of fuel had curtailed the trips of their community health team, but patients found their way to the hospital from all directions. The hospital at the Kuba capital at Mushenge was virtually nonfunctioning. During our stay, guest facilities on the station were occupied by members of the royal family who came for medical care. Many patients came from the rail center at Mweka. As already mentioned, the problems were accentuated by the flood of refugees from Shaba.

Another problem which had not seemed acute during our earlier stays at Bulapé was that of ethnic conflict. Whereas the local population was largely Bakete, who were formerly subjects of the Bakuba, these groups had dwelt and worked together for decades in relative peace. Now that Zaïre's political situation is chaotic from the national level down, this balance is in question, and mistrust is rampant.

In the face of all these unfavorable circumstances, we were impressed by the local efforts to maintain the station. The hospital staff, of mixed ethnic origins, cooperated and worked valiantly to meet the needs of all patients. Katie taught in the nursing school, and applauded Director Luboya and his teaching staff for their diligence. We were overwhelmed by the generosity and loving concern for our needs.

One of my patients was Kueta Busheba, an old friend who had served for many years as the head operating room nurse. He was diabetic and had developed gangrene of one foot and ankle. He would not accept amputation and eventually died. We, along with a number of the hospital staff, attended his funeral. We had attended the funeral of one of the tribal elders many years before. There were similarities, but also some marked differences. At Kueta's funeral, the women were all sitting under a couple of sheds erected

Women dancing at funeral of village leader, Bulapé 1953.

for the purpose, and the men sat together a short distance away. A man was dancing in traditional costume when we arrived, but there was none of the traditional wailing. A choir of women came and sang hymns, and there was dancing, but all were fully clothed. In the past, the women dancers were often bare to the waist. A pastor led in prayer, gave a short eulogy, and preached a sermon. Everyone was relieved that Kueta's suffering was over and gave thanks for his many years of service. Seven of Kueta's eight children were living, and a number of the grandchildren were there for a family photograph.

While at Bulapé, we worshiped at the two churches in Bansueba village and also at the big station church. All of them were well attended. We were especially impressed with the large number of children, who occupied the front of the church, many sitting on the floor. It was amazing how attentive and well behaved they were, especially since the services lasted up to three hours. There were four or five choirs at each of the churches, and each of them sang four or five numbers. Some of the choirs used guitars, drums, and other percussion instruments for accompaniment. Sermons usually were not more than twenty minutes. There were usually two offerings, which were taken by having the congregation march up to drop the offering in a box. The reason for two offerings was that a percentage of the regular offering was shared with the Presbytery. The second offering was for special local projects.

The plane that came to get us brought Dr. Hank Watt and Mr. Khanh Dinh, a Vietnamese-American engineer. With funding from Medical Benevolence Foundation, Mr. Khanh had invented a solar autoclave. The two of them had just been to Embangweni in Malawi to install the first of these. They then came to Bulapé to install one there. The old autoclave at Bulapé was heated with charcoal or wood. It had a small leak in the jacket so was in need of replacement. Mr. Khanh had developed some very efficient air-conditioning equipment, using some newly developed material that conducts heat in a superior fashion. This material was used in producing the solar autoclave. I'm sorry that we were not there to see it in operation. We saw Hank and Mr. Khanh at Tshikaji after the installation was complete. The test runs had shown it capable of completing a sterilization cycle in twenty minutes and running three successive cycles without difficulty. It should prove to be a great boon in institutions where electrical power is not available and where fuel is a problem.

IMCK Tshikaji

On arriving back at Tshikaji, we stayed in house Number 10. Dick and Judith Brown had been the last occupants and it still contained some of their beautiful ironwood furniture, carved with Kuba motifs. One wall of the bedroom had a large mural of coconut palms gently swaying in a breeze on the shore of a bay, reputedly Dr. Richard (Dick) Brown's handiwork. On those occasions when I could hit the horizontal after lunch, I found it restful to lie watching for the coconuts to fall!

The patient load at Tshikaji was even heavier than at Bulapé, because the hospital functions as a referral center for the entire central portion of Zaïre. I inherited a number of problem cases. Most of these were orthopedic problems resulting from open fractures. External fixation devices were used for a number of cases, including one patient with a widely separated fracture of the pelvis. Dr. John Terry, a plastic surgeon, arrived for a three-week stay while we were there. His special skills were a tremendous help. I assisted him in a number of plastic procedures, and he helped me with a number of my operations. He was especially interested in harelips. We also did a number of procedures on children with urinary tract abnormalities.

Our concession at Lake Munkamba was due to expire in the year 2000 and our need for it had passed. We decided to offer it to the IMCK, as they have annual retreats for the students there and could use it for vacations of the staff. The offer was accepted. There had been problems with the sentry. As he was our employee, this was the time, both logically and legally, to discharge him. Elder Shamba Manenga, the hospital administrator, accompanied us to the lake to help us do this and to arrange for a new sentry in the employ of the institute. We spent a weekend there and were able to accomplish it all satisfactorily.

Katie had an opportunity to go to Lubondai in the Lubondai hospital vehicle. She was there for five days, during which time she divided her time between Lubondai and Tshiondo village where she researched child rearing patterns during the sixties. I was able to go down in the plane that went to get her. Several of the old staff came to the landing strip to greet me. While there, Katie was the guest of Dr. Kabongo Nvita and his wife Agnes.

Good Shepherd Hospital
  A. Administration
  B. Outpatient, lab and X-ray
  C. Obstetrics
  D. Operating rooms and
     Sterilizing
  E. Men's Ward
  F. Pediatric Ward
  G. Women's Ward
  H. Ophthalmology
  I. Kitchen, Laundry and
     Drug stores
  J. Maintenance and White
     Cross
  K. Fuel Depot
  L. Generators
  M. Water Tank
  Nutritional Center
  Extended Care
Continuing Education
Nursing and Lab Tech School
Boys' and Girls' Dorms
Faculty Houses 1-11
Staff Houses 12-17

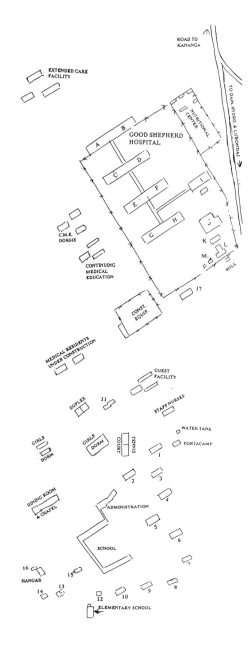

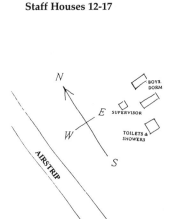

I.M.C.K. Tshikaji
1993

Remembering our own struggles at that difficult post in the sixties, she was impressed by the valiant efforts of the hospital staff in the face of dissension over the local chieftainship, the pressure of more than a thousand refugees on the patient register in addition to the usual load, the difficulty of procuring food, and the lack of an adequate water system. When she asked Dr. Kabongo about the one most pressing need at the hospital, he answered simply, "Water!" The old hydroelectric system is long defunct. In the present chaotic state of the country, fuel, building materials, and transportation facilities are virtually unavailable at isolated posts. It was inspiring to see our IMCK graduates trying "to make bricks without straw" and succeeding to a marked degree, but heartbreaking to know that a rotten political system had cheated them of their birthright.

During our weeks at Tshikaji, we were privileged to worship there and at two other places. One Sunday we went to Ndesha, near Kananga to worship. The church was packed, and the service similar to the ones we attended at Bulapé, with several choirs. The Rev. Dr. Lamar Williamson was retired and had returned for a couple of years to teach at the theological school. He and Ruthmary had graciously invited us to have dinner with them. On Sunday, November 28, we attended the French service at the Protestant Center in Kananga and had dinner with Elder Shamba Manenga and his family. Following the service, Shamba gave a short explanation of the work of the Gideons. He is a member of a group of Zaïrian businessmen in Kananga who belong to the Gideons, and they were distributing New Testaments.

As inflation continued to increase, the exchange rate fluctuated madly and reached over thirty million zaïres to one U.S. dollar. Mobutu issued a new zaïre which would knock off six zeros; however, the people in the two Kasai regions and Shaba were refusing to accept the new bills. Mobutu sent one of his ministers to Kananga to see if he could solve the problem. Riots resulted and we spent our last day there in an effort to salvage lives of victims.

Our reservations to leave Kinshasa and continue on to China were for Friday, December 3. We were scheduled to leave on Shabair on Wednesday, but the scheduled flight to Kananga was in doubt. An opportunity was found for us to go on Tuesday, on the charter flight of another air service, ATO, that was coming to evacuate the Italian engineers of the road building company. The Italians told us that they were leaving and were definitely not planning to return.

Kinshasa

When we arrived back in Kinshasa, we stayed at MPH along with Dr. John Terry. Our friend Kalonji Matadi was in charge. He put us in touch with other friends from the Kasai, with whom we had good visits. As always, we were overwhelmed by their gracious hospitality. Throughout our stay, we were amazed at the courage with which our friends face problems of ethnic and political conflict and of economic chaos.

We left Zaïre encouraged by the way in which individual Christians are trying to meet the needs of refugees, by the efforts of Zaïrian medical personnel to solve overwhelming health problems, by the potential for leadership among young men and women, and by the courageous stand of the church in opposition to ruthless oppression, wherever it occurs. We left reluctantly, realizing that short-term assistance was not enough, but we left inspired by the lives of Zaïrian Christians who are seeking to follow in the footsteps of Christ.

Appendix A

Chronology of Years Abroad

Africa	Dates	China
	Jan. 1923-Dec. 1926	Huzhou, Zhejiang: childhood
	Sept. 1947-Jan. 1948	Jiaxing, Jiangsu
	Feb. 1948-Aug. 1949	Beijing: Language study
	Sept. 1949-Jan. 1951	Taizhou, Jiangsu

Belgium: Study
   Brussels: French
   Antwerp: Tropical medicine
	Sept. 1951-Nov. 1952	

Zaïre: Sona Bata, Bulapé, Luebo	Dec. 1952-June 1956	
Zaïre: Luebo	Aug. 1957-May 1961	
Zaïre: Lubondai	Aug. 1964-June 1967	
Zaïre visit	May 1971	
Zaïre: IMCK Kananga, Tshikaji	July 1972-June 1974	
Zaïre: IMCK Tshikaji	June 1978-June 1982	
Zaïre: Bulapé, IMCK Tshikaji	Dec. 1983-Apr. 1984	
	Aug. 1986-June 1989	Zhenjiang, Beijing, Xian
Malawi: Embangweni	Oct. 1989-Mar. 1990	
	March-May 1990	Beijing
Zaïre: Bulapé	May 1991	
Cameroon: Enongal Hospital	Aug.-Sept. 1991	
	Oct.-Dec. 1991	Beijing, Fenyang
Zaïre: Bulapé, and IMCK Tshikaji	Sept.-Dec. 1993	Return via Hong Kong, Nanjing, Zhenjiang, Taizhou, Beijing

Appendix B

Nelson Family Tree

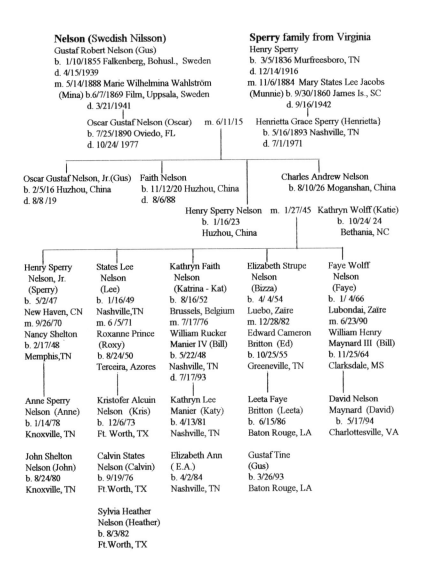

Nelson (Swedish Nilsson)
Gustaf Robert Nelson (Gus)
b. 1/10/1855 Falkenberg, Bohusl., Sweden
d. 4/15/1939
m. 5/14/1888 Marie Wilhelmina Wahlström
(Mina) b.6/7/1869 Film, Uppsala, Sweden
            d. 3/21/1941

Sperry family from Virginia
Henry Sperry
b. 3/5/1836 Murfreesboro, TN
d. 12/14/1916
m. 11/6/1884 Mary States Lee Jacobs
(Munnie) b. 9/30/1860 James Is., SC
            d. 9/16/1942

Oscar Gustaf Nelson (Oscar)   m. 6/11/15   Henrietta Grace Sperry (Henrietta}
b. 7/25/1890 Oviedo, FL   b. 5/16/1893 Nashville, TN
d. 10/24/ 1977   d. 7/1/1971

Oscar Gustaf Nelson, Jr.(Gus)   Faith Nelson   Charles Andrew Nelson
b. 2/5/16 Huzhou, China   b. 11/12/20 Huzhou, China   b. 8/10/26 Moganshan, China
d. 8/8 /19   d. 8/6/88

Henry Sperry Nelson   m. 1/27/45   Kathryn Wolff (Katie)
b. 1/16/23   b. 10/24/ 24
Huzhou, China   Bethania, NC

Henry Sperry Nelson, Jr. (Sperry)	States Lee Nelson (Lee)	Kathryn Faith Nelson (Katrina - Kat)	Elizabeth Strupe Nelson (Bizza)	Faye Wolff Nelson (Faye)
b. 5/2/47	b. 1/16/49	b. 8/16/52	b. 4/ 4/54	b. 1/ 4/66
New Haven, CN	Nashville,TN	Brussels, Belgium	Luebo, Zaïre	Lubondai, Zaïre
m. 9/26/70	m. 6 /5/71	m. 7/17/76	m. 12/28/82	m. 6/23/90
Nancy Shelton	Roxanne Prince (Roxy)	William Rucker Manier IV (Bill)	Edward Cameron Britton (Ed)	William Henry Maynard III (Bill)
b. 2/17/48	b. 8/24/50	b. 5/22/48	b. 10/25/55	b. 11/25/64
Memphis,TN	Terceira, Azores	Nashville, TN	Greeneville, TN	Clarksdale, MS
		d. 7/17/93		
Anne Sperry Nelson (Anne)	Kristofer Alcuin Nelson (Kris)	Kathryn Lee Manier (Katy)	Leeta Faye Britton (Leeta)	David Nelson Maynard (David)
b. 1/14/78	b. 12/6/73	b. 4/13/81	b. 6/15/86	b. 5/17/94
Knoxville, TN	Ft. Worth, TX	Nashville, TN	Baton Rouge, LA	Charlottesville, VA
John Shelton Nelson (John)	Calvin States Nelson (Calvin)	Elizabeth Ann (E.A.)	Gustaf Tine (Gus)	
b. 8/24/80	b. 9/19/76	b. 4/2/84	b. 3/26/93	
Knoxville, TN	Ft.Worth, TX	Nashville, TN	Baton Rouge, LA	
	Sylvia Heather Nelson (Heather)			
	b. 8/3/82			
	Ft.Worth, TX			

Appendix C

Chinese and African Names of Nelson Family

	Chinese Names		**African Names**	
Oscar Gustaf Nelson	倪尔迅	Ni Er Xun (Humble)		
			Kuba Names	
Henry Sperry Nelson	倪恩义	Ni En Yi (Kindness & justice)	Kueta Mabintshi	
Kathryn Wolff Nelson	倪克仁	Ni Ke Ren (Able & Sensitive)	Tshiekueta	
				Luba Names
Henry Sperry, Jr. (Sperry)	倪爱理	Ni Ai Li (Love the Truth)	Mingashanga	Kalala
States Lee (Lee)	倪信理	Ni Xin Li (Faith in Truth)	Mikobe	Mulumba
Kathryn Faith (Kat)	倪望理	Ni Wang Li (Hope in Truth)	Tshieshanga	
Elizabeth Strupe (Bizza)	倪美理	Ni Mei Li (Beautiful Truth)		Mujinga
Faye Wolff (Faye)	倪安理	Ni An Li (Peace & Truth)		Mbumbu Esther

Bibliography

China

Brown, Frank A. *Charlotte Brown, A Mother in China: The Story of the Work of Charlotte Thompson Brown in China from 1909-1949*. U.S.A.: Brown, 1953.
Mission Yearbook for Prayer & Study (1986-95). Louisville, KY: Presbyterian Church (U.S.A.).
Mizell, Marguerite. *The Marguerite Mizell Story: An Ordinary Woman on Whom the Lord Laid His Hand, As Told to Ernestine Van Buren*. Dallas, Texas: First Presbyterian Church, 1987.
Richardson, Agnes R. *The Claimed Blessing: The story of the lives of the Richardsons in China, 1923-1951*. Cincinnati, OH: The C. J. Krehbiel Co., 1970.
Tsao Hsueh-Chin and Kao Ngo. *A Dream of Red Mansions, Vols. I, II, and III*. Peking: Foreign Language Press, 1978.
Wickeri, Philip L. *Seeking the Common Ground: Protestant Christiantiy, the Three-Self Movement, and China's United Front*. Maryknoll, NY: Orbis Books, 1988.

Africa

Anderson, Vernon A. *Still Led in Triumph*. Nashville, TN: Board of World Missions, Presbyterian Church, U.S., 1959.
Longenecker, J. Hershey. *Memories of Congo*. Johnson City, TN: Royal Publishers, Inc., 1964.
Nelson, Kathryn Wolff. *Child Rearing Patterns in a Lulua Village of South Central Congo*. Ann Arbor, MI: University Microfilms, Inc., 1969.
Phipps, William E. *The Sheppards and Lapsley: Pioneer Presbyterians in the*

Congo. Louisville, KY: The Presbyterian Church (U.S.A.), 1991.

Pruitt, Virginia G., and Winifred K. Vass (eds.). *A Textbook of the Tshiluba Language*. Revised Edition. Luebo, Democratic Republic of Congo: American Presbyterian Congo Mission, 1965.

Roseveare, Sir Martin. *Joys, Jobs, and Jaunts: Memoirs of Sir Martin Roseveare*. Blantyre, Malawi: Blantyre Print and Packaging, Preface 1984.

Rule, William. *Milestones in Mission*. Knoxville, TN: Rule, 1991.

Traveler's Guide to the Belgian Congo and Ruanda-Urundi. Brussels: Tourist Bureau for the Belgian Congo and Ruanda-Urundi, 1951.

Vass, Winifred K. *Doctor Not Afraid: E. R. Kellersberger, M. D.* Austin, TX: Nortex Press, 1986.

Wharton, Ethel T. *Led in Triumph*. Nashville, TN: Board of World Missions, Presbyterian Church, U.S., 1952.

Resources for Further Information

China

Amity Newsletter, The Amity Foundation, 17 Da Jian Yin Xiang, Naning 210029, People's Republic of China; or The Amity Foundation, Overseas Coordination Office, 4 Jordan Road, Kowloon, Hong Kong.

China News Update, China Program, Room 420, Presbyterian Church (U.S.A.), 475 Riverside Drive, New York, NY 10115; or Presbyterian Church (U.S.A.), 100 Witherspoon Street, Louisville, KY 40202.

China Connection Narrates: China Chronicles, 458 S. Pasadena Ave., Pasadena, CA 91105.

Africa

Information on Presbyterian medical work in Africa and elsewhere, Medical Benevolence Foundation, 1412 N. Sam Houston Pkwy E. #120, Houston, TX 77032-2946.

Worldwide Ministries, Africa Office, Presbyterian Church (U.S.A.), 100 Witherspoon Street, Louisville, KY 40202-1396.

General

Newsletter, Association of Presbyterians in Cross-Cultural Mission, 221 Mt. Vernon Drive, Decatur, GA 30030.

Index